IN EVERY STYLE OF PASSION

The Works of Leonard Cohen

IN EVERY STYLE
OF PASSION

The Works of Leonard Cohen

Jim Devlin

OMNIBUS PRESS
LONDON · NEW YORK · PARIS · SYDNEY

Copyright © 1996 Omnibus Press
(A Division of Book Sales Limited)

Edited by Chris Charlesworth
Cover designed by Michael Bell Design
Picture Research by Nikki Russell

ISBN 0.7119.5496.8
Order No. OP47811

Exclusive Distributors
Book Sales Limited,
8/9 Frith Street,
London W1V 5TZ, UK.

Music Sales Corporation,
257 Park Avenue South,
New York, NY 10010, USA.

Music Sales Pty Limited,
120 Rothschild Avenue, Rosebery,
NSW 2018, Australia.

To the Music Trade only:
Music Sales Limited,
8/9 Frith Street,
London W1V 5TZ, UK.

Photo credits
Front & back cover pictures by Robin Francois/Retna.
Picture Section: Christof Graf: 7t&b; Lars Hols: 5; LFI: 2,3,4,8;
David Redfern: 1; Ebet Roberts/Redferns: 6

Every effort has been made to trace the copyright holders of the
photographs in this book but one or two were unreachable. We would
be grateful if the photographers concerned would contact us.

Printed in the United Kingdom by Hartnolls Limited, Bodmin, Cornwall.

A catalogue record for this book is available from the British Library.

Contents

Dedicated to the memory of my parents

Introduction

This book aims to focus on Leonard Cohen's musical output in terms of his songwriting, and performance both in the recording studio and on the concert stage. It does not attempt a day-by-day chronology though, of course, I have included the major biographical facts. His life as a performing artist began in the mid-1940s when he played clarinet in his High School Band, since when his talents in other artistic areas have been on public display for more than 50 years – as a poet, novelist, public speaker, screenplay writer, film narrator, singer, video-star, presenter, interviewer, interviewee, watercolour artist and in more recent years, computer graphicist, as evidenced, for example, in his 1993 Tour programme.

Leonard's first recording dates from 1957, at a time when he was fêted as Canada's literary 'wunderkind' rivalling well-established writers like Irving Layton and Louis Dudek. The accolades were many and generous, but his royalties were small potatoes. He decided to write songs in the belief that more money could be made in Tin Pan Alley. I have attempted to trace the steps of that musical journey from his well-to-do Montreal family home to New York, to Hydra, to Los Angeles and his Zen retreat on Mount Baldy, and back and forth again, through his 118 album tracks, 18 tours, and scores of television/radio/newspaper interviews. En route, this 'lonely heart', 'depressed writer', 'committed Jew', 'incorrigible ladies' man', 'gloomy poet', 'famous drinker', '60s refusenik', 'devoted father', 'disciplined Zen devotee', 'old folkie with a young appeal', 'blocked songwriter prone to breakdown', 'ascetic and tequila drinker', 'crooner with a gravelly voice', 'witty and charming man', 'Jacques Brel sound-alike', 'restless pilgrim', 'existential comedian', 'durable hipster', to cite just a few of the Cohen-clichés, has worked indefatigably to express himself in songs which, thus far, have eluded musical analysis in any detail. The reader will find much evidence in the bibliography of studies which have, for the most part, concentrated on Leonard's poetry and prose, often viewing the songs merely as an extension of his wordsmith's craft and guile. I have preferred to *hear* them as the natural fusion of melody and lyric. In so doing, I have tended not to examine, nor even point out, every single instance of Leonard's thematic and intoxicated leitmotifs: religion, sex, love, life and death – the reader is invited to pursue these at leisure through listening again to the songs and re-reading the lyrics.

In an interview published in *The Sunday Times* in October 1991, Leonard said: "You never set out to write an obscure or unlovable song . . . they're all started with the same panicked good intentions." A month later, *Q* magazine quoted him thus: "I'm fond of saying that my songs last just as long as a Volvo – 30 years." This book explores his well-intentioned aspirations and resultant compositions in the former, while giving the lie to the latter – since 'Suzanne', 'So Long, Marianne' and 'Sisters Of Mercy' (and a good many others) will ensure that Leonard Cohen's name-plaque will continue to gleam brightly for many more years on the front door of music history's Tower Of Song.

Acknowledgements

I would like to express my thanks to everyone who has helped me in completing this book. First of all, to my wife, Jeannie, and my daughter Imogen, whose encouragement and patience have eased my task in no small measure. I also want to thank Gerhard Schinzel and Michael Lohse without whose painstaking and pioneering research to collate Leonard's concert set-lists, recordings and interviews over the years, together with their continuing friendship and reliability to 'come up trumps', I would never have embarked upon writing this book in the first place.

Many sincere thanks also to: Steve Goldstein, Martine Moreau, Patrick Sexton, Jarkko Arjatsalo, Mike Hollis, James Ryan, Ron Mura, Lars Hols, Christina Briem, Seamus Curley, Martin Rupps, Ron Scarlett, Bill Ginn, Johannes Knapp-Menzl, Espen Havaldsen, Camilla Oey, Gogo Krampota, Joachim Wacker, Tatjana Richter, Josephine Hogan, Olivia Chevalier, Maryse Balard, Nadège Laburthe, Yvonne Hakze, Ed Casey, Jurgen Jaensch, Håvard Rem, Geoffrey Wren, Paul Ostermayer, Soheyl Dahi, Frank Robinson, Vlad Arghir, Emmanuel Klein, Joe Curzi, Lorenzo Conci, Christof Graf, Flemming Schmidt, Perla Batalla, Ken Norris, Ira Nadel, Tom Layesman and Brendan Dignam for the steady and reliable flow of 'Par avion' envelopes, packets, and parcels with all the LC items that you have sent me since our correspondence first began more than ten years ago.

Closer to home, I wish to express my gratitude to John Etherington for his many insights and enthusiasm to keep going; also to: Rob Huntley, Lynne Sweetman, Bob Lewis,

Susan Porter, Jeannie Barrett-Klaasen, Sarah Finch, Trevor Neal, Ziyad Georgis, Neil Watson, Ray Neapolitan, Norman Maycock, John & Linda McDonald, Dave Carlin, Ellen Ley, Chris Firth, Phillip Smith, Val Corbett, Andy Jones, Gordon Fraser, Frank Robinson, Elaine Christmas, Denise Knowles, Michael Corney, Walter Maynard, Dave Drewett, James Finch, Dave Johnson, Brian Webb, J.P. Bean, Glyn Pope, Brian Webb, Jennifer Mills, Phyl Wearne, Philip Webb, Brian Rooney, Carmel Agnew, Pete Jackson, Dave Lindon, Mark Badger, Pierre Borms and Tony Palmer for their stimulating conversations and correspondence, clippings, tapes, translations and visuals – I have endeavoured to make diligent use of their important source material throughout the book.

I am indebted to Gerhard Schinzel and Michael Lohse for their co-operation to reproduce their 1970–1985 lists in the Appendices. I owe several debts of gratitude to Joan Lynch at Stranger Music in Los Angeles and Joe Donnelly at CBS/Sony in London for their timely advice. Also to my Editor, Chris Charlesworth for his guidance and perseverance throughout this project, I offer many thanks.

Finally, I would stress that any merit in this book can be attributed to all those who have informed and assisted me so generously – any errors are all mine.

Jim Devlin, Sheffield, July 1996

I

It Seems So Long Ago

Leonard Norman Cohen was born on September 21, 1934, the second child of Nathan and Masha who were married in 1927. Leonard's sister Esther was born in 1929. They lived comfortably in the middle-class Westmount district of Montreal, employing a chauffeur-cum-gardener and an Irish Catholic nurse ("nursie" Anne Smith). Religious duties – celebrating the Jewish Sabbath, attending the Synagogue, lighting candles and reciting prayers – were all observed without, as Leonard himself has recounted, fanaticism. "Religion structured our life . . . it was all friendly, ordinary. It was never mentioned, no more than a fish would acknowledge the presence of water," he told *Les Inrockuptibles* in 1991.

Nathan Cohen's family had emigrated from Poland in the early 1870s and established themselves as leading Jewish citizens in Montreal. His father, Lyon, helped found the Zionist Organisation of Canada, and the Hebrew Free Loan Association of Montreal, among several other notable enterprises. Masha's family came to Canada from Lithuania in the 1920s. Her father, Rabbi Solomon Klinitzky-Klein, wrote two books, *The Thesaurus Of Talmudic Interpretation* and *A Lexicon Of Hebrew Homonyms*.

Nathan Cohen and his brother Horace served in the Canadian Army, the first commissioned Jewish officers to do so, in World War 1. Nathan returned from Europe partially disabled. When he died in January 1944, nursed of course to the end by Masha, a Red Cross Worker, Leonard was 9 years old. (His mother's subsequent re-marriage was not a success.)

Growing up in Montreal, Leonard attended Roslyn Junior

High, then Westmount High School (the backdrop for 'Memories'); he had piano lessons with Miss McDougall, three guitar lessons from a teenage Spanish boy and played clarinet in the School Band. His bar mitzvah, at age 13, was in 1947. Leonard graduated from Westmount High in 1951 and on his 17th birthday enrolled at McGill University.

That same year he teamed up with a couple of fellow buckskin jacket-owning friends to play music in Church and School halls and basements; Leonard on rhythm guitar, Mike Doddman on harmonica and Terry (surname unrecorded) on bucket bass – The Buckskin Boys were in business. They lasted a couple of years. In the course of four years at McGill, Leonard studied Arts in the first, third and final, with Business Studies (as it would probably be called today) engaging him in the second. At McGill his teachers included Hugh MacLennan and Louis Dudek; and he met Irving Layton who became like a mentor to him, a status rigorously denied by Layton himself. "Leonard was already a genius when we met," Layton has claimed. The two have remained the closest of friends to this day; indeed, Leonard is godfather to Layton's son David. In his own day, Layton was more the bruiser '*poète terrible*', Leonard the browser, of style and form.

Yeats, Eliot, Rimbaud, Shakespeare, Hemingway, Auden, Frost, Baudelaire, Steinbeck and many others were on his University's reading-list; Lorca, too, as it happened, which must have thrilled Leonard since he had himself first dis-covered the work of the Spanish poet six years earlier in 1949, in a Montreal bookstore. Leonard: "This was the man who ruined my life." Ira Nadel's contribution in *take this waltz*, a celebratory collection of articles published in 1994 for Leonard's 60th birthday, explains in some detail the creative links between Cohen and Lorca, and they are certainly more substantial than many critics have hitherto realised. Leonard went on to win the Chester MacNaughton Prize for Creative Writing and the Peterson Memorial Prize for Literature in his final year. As President of the McGill Debating Union Society in 1954, he later banned all debates. (Ten years later, he would be embroiled in a widely reported debate on 'The Future Of Judaism in Canada'.) In 1955, Leonard graduated with a B.A. degree. He was undecided as to what he should do next: continue his studies, go into the family clothing business, drop out . . . While he pondered, he went to Law School for a short period, and this allowed him the time to supervise the publication of his first book of poetry.

Leonard has often told of the first time he wrote a poem. After his father's funeral, he wrote some lines on a piece of paper, folded it into one of his father's bow-ties and buried it in the garden. *Let Us Compare Mythologies*, dedicated to the memory of Nathan B. Cohen, was Leonard's first book and the first publication in the McGill Poetry Series, overseen by Louis Dudek. (This was not the first time Cohen's poetry had appeared in print: several of the *Mythologies* poems were published in various magazines during 1954-56.) The book contained 44 poems, written between the ages of 15 and 20 (between 1949 and 1954). Five have the word 'song' in their titles and two are simply called 'Ballad'. That there are musical overtones in so many of these lines should not surprise since Leonard was so often seen with a guitar over his shoulder. Leonard: ". . . writing grew out of my interest in folk music and the lyrics of folk music . . . I've never really separated the two activities – writing and music, and I've always felt there was an invisible guitar behind the verse that I've done." (WNEW FM interview, New York, July 1988.) Five hundred copies of *Let Us Compare Mythologies* were printed, and the edition sold out. McClelland and Stewart, Cohen's Canadian publishers since 1961, reprinted it ten years later without Freda Guttman's six original line-drawings.

"This is Leonard Cohen reading some poems from my book *Let Us Compare Mythologies*" were Leonard's first words on 'Six Montreal Poets', an album of poetry readings by A.J.M. Smith, Irving Layton, F.R. Scott, Louis Dudek and A.M. Klein – auspicious company, indeed. Leonard, shooting from the lip, recorded eight texts: 'For Wilf and his House', 'Beside The

Shepherd', 'Poem', 'Lovers', 'The Sparrows', 'Warning', 'Les Vieux', and 'Elegy', making up track two on the disc, issued by Folkways Records in 1957. His tenor delivery is pacey and declamatory.

In the autumn of 1956, Leonard continued his studies at Columbia University in New York. He stayed less than a year; but New York would figure large in his future career. Meanwhile, back home in Montreal he went on the road to read poetry in cafés and coffee shops. Dunn's Famous Steak House on Saint Catherine Street had a top floor room called Birdland, like a poet's pub, where Leonard would appear around midnight and 'perform'. Maury Kaye was the resident pianist/bandleader and a radio tape exists of Leonard reciting 'Gift' (from *The Spice-Box of Earth*), on April 8, 1958, over Kaye's sympathetic accompaniment. Quite how Leonard's stuff came across with a larger ensemble was not recorded.

A $3,000 Scholarship allowed Cohen to travel; he flew to London. He had been working for a while in his uncle's brass works (as described in 'Priests 1957' in *The Spice-Box Of Earth*), followed by a spell in the clothing factory. Leonard: "I was learning how to work a sewing machine." Shortly before he left, he shared an evening's poetry reading with Irving Layton and F.R. Scott in New York. Such joint public readings would become common for Cohen and Layton in the mid-Sixties; a film crew followed their October 1964 tour of universities, libraries and theatres in and around Toronto, London and Montreal – from which the Cohen footage was extracted and turned into a major feature documentary which boosted Leonard's career significantly.

London was cold and rainy. That's why and where he bought his blue raincoat. He stayed in Hampstead, a leafy north suburb, in the house of Mr and Mrs Pullman. (His Montreal sculptor friend Mort Rosengarten had stayed in the same area when he came to London.) After speaking to a suntanned Bank of Greece bank teller who told him where the sun was warm and the soft winds rode, Leonard booked a flight to Athens, leaving behind his London girlfriend. He settled on the small island of Hydra where he rented a house for $14 a month. He eventually bought one, for $1500, and maintains it to the present day.

'Hydra 1960' and dozens of other poems flowed from his pen during his seven-year (on-and-off) stay, resulting in the next three collections: *The Spice-Box Of Earth* (1961), *Flowers For Hitler* (1964) and *Parasites Of Heaven* (1966.) His two published novels: *The Favourite Game* (1963) and *Beautiful Losers* (1966) were completed there too. And he met Marianne, the estranged wife of Norwegian novelist Axel Jensen, and her infant son Axel (today a novelist himself). Leonard had met his Muse and she brought a sense of order and security to his somewhat chaotic *modus operandi*.

Shuttling back and forth from Hydra to Montreal for short bursts of remunerative journalism (and poetry readings – e.g. Toronto, May 1961) to pay for his new life on his Greek island with Marianne became an irregular routine. The second Canada Council Arts Scholarship he was awarded in 1960 for $1000 helped also. (In the mid-Sixties, Leonard interviewed for a job as a broadcast journalist with CBC; he did, in fact, interview the pianist Glenn Gould.) In an autobiographical short story called *Luggage Fire Sale*, dated 'Hydra, Greece, 1964' but not published until 1969, Leonard refers to having read several books in advance of a CBC programme he was recording in Paris. He and Irving Layton wrote some plays together in late 1960: *Enough Of Fallen Leaves* and *Lights On The Black Water* remain in manuscript; *A Man Was Killed* was finally published in 1977 and premièred in Montreal in 1983.

In April 1961 Cohen was arrested during a trip to Cuba. *The Spice-Box Of Earth* entered the bookshops in May. If it wasn't already evident in his first book, autobiographical elements were to become so in every Cohen book since – far too many references to quote in this brief study. The same is true, of course, for the novels and many of his songs. Reviews of this second collection of 58 poems (six with 'song' in the title) and a six-page 'Lady's Man' type piece 'Lines from My Grandfather's Journal', were mixed. The book is more erotic, insistent, elegant and accomplished; there is a whispered lyricism lacking in the more staid *Mythologies* book. Several texts were oft-recited in his Seventies concerts (e.g. 'Dead Song', 'Celebration'), and most of 'As The Mist Leaves No Scar' later became a song lyric in its own right.

Leonard spent the rest of 1961 and most of 1962 working to complete his 'next' novel (his earlier effort *Beauty At Close Quarters* having been rejected), which was eventually published in September 1963 with the title *The Favourite Game*. The book was in three parts, with no chapters, just numbered sections, representing different periods in the life of a Jewish man, the only son of wealthy parents, and his coming of age in Montreal. (The lack of 'formal' structure in so many pieces of prose or poetry was an early and distinct Cohen trademark; and indeed, one of his most recent poems, 'When Even The', in 'Stranger Music', 1992, demonstrated his continuing penchant for experimentation.) In October he collected a $500 1st Prize in Montreal from CBC in a Poetry Competition. A year later, he received nearly ten times as much for the Prix Litteraire du Quebec ($4000) for *The Favourite Game*.

Two more collections and his next novel were published while he continued living on Hydra. The island itself did not constitute a major element in his writings: women, religion, sex, death, blood, friends and friendship, loving and losing, guilt, pain and longing blackened page after page after page. *Flowers For Hitler*, dedicated to Marianne, was published in October 1964 – with Queen Victoria, Churchill, Eichmann, Rimbaud, Hitler, Goering, Goebbels, Marco Polo and Marianne covering pages of belligerent symbolism, piquant imagery and sentimentality: these are his Poems of Love and Hate. 'Style' has the lines "I will forget my style/ I have no style" and contradicts the plethora of styles in these 94 pieces: formal rhyming poems, prose-texts, lists, a Ballet-Drama in One Act (unperformed until 1993) and three line-drawings. (It was to be another 14 years before Cohen the Artist offered any more 'visuals'.) 'The Music Crept By

Us' became his most oft-quoted poem in concert. 'Queen Victoria' became a song lyric. Was it all Leonard's attempt to build his Tower of Poems? Using a wide variety of building blocks? Or was he dismantling it brick by brick ("I have no style") before it was toppled over in order to start again, somewhere else: "There is a whitewashed hotel waiting for me somewhere, in which I will begin my fast and my new life." ('The True Desire.') These latter sentiments indicated some dissatisfaction with his own personal *ménage à trois* on Hydra as he and Marianne (and Axel) spent less time in each other's company.

Leonard's early life was often captured on home-movies by his father; some were included in Don Owen and Donald Brittain's film-documentary *Ladies and Gentlemen . . . Mr Leonard Cohen* broadcast in 1965. The original intention was to promote the poetry tour (Toronto, Kitchener, London, Kingston and Montreal) in October 1964 by Cohen, Layton, Earle Birney and Phyllis Gotlieb – again, auspicious company for a 30-year old, but 'technical problems' meant that, in post-production, the focus was diverted to concentrate on Leonard's work on the tour. This film marked his first real entry onto the public platform as a writer of some distinction – and as a 'performer'. He is the first character we see on the screen – walking onto a stage in front of an applauding audience; many different scenes, both formal and informal, follow in the next 45 minutes: in the street, in shops, restaurants, hotels, a television studio round-table discussion, book-signings etc. Opinions on vegetarianism and the *I Ching* and sexuality are swopped with friends, and we hear recitations (some complete, most not) of poems from all his three published books and one, 'Here was the Market', later included in *Parasites Of Heaven.* Two versions of 'Twelve O'Clock Chant' are offered: the first as a poem, the second as a song (sounding much like a nascent 'Teachers'), the earliest footage of Cohen The Singer. "The film suggests . . . Cohen's sense of vulnerability and humbleness before the responsibility of his vision," wrote Ira Nadel – to which should be added Leonard's humour and candour.

19

1966 was certainly an *annus mirabilis* in Leonard's life. On February 14, he and Irving Layton read poetry and prose at the famous 92nd Street YM-YWHA Hostel. Leonard's selections were of four passages from his forthcoming novel *Beautiful Losers* and three poems: 'You All In White', 'For E.J.P.' and 'You Have The Lovers'. By now a seasoned performer, his delivery was confident, well-timed, clever. He was a 'voice-over' in *Angel*, a seven-minute film directed by his friend Derek May, one of his companions in *Ladies and Gentlemen* . . . and he made his Canadian national TV musical début on May 23 in *Take 30*, hosted by his friend Adrienne Clarkson, during which he sang 'The Stranger Song'. He sang no songs during a Canadian TV interview with Berly Fox, though he admitted: "I always thought of myself as a singer." Two books were published, *Beautiful Losers* (working titles had been *Plastic Birchbark* and *The History Of Them All*), and *Parasites Of Heaven*, his fourth collection of poems. The novel, "written to the sound of the Armed Forces radio station in Athens" was completed during 1965 with Leonard high on drugs most of the time and it is probably his best-known, if not his best, book. An earlier version called *Ballet Of Lepers* had been withdrawn. *The Listener* found it "extraordinary . . . a wild psalm to all the beautiful losers of sexual, racial and political exploitation." *Book Week* described it as "swirling, hallucinatory, squirty, intensely physical." The integration of various styles within the novel mirrors his attempts to do so poetically in *Flowers For Hitler*. It is far beyond the scope of this study to provide an in-depth analysis of *Beautiful Losers* – the reader is advised to seek out Buffy Sainte-Marie's recording of the 'God is alive. Magic is afoot' passage (from Book Two: 'A Long Letter From F') on her 1971 album 'Illuminations' (she has since released a 1995 re-recording) for a sound-world toe-dip into this 'love story, orgy, prayer, black mass, shriek, satire, joke, hallucination and religio-sexual epic.' Autobiographical too.

Parasites of Heaven, dedicated to Irving Layton, contained 58 pieces: 47 'conventional' poems and eleven prose-poems, with lines from as far back as 1957. Five poems were later incorporated into the songs 'Fingerprints', 'Master Song',

'Teachers', 'Avalanche' and 'Suzanne'. Gone are the effusive and hysterical tirades against politicians, mass-murderers, saints and sinners; Leonard targets 'you', 'we' and 'I' in over 70% of these title-less pieces which read more rhythmically and with a more distinct metre than any previous collection. It is an underestimated book, overshadowed by the reputations of earlier publications and his later song recordings.

Cohen's second poetry recording was issued by CBC on a double album, 'Canadian Poets 1', shared with Phyllis Webb, Earle Birney, John Newlove, Alfred Purdy, Irving Layton, George Bowering and Gwendolyn MacEwen. Described as "one of the most lyrically sensuous love poets of our time" (the hype was beginning to breed its own hybrid, you could tell), Leonard read seven poems: 'These Heroics' from *Let Us Compare Mythologies*, 'You Have The Lovers' and 'Now Of Sleeping' from *The Spice-Box Of Earth*, 'What I'm Doing Here' and 'Style' from *Flowers For Hitler*, and 'Two Went To Sleep' and 'Nothing Has Been Broken' from *Parasites Of Heaven*, still unpublished at the time. It's a serious and sober-toned ten-minute reading though still a little quick in the delivery compared to, say, Leonard's *Book Of Mercy* readings in 1985.

By July 1966 the restless pilgrim in his soul had tired of the to-ing and fro-ing between the climatic and domestic cauldron on Hydra and the 'frozen North' of North America. The *Toronto Star* reported him "hard at work writing songs". 'Tonight Will Be Fine' (acknowledged by Leonard as his first song), 'Rivers' ("All the rivers in the world couldn't wash away the tears in my eyes"), 'Store Room' and 'Everybody's Child' (neither performed until 1976, and sounding remarkably similar to 'Do I Have To Dance All Night' from that same year!) could be traced to his early songwriting days. In New York, where he recorded some 'demos' of these songs in the Vanguard Studios, there was talk of Garth Hudson – organ player in The Band – producing an album with Leonard after they had recorded some tracks together. His original plan had been to head down south to Nashville to make a record but, to use his own word, he got "hijacked" by the scene in New York

21

City. Leonard: "I became aware that there was something going on here ..." There were, admittedly, a few others hanging around: Dylan, Baez, Ochs, Blue, Joplin, Nico, Collins, Reed, Sedgwick, and during his initial stay at the Chelsea Hotel, Leonard saw and met most of them. He sang some songs for Judy Collins and she asked him to call her back when he had some more. He met John Hammond, the legendary A&R man who brought Billie Holiday, Bob Dylan and others to CBS. They had lunch. Back at the Chelsea, Leonard sang 'Suzanne', 'The Stranger Song', 'Master Song' and several others for him. Within a week, Leonard was in Columbia's Studio E, 49 East 52nd Street, recording his first album with John Hammond at the controls.

II

I Found My Place In The Chain

Long before Columbia had released Leonard's début album, his songs were being recorded by other singers. This practice has continued and today, thirty years later, there are near to 200 recorded 'covers' by different artists, in various languages, from all over the musical spectrum: the 'A to Z' includes Aaron Neville, Joe Cocker, Neil Diamond, Roberta Flack, Emmylou Harris, James, R.E.M. and Jennifer Warnes. Leonard's earliest, and probably best known, champion was Judy Collins who included 'Suzanne' and 'Dress Rehearsal Rag' on her late 1966 album 'In My Life'; and followed this a year later with 'Sisters Of Mercy', 'Priests' (to this day, still unrecorded and unperformed by Cohen, though also covered in 1969 by Richie Havens) and 'Hey, That's No Way To Say Goodbye' on 'Wildflowers', which was released a month or so before the public heard 'The Songs Of Leonard Cohen' for themselves. English singer Noel Harrison, son of actor Rex Harrison, sang 'Suzanne' on the *Ed Sullivan TV Show* and his cover got to No 56 in the US chart in October 1967. He had greater success in Britain early in 1969 with his Top Ten hit 'Windmills Of Your Mind'.

On April 6, Leonard read from *Beautiful Losers* to a capacity crowd in the Fillmore Room at the University Of Buffalo, sharing the evening's presentation as so often before with Irving Layton. With the stage to himself he sang 'Suzanne', 'The Stranger Song', 'Master Song', 'The Bells' (or at least an early version of 'Take This Longing') and 'Love Calls You By Your Name'. A report published in *Introspectum*, on April 11, also noted: "Spurred on by a receptive audience, Cohen performed three encores." Leonard must have felt it time to 'go public', for real.

His first acknowledged 'bona fide' appearance into the 'racket' (as he himself often called it) of musical performance in front of a paying audience took place three weeks later and was all down to Judy Collins. She persuaded him to go onstage during her anti-Vietnam Benefit Concert in New York's Town Hall, on April 30, 1967. They both tell the story of his breaking down as he sang 'Suzanne', leaving the stage, retuning his guitar and going back to finish the song.

Leonard sang at Newport in July 1967 on a bill that included Judy Collins, Pete Seeger, Arlo Guthrie, Gordon Lightfoot and Buffy Sainte-Marie. Photographs of the event by David Gahr have appeared in many publications – those with Leonard include his well-known hug with Joni Mitchell. A few days later, in New York's Central Park, he performed two evening shows. In August, he sang at the 7th Annual Mariposa Folk Festival at Innis Lake, near Caledon East. Other performances that year were at Canada's Expo '67, the Big Sur Festival in California, and on CBS's Sunday morning cultural affairs programme, *Camera Three*, in September which, according to the *New York Times*, elicited "the greatest audience response in the show's 14 year history." (His appearance on *Austin City Limits* in 1988 was to effect a similar reaction.) It's probably safe to assume his song-choice comprised many of the titles heard in Buffalo and New York. Leonard's other television spot in 1967 was as Julie Felix's guest on her BBC show *Once More With Felix* in London. Her gracious introduction mentioned that *Beautiful Losers* had still not been published in England. (Jonathan Cape published it in 1970.) Leonard sang an entrancing solo 'The Stranger Song' (and I'm sure that's a tear in his hazel eye at the end), then they duetted comfortably on 'Hey, That's No Way To Say Goodbye': Leonard on verse 1, Julie on 2, together on the last. It is worth bearing in mind that after those early 1967 appearances with Judy Collins (echoing Joan Baez's sponsorship of Bob Dylan), Leonard has never since been a guest in any other singer's concerts, nor has he himself invited anyone else onstage with him!

Leonard wrote some music for Don Owen's 1967 film *The Ernie Game* and appeared in it himself, at a party, singing 'The Stranger Song'. Another Cohen-related film was also televised that year: *Poen* – a 5-minute feast of various strikingly graphic images, both sacred and secular, edited/directed by Josef Reeve, to a passage from *Beautiful Losers* (Book One, section 9, beginning "my mind seems to go out on a path" to "we are part of a necklace [pronounced 'neck lace'] of incomparable beauty and unmeaning"), read on the soundtrack by Leonard himself.

And then finally, came the real thing: 'Songs Of Leonard Cohen', with the Canadian songwriter-now-singer looking older than his 33 years, gazing out from the sepia-coloured photograph (by 'Machine' – was it really taken in a photo-booth?) which adorned the front cover, was launched at the turn of 1967-68 into a market already offering 'Sergeant Pepper's Lonely Hearts Club Band' from The Beatles, 'The Last Waltz' from Engelbert Humperdinck and 'Their Satanic Majesties Request' from The Rolling Stones. LPs from Tom Jones, Val Doonican, The Supremes and The Four Tops were all high in the charts too. Bob Dylan's 'John Wesley Harding' had a catalogue number just 11 digits on from Leonard's CBS 63421. In the singles' chart, Louisiana's John Fred & His Playboy Band, named after Hugh Hefner's girlie magazine, with their good time stomp 'Judy In Disguise' was the only act common to both UK and US listings in January 1968. Several Cohen songs from this first album were chosen as singles: 'Suzanne', of course, 'Sisters Of Mercy', 'So Long, Marianne', in many different countries: Canada, France, Holland (and in later years too with a variety of couplings from other albums) but none made any impression at all. Leonard Cohen has never had a 'hit single'.

The album leads with 'Suzanne', still Leonard's most famous song. And probably his most written-about song too –

though more from the lyrical point-of-view than the musical. 'Suzanne' was not the Suzanne with whom he later lived, after he had left Marianne, and therefore not the mother of their children Adam and Lorca. (That was Suzanne Elrod.) This Suzanne was Suzanne Vaillancourt, wife of a sculptor friend of Leonard's in Montreal. Their time together was platonic; they drank tea – 'Constant Comment' tea, a blend of orange rind and tea leaves. She lived near the St. Lawrence river which runs through Montreal. The song was merely (to use Leonard's word) "reportage". It's great poetry too. In fact, that was its first incarnation – as a poem in 'Parasites of Heaven' published the previous year. (An earlier poem, 'Suzanne wears a leather coat', from 1963, appeared in the same collection.) But it doesn't sound like a poem set at a later date to music. Each image and every line offers its own interpretation; ultimately though it's a *song* – "in which all the loneliness and pain of the beautiful loser is transmuted into joy", as Stephen Scobie judged in his 1978 Cohen study. Leonard later mused that perhaps 'his' Suzanne was in some way summoned by the spirit of the song, which was written over a 4-5 month period in Montreal.

The melody flows as easy as the river and the sun pouring down like honey. There's even an inevitability in Cohen's use of the four consecutive chords – E, F sharp minor, G sharp minor and A – which is certainly not 'Classical' by any means but it is *the* Cohen classic. From Leonard's gentle combination of slightly cautious tenor and assured acoustic guitar picking to the cooing female backup vocals, provided by producer John Simon's girlfriend. Simon's own contribution on piano was left out of the final mix which Leonard himself prepared for the album.

The second verse introduced Jesus for the first time in a Cohen song; He had previously been presented in 'For Wilf And His House' (and others) in Leonard's first book, *Let Us Compare Mythologies*. In the 1980 documentary *Song Of Leonard Cohen*, directed by Harry Rasky, Leonard explained thus: "Notre Dame de Bon Secours [the church that overlooks

Montreal harbour] is a church for sailors. Inside the church there are models of ships hanging and the sailors are blessed from that church. So the very next verse moves very easily to the idea that Jesus was a sailor . . ."

No doubt we all have our own personal image of Suzanne. Leonard's was included in his 1983 video-drama *I Am A Hotel.* The real Suzanne has since left Montreal. In 1992, she and her 19-year old son Kahlil were reported (by Jack Todd in *Montreal Gazette*, May 21) to have headed off "on an indefinite journey through the United States."

Leonard's voice sounds tired and choked at the beginning of the next track 'Master Song', but it improves as it goes on. The original version of these lyrics was in *Parasites Of Heaven*, but unlike the previous masterpiece, this *does* sound like a poem set to music. It is more of an 'Art Song', almost a technical exercise with clever chords, verse after verse and no chorus, and a complicated *ménage à trois* to follow involving a master, a pupil and a prisoner. There's fine use of stereo in the production including bass and strings.

The eight-second fade-in for 'Winter Lady' is a non-intro but it is a splendid little song. Another guitar, flute and bells are added to flesh out Leonard's wistful vocals filled with longing and wanting, memories and regret. All in just two verses. And basically just two chords – D and A, with a couple of bars in C and a few more in A minor. Robert Altman used this song to great effect in his movie *McCabe & Mrs Miller* a couple of years later. Apart from 'Minute Prologue' on 'Live Songs', this is Cohen's shortest song.

Leonard's sense of loneliness continued in 'The Stranger Song', perpetuating the theme evident in his earlier poems. He'd been singing this song for a couple of years before recording it and has sung it on every concert tour since except in 1993. He'd even sung it on national television in Canada in 1966, long before his credentials as a singer and songwriter, had been formulated. And it's a theme that he would continue to promote in many more songs.

There is much powerful imagery in these ten verses and it is a style of performance that has remained unchanged for 30 years. The whole of Altman's film *McCabe & Mrs Miller* has been described as the perfect two-hour promo video for this song.

In many concerts, and interviews too, Leonard himself has supplied the visual commentary for the fifth track, 'Sisters Of Mercy' – namely Barbara and Lorraine, two girls he met one night sheltering from a snowstorm in Edmonton, Alberta, who went back to his room. As they slept, by the light of the moon on the Saskatchewan river, he wrote this song and it was ready next morning. (He'd already had the melody beforehand.)

In the days of vinyl, side two immediately offered a sadder scenario with two songs of parting: 'So Long, Marianne' and 'Hey, That's No Way To Say Goodbye', yet both are bitter-sweet with a musicality that defied the oh-so-obvious minor key and slow lament formula. The former turns on its upbeat tempo, whilst the songbook includes a seventh verse not on the record. Leonard has sung it in concert, rarely though – Stockholm and Frankfurt in 1972 and Toronto 1993 are known for sure.

Leonard wrote 'Hey, That's No Way To Say Goodbye' in the Penn Terminal Hotel in New York in 1966. It is a simpler four-chord farewell in three verses. Two lovers are parting and the man is keen to make the break a gracious one while still harbouring mutually fond memories. Leonard (as ever, the Master of his own Density): "I was living in a brown hotel room . . . I was with the wrong woman, as usual . . . but as you Eastern Metaphysicians know, just as from the darkest mud blooms the whitest lotus, so from the brownest hotel room, you occasionally get a good song." (Montreux, 1976.) The story is told that Marianne saw Leonard's rough drafts of this song on his desk and questioned him as to who it was for.

There's a hard edge to the next couple of songs providing stark contrast to the preceding love-songs. 'Stories Of The Street', stories from the street more like, as viewed from his hotel room (itself a recurring leitmotif in Cohen's personal and professional lives) presents a bleak picture of Cohen's present situation (poison gas, suicide, war) – even back then his future was murder. His voice is desperation in these lines backed by strong acoustic strumming and various guitars and keyboard. No girls needed this time. There *is* a crack though in verse five where the light gets in, when he imagines a domestic scenario that is safe and warm, his shelter from the storm, but it doesn't last long. The ending is quite abrupt too after the A to A minor chord change. The lyrics are omitted in the 1993 'Stranger Music' collection.

'Teachers' was the third and last of these songs to have first been published in *Parasites Of Heaven,* and is similar in form to 'Master Song'. It's another angle on the Master/Pupil theme too. Leonard chants each of the 13 verses in a steady, unfaltering voice. The only known live version of this song was given before a BBC television audience in the summer of 1968 and it's a better performance: Leonard varied the vocal line a little more and his double bass and keyboard back-up added a nice sense of involvement which is missing from the original's relentless repetition.

We know from John Hammond's reminiscences of his working with Leonard, before he became unwell and was replaced by John Simon, on this first album that candles, incense and mirrors were important elements present in Studio E as Leonard recorded these songs. The final track, 'One Of Us Cannot Be Wrong', one of very few Cohen song titles not extracted in some way from a line in the lyric, brings this whole set-up to life. Leonard calls it 'Thin Green Candle'. It's a finely crafted song (written in the Chelsea Hotel), well within Leonard's vocal range, featuring just him and his guitar, but it hardly provided the album with a convenient happy ending since after four highly personal verses, full of strong imagery, Leonard's pained screams are the last noises heard on the fade-out. Yet it leaves the listener in suspense for some kind of resolution in the 'next episode', as it were. Some concert performances in the Seventies involved Leonard blowing through his hands as the instrumental 'coda', so to speak, and he would often warn his audiences not to be alarmed at the sight of his hands leaving his guitar.

Leonard expressed some dissatisfaction with his first album. Not with the words – the mystical eloquence of his lyrics provided an intellectual foil for the still rampant (though waning) late Sixties psychedelia. He has always been Alternative. In an interview with Ritchie Yorke for *Toronto Globe and Mail* in February, 1969, he remarked: ". . . the music got a little away from me." It was not, as we shall hear, a mistake he repeated on his second album.

III

The Heart Has Got To Open

Words remained Cohen's main métier. *Selected Poems 1956-1968* was published later in mid-1968 by Viking Press (USA) and the following year by Jonathan Cape (UK), containing selections, actually made by Marianne, from each of Leonard's four previous volumes as well as some twenty 'New Poems'. This latter material provided as good a promotional package of Leonard's notions on loving and losing as most of the songs on the début album. (The second verse of 'Who Will Finally Say' is the third verse of 'A Bunch Of Lonesome Heroes'. Also, though out of context here, 'Joan Of Arc' is summoned in 'I Met You', and 'Edmonton, Alberta' reads like a non-identical twin of 'Famous Blue Raincoat'.) The book's success was immediate – Ira Nadel quotes figures of almost 200,000 copies in the first three months after publication. It won for Leonard the Canadian Governor General's Literary Award for Poetry in 1969. He refused it, telegramming: ". . . the poems themselves forbid it absolutely."

Leonard flew to London for some BBC work. 'You Know Who I Am', 'Bird On The Wire', 'Hey, That's No Way To Say Goodbye', 'So Long, Marianne' and 'Dress Rehearsal Rag', the last included at the request of Fairport Convention singer Sandy Denny who was present in the studio at the time, were recorded on July 9 for John Peel's *Top Gear* Radio 1 programme. John Peel: ". . . it really was one of the nicest sessions we've ever had, it was just incredible." The first four songs were broadcast five days later; 'Dress Rehearsal Rag' was aired on August 11. With Dave Cousins of the English group The

Strawbs on banjo, three unidentified backup singers, drums, piano and bass, Leonard sounds relaxed, particularly on 'Bird On The Wire', taken at quite a nifty pace. (A few more background details are in the splendid book *In Session Tonight*, a comprehensive run-down of the Peel sessions, by Ken Garners.) John Peel: ". . . if Leonard Cohen ever comes back to this country I vote that they give him an entire *Top Gear* to himself." It was not to be.

Leonard went on to record 12 songs for television, in front of a studio audience, broadcast on BBC 2 on consecutive Saturdays, August 31 and September 7, but it would be another 25 years before he sang on the BBC again, on BBC 2's *Later With Jools Holland* in May 1993. His 1968 TV choice comprised 'You Know Who I Am', 'Bird On The Wire', 'The Stranger Song', 'So Long, Marianne', 'Master Song', 'Sisters Of Mercy', 'Teachers', 'Dress Rehearsal Rag', 'Suzanne', 'Hey, That's No Way To Say Goodbye', 'Story Of Isaac' and 'One Of Us Cannot Be Wrong', thus eight songs from the first album, three from the as yet unreleased (and unfinished) second, and 'Dress Rehearsal Rag' which would not be issued until 1971, on the third album. A non-official CD, 'Leonard Cohen At The Beeb' was issued in 1993 containing 11 of these dozen songs. He's in confident vocal form. The arrangements are pretty similar to the album versions, but you can just tell it was a live gig. At one stage, he improvised a charming little good-humoured self-deprecating refrain, inviting the audience to join in – "No, it wasn't any good/ There's no reason why you should/ Remember me."

Leonard met 61-year old Joshu Sasaki, aka Roshi (= 'teacher'), in 1968. They were introduced to each other by Steve Sanfield, a friend from the mid-Sixties on Hydra. (Leonard wrote 'to' Steve in his 1963 poem "I see you on a Greek mattress.") Sasaki, a Zen Buddhist, had come to the USA in July 1962 and was now running a monastery dedicated to Rinzai Buddhism (a discipline "demanding genuine insight, not mere lip-service, in the scriptures, with a life consonant with that insight" – Dorman & Rawlins), at Mount Baldy, 6,500 feet up in the San Gabriel Mountains, in the middle of a national forest, about 50 miles east of Los Angeles. (All three were photographed together, by Don Farber, in 1993 at celebrations of Roshi's 86th birthday and his 30th year of teaching in the USA.) Leonard, the inveterate disciplinarian – think of his self-imposed regime on Hydra while writing *Beautiful Losers*, and years before in London when Stella Pullman ensured he had written his three pages per day – tried it out for a few weeks, but didn't really take to it. Not at first. He went back for a few months at a time every year for nearly 25 years! Just as in the Sixties he kept going back to Montreal to "renew his neurotic affiliations", his habit of going back up the mountain to Mount Baldy became a dominant feature of his Eighties and Nineties life-style. He did it more for the physical exertion – "shovelling snow, scrubbing floors, cooking and working in a communal kitchen" according to *People* magazine, March 25, 1996 – and meditating than for any sort of 'religious' education. As if to debunk his own Zen credentials completely, Leonard often credits Roshi with merely teaching him how to drink! In 1994, he finally 'moved in'. References to Leonard's teacher have appeared occasionally in his writings, most obviously in *Death Of A Lady's Man*, and *Book Of Mercy* is dedicated to Roshi.

While he may have wanted to go to Mount Baldy for some sort of rest, his record company was not content to let him rest on his laurels. The success of his début album in the USA was unspectacular, only reaching No 83 in the charts, while in Britain it climbed to a heady No 13 and remained in listings for over 70 weeks. Leonard confessed to *Zigzag* magazine in March 1970 to not planning to record another album, thinking it unnecessary. But pressure from Columbia and his manager prevailed. He went to Hydra for a while; then holed up for a few months writing songs in a hotel bedroom in California. Then he met Bob Johnston, who had recently worked with Bob Dylan on 'John Wesley Harding' and 'Nashville Skyline', and later in 1969 again on 'Self Portrait'. (Johnston subsequently joined Leonard's band The Army and played concerts in Europe in May 1970 and again in March/April 1972.) They went to Nashville and recorded some songs. But Leonard was unhappy with the initial results. The *Zigzag* interview related how he went back to his hotel room, depressed . . . but after some days spent rewriting, went back into the studio and completed the album as we now know it.

At the time, Leonard was renting a cabin and some farmland in Franklin, Tennessee, from the songwriter Boudleaux Bryant for $75 per month. He had separated from Marianne and was now living with 19-year-old painter Suzanne Elrod whom Leonard had met in an elevator in Manhattan. He may well have been out of sight but thousands upon thousands did not forget him. Sales of his second album 'Songs From A Room', released in Spring of 1969, boosted it to No 2 in the UK charts. In the US it fared rather worse, peaking at No 63. The room in question was in Leonard's house back on Hydra and in which, for the album's rear cover, a smiling Marianne was photographed, sitting at one of two tables, hands poised on the typewriter he had bought in London. The shutters are closed. The walls are bare. There is only one bed, only one chair.

'Songs Of' presented certain doom-laden and crestfallen situations; this new collection of songs sought to soothe. Whereas 'Songs Of' seemed at times to delight in mental anguish, these new songs were a less than glorious paean to pain. Bleak may have been their colour, but the final song 'Tonight Will Be Fine' seemed an attempt to leave the listener with a less dismal scenario. The album acknowledges a more sentient viewpoint, e.g. "Sometimes I *need* you naked/ Sometimes I *need* you wild" ('You Know Who I Am'), "*None* of us were strong" . . . "We *told* her she was beautiful" ('It Seems So Long Ago, Nancy' – my emphases).

Most Cohen followers would claim this to be his best album. Yet, as was the case with his next, 'Songs Of Love And Hate', it is represented in 'Stranger Music' with only five out of the ten tracks printed.

Just as the début album ended with Cohen's unaccompanied voice, so did the follow-up begin, with 'Bird On The Wire', on a two-note phrase that precedes the instrumentation. It was probably not the first song they recorded. Leonard's voice is gentle, but it sounds cracked and tired; apt indeed. He has to stretch for some notes in the chorus. His sleeve-notes for the song on the 'Greatest Hits' collection admit to not getting the song 'perfect', but bearing in mind the quite prosaic circumstances which first inspired him to write the song (Leonard: ". . . and outside my window the telephone company had put up a wire, and on that wire sat a bird . . ."), it'll do nicely. 'Bird On The Wire' opened almost every European concert on every tour from 1970 to mid-1988. It was released as the album's lead-single in the UK (c/w 'Seems So Long Ago, Nancy', CBS 4262), but on French and Dutch vinyl it was relegated to the B-side for 'The Partisan' as the A-side.

From one Cohen theme of an individual and his struggle to be free to another: Religion. In 'Story Of Isaac', Leonard used the Abraham and Isaac story to express concern about how an individual can be sacrificed to an Idea – a "scheme", a "vision", thereby also revisiting familiar themes of the wounded victim (also later in 'Field Commander Cohen') and the 'soldier as loser' (in 'The Captain'.) The Father and Son theme was also later evident in, among others, 'Queen Victoria', 'Lover Lover Lover' and 'Night Comes On'.

There's a clipped delivery in this song. The voice is steady, unfaltering, the "very cold" of line six, backed by acoustic guitar, Jew's harp and bass as in the first song. Thin high synth chords hover in verse two over the mountain, the broken bottle of wine and the altar, through to the end. One is tempted to concur with Stephen Scobie's assessment that 'A Bunch Of Lonesome Heroes' "remains intriguing but inconclusive." It doesn't start that way though – there's the confident 'Marianne'-esque strumming (in the same strong key of A major too) and Leonard's matter-of-fact opening lines printed as 'spoken rather than sung' in the songbook. With 'military' and 'loser' themes, the song has become a predictable Cohen-on-guitar with Jew's harp and bass vehicle, this time with the added colouring of a 'kazoo'-sounding instrument which may well be an electronic keyboard contraption. The unexpected cymbal crash and drums at 2'30" emphasise the soldier's repeated desire to tell his story; and then you realise he's only readvertising the 'gold' reference in 'The Cuckold's Song' from *The Spice-Box Of Earth*. There are no reports of this song ever having been sung in public.

'The Partisan', on the other hand, featured in most concerts from 1970 until 1988. It was not included in 1993. This is the first non-Cohen song on disc. It was not included in the songbook. (Unlike another 'cover', 'Be For Real' by Frederick Knight which *was* printed in the 1993 'The Future' songbook.) Leonard: "I learned this from a friend when I was 15. He was 17 . . . We were working at a camp in Ste. Marguerite, Quebec. We sang together every morning, going through The People's Song Book from cover to cover. I developed the curious notion that the Nazis were overthrown by music" (from his sleeve-notes to 'Greatest Hits'). The song certainly had anti-Nazi credentials. The words and music were written in 1944 by Anna Marly who ran a hostel in London for French nationals during the war. She herself had recorded it but the tapes, en route to the French Resistance, were accidentally destroyed after a parachute drop; it was then simply passed on in the old oral tradition, by word of mouth.

It sounds like a song Leonard could have written – a Song Of Lamentation with acoustic guitar accompaniment. He sings the English translation by Hy Zaret (of 1950s classic 'Unchained Melody' fame) omitting verse two (out of six), and altering "Germans" in his third verse to just "soldiers". Charlie Daniels' bass never throbbed better and producer Bob Johnston's inclusion of a French accordion into the mix was a great touch. Even better though, just when you think the song is over Corlynn Hanney and Sue Mussmano join with Leonard to reprise the first three verses in French. This combination compounds the sadness with its specific mention of "Les All'mands" . . . and *that* accordion!

'Seems So Long Ago, Nancy' is another sad song, sung sadly. Leonard: "A song I wrote for a young woman in Montreal." Similar in style to 'Winter Lady'. Play them back to back and Leonard's fingerprints are scattered all over them like confetti: slightly distant miking, touch of echo, nostalgic, regretful – with (by now) typical guitar picking, of course, but with a more sophisticated chordal structure making it quite distinctive if you *listen* out for the major-minor-major interplay. The year 1961 is identified: Leonard was in his 27th. Now that was some year: *The Spice-Box Of Earth* was published and the Cuban Bay Of Pigs fiasco with Castro!

Such lyrics as "so long ago", "alone", "no one at all" (repeated) in just the first verse are the real backdrop of the song. It's a song about suicide; in its own way it's as brave a song about such subject matter as was Cohen's inclusion of 'The Partisan' in his German concerts. It's a reportage song not unlike 'Suzanne' and 'Sisters Of Mercy' and shares with them both a 'happy' ending – in that the 'spirit' of Nancy is evoked in such a way as to leave the listener in some degree of comfort, with the realisation that her corporeal ordeal is indeed long gone. Remember, this guy is a poet. The song should have made it onto 'Greatest Hits'.

Images of soldiers, killers, war and death recur in 'The Old Revolution'. Not in the literal sense: Leonard uses them this time to clothe his theme of "The Daily Struggle" in a variety of forms: eg. Rich vs. Poor. Leonard offered no solution, preferring to invite the listener to share his suffering. The music is warm, employing the album's now standard quartet: bass, Jew's harp, Leonard's guitar and Bob Johnston's adeptly minimalist keyboard work, especially effective with its higher register contributions on verse four. Cohen's well-phrased singing *combines* with this, as opposed to singing *over* it – the sublime effect contrasting, as earlier on 'The Story Of Isaac', with the violent lyrics.

'The Butcher' is Leonard's first song about drugs, but far from hyping the hypodermic, the whole lyric seems to be a self-engendered hallucination, at times confused, at others pitiful. "I think that drugs without a sacrament, without a ritual, without a really great understanding of their power are dangerous," Leonard told Zig-Zag's Robin Pike in September 1974. The voice sounds tortured, tired, troubled, struggling to get to the heart of some notes. Marked "very slow" in the songbook, Leonard begins at about 80 beats-per-minute but by the end he has accelerated into the mid-90s, perhaps to keep apace with his desperate last verse. Aptly too, it's just Leonard and his guitar – "broken down". In live performances during the mid-Seventies tours, this song was subjected to a raucous mauling quite unlike any other Cohen song before or since. One 1976 outing (Paris, June 6) was issued as the B-side of a 7" single (A-side: 'Do I Have To Dance All Night?", also live from Paris, and likewise, not on any Cohen album).

The affirmation of "I am what I am" in 'The Butcher' is extended in 'You Know Who I Am', a vignette of contrariness, in which a seemingly dead-end liaison is given no hope in one verse after another, only for it to be resuscitated in the intervening choruses. A pervasive sense of resignation gives way, albeit briefly, to hope at the end of verse three. Corlynn Hanney and Sue Mussmano, where were you?

'Lady Midnight' attempts a waltz-like personification of "The Darkness" (making it a distant relative of 'Our Lady Of Solitude' on 'Recent Songs' in 1979). Musically straightforward, as the mourning becomes the morning, Leonard's comfortable melody line and the repeated "You've won me" seem to suggest, and on this album not for the first time, some degree of assurance.

As if to confirm, and then to further underline, the album's *raison d'être*, the final song 'Tonight Will Be Fine', another three-chorder, recapitulates the themes of self-will, loving and losing, desperation and hope with the singer mulling over a past and failed relationship, inside the very room itself, described in some detail in verse two. (Leonard sings "almost bare" instead of "must be bare.") Leonard may well have had recourse to think of the past as he, Marianne and Axel, after all his to-ing and fro-ing between Montreal, Hydra, Tennessee and New York, had now finally parted company. They subsequently returned to her native Oslo. The song was written in the Hotel de France, on Saint Catherine Street, Montreal and Leonard acknowledged it as his "first song" as such, as opposed to his previous poetry- and prose-writing. Stephen Scobie remarked that the penultimate line "suggests the same desperate attempt to escape history as is found in *Beautiful Losers*." With the final line itself and the long 'da daa' into the hands-and-whistling fade-out, Leonard signed off for the second consecutive time on a non-verbal 'note', though in comparison to the début disc's, it's less abrasive. Live performances transformed the song into a countrified clap-along – the 1970 version from the Isle Of Wight Festival on 'Live Songs' is a fair example, as are later versions, often including extra lyrics, where the verses are sung a shade less exuberantly than the intoxicating chorus.

Leonard and Suzanne lived for a while in the Tennessee backwoods and then headed for the Greek district of Montreal; a few years later they moved across to a house on rue Vallières, opposite Parc du Portugal. And so began another long chapter in Leonard's own Book Of Changes which would see him blacken more pages (and blot his copybook too), producing in the next decade or so, two books and four albums, and give more than 200 concerts – mostly in Europe (tours in alternate years between 1970–76 and again in 1979) where his popularity and fame far exceeded that in North America. Indeed, at the time of writing (1996), this situation still prevails, though unlike in the Seventies when Leonard was seemingly quite content to concentrate his efforts in Europe, and ignore his home audience, he certainly set about making his music more widely known and accepted in Canada and America with major tours there in 1988 and 1993 (over 60 concerts combined compared to about half that number in the years 1975-85).

With his domestic arrangements now in less disarray, Leonard began work on the songs for his next album (one of four to be released in the Seventies) in March 1970. He teamed up again with Bob Johnston in Nashville.

Given Leonard's self-confessed propensity to "want to show off", it was only a matter of time before he took his show on the road. In May 1970, he and his 'Army' gave his first 'real' concerts in Europe and straightaway we heard what had become the typical Cohen 'sound': Leonard strumming away on acoustic guitar, female backup singers and an emphasis on melody and lyric – scene-setting and story-telling – which in his case, therefore, meant no distracting drum kit! It wasn't until the late 1975 dates in the USA that drums were introduced. The 'Army' came with a good pedigree: Ron Cornelius, Charlie Daniels and Bubba Fowler had, along with producer Johnston who put the band together, all recently recorded with Bob Dylan; bassist Daniels would later form his own band.

With only two albums behind him, there weren't that many songs for Leonard to choose from. At least 20 were performed every night, almost without any variation. From 'Songs Of Leonard Cohen', he chose six: 'Suzanne', 'The Stranger Song', 'Sisters Of Mercy', 'So Long, Marianne', 'Hey, That's No Way To Say Goodbye' and 'One Of Us Cannot Be Wrong'; while seven were from 'Songs From A Room': 'Bird On The Wire', 'Story Of Isaac', 'The Partisan', 'Seems So Long Ago, Nancy', 'You Know Who I Am', 'Lady Midnight' and 'Tonight Will Be Fine'. Their arrangements were quite similar to the album versions – just a bit louder. Already they had become self-chosen 'Greatest Hits'! The new songs (some as yet unrecorded, but all later released on the 1971 'Songs Of Love And Hate') were 'Avalanche', 'Diamonds In The Mine', 'Famous Blue Raincoat', 'Sing Another Song, Boys' and 'Joan Of Arc'. The other two were 'Un As Der Rebbe Singt', an old Jewish traditional 'chant', on which Leonard accompanied himself on guitar, and the full band finale 'Please Don't Pass Me By'. Leonard also recited some poem or other during every concert: 'Dead Song', 'Celebration', 'Travel' and 'For E.J.P.', thus initiating a practice he was to continue throughout the Seventies.

But Leonard, lest we forget, was no novice concert performer. True, his appearances at the 1967 Festivals and on BBC Television in London (1968) were somewhat less arduous than the rigours now demanded of him on stage for the performance of 20 songs (usually in two more or less equal sets), but they will have provided him with some resilience against the rigours of staying on for up to 90 minutes, and often more, in this, his first, series of full-length concerts. 'He who dares, wins'.

For the 1970 Frankfurt show Cohen was really 'clear'; he and the Army hit a groove and rolled along it with 'So Long, Marianne' and 'Hey, That's No Way To Say Goodbye' framing the evening's session, which was crowned by 'Suzanne', and then insummarily dethroned by the unexpected 13-minute encore 'Please Don't Pass Me By'. Lots of the audience ended up onstage. (Burr Snider caught it all for *Gypsy I, No 1*, reprinted in Michael Gnarowski's 1976 anthology.) The recording deserves official release.

Reviews in *New Musical Express* and *Record Mirror* praised his London concert as much for his words as for the music. The tapes reveal a simple and uncluttered approach to the songs, similar to his 1968 BBC Television performances. There was a good rapport with the audience too. Many songs were introduced, briefly, which afforded them a touch of dignity, especially the new ones, of which only 'Joan Of Arc' (no applause at the beginning, of course) featured in the first set each night. Only the London audience heard 'Avalanche' (also greeted in silence, of course), but it has since featured as an acoustic highlight (except in 1974 and 1975). 'The Stranger Song' was also included in the first set and has been performed in almost every concert on every tour ever since, except in 1993. The first set closed, in contrast to its muted opening, indeed to the whole session thus far, with a rousing 'Tonight Will Be Fine'. This performance must have sent out seismic psychic shockwaves to Cohen followers (and to the curious alike each night!) since it was *such* a departure from both his intimate concert style and from the version on 'Songs

From A Room'. (By the time they got to hear, never mind see, him singing it in his Isle Of Wight appearance in August of that year, and then bought 'Live Songs', it won't have come as such a surprise.)

Normality was seemingly restored after the interval with a second set which began with a couple of less frenzied tales: Corlynn Hanney and Sue Mussmano were typically effective in 'The Partisan' (not one to shirk the political jibe – cf. Cuba 1961; Greece and the military coup, 1967 – Leonard dedicated this song to the memory of the four students shot dead by the National Guard at Kent University for protesting against the USA's involvement in the Vietnam War), and 'Sisters Of Mercy'. There then followed, in the words of Dana's winning effort in the recent 1970 Eurovision Song Contest, "all kinds of everything" – one up-tempo Song of Hate, two low-key Love Songs, and then the same combo again, before the show concluded with the biggest rabble-rouser of the evening, and of Leonard's entire career, ever: a 13-minute diatribe called 'Please Don't Pass Me By'. This song, despite its seemingly and interminably complex structure as printed in the 'Greatest Hits' songbook is partly sung, partly rapped, partly chanted and the rest just improvised with a verve, and a nerve, that positively confounded the stereotypical Cohenite. In the song, Leonard bared himself as never before, or since, and expressed an urgent desire to his audience to empathise with his suffering on behalf of the "Jews . . . Gypsies . . . children of England . . . a Saviour with no-one to save . . . blonde beasts . . . freaks . . . cripples . . . hunchbacks . . . the burned . . . the burning . . . maimed . . . broken . . . torn . . . those that get talked about . . . the hunted . . . the down . . ."

He was still not a happy man when interviewed during the following day's party according to Caroline Boucher in *Disc and Music Echo*, May 16, and a week later by "The Crawling Eye" in *Record Mirror*. The Poetry Reading he gave later that evening at the Institute for Contemporary Art (admittance was limited to ICA members only) was a happier affair though.

Norman Maycock was there: "Leonard started off by asking the audience, probably no more than a couple of hundred, what they wanted him to read! He read for about an hour at the most from his poems and also from *Beautiful Losers* . . . I'm sure the whole ICA crowd were just longing for him to reach for a guitar and sing a few songs; someone asked him to, but he said he wasn't allowed to for contractual reasons; someone in the audience offered him a guitar but he still wouldn't; someone suggested we should all go across the Mall to St. James's Park and then he could sing, but to no avail. It was all very good-humoured . . ." Plans for another BBC 'special' later in the month also met with no success.

A couple of days later Leonard and The Army stormed the Olympia in Paris. As at Frankfurt, the audience stormed the stage. The police were called. *Le Nouvel Observateur* later hailed him 'le folksinger de l'année'.

The following month, Parisian audiences heard more Cohen, this time in the form of Brian Macdonald's reading of nine poems (mostly from *The Spice-Box Of Earth*) as part of the soundtrack for a new ballet *The Shining People Of Leonard Cohen*, performed by The Royal Winnipeg Ballet Company. Macdonald, a fellow-graduate of McGill University, had met Leonard back in 1964 and discussed with him then the idea of doing a ballet to his verses. In later years, other artistic endeavours (plays, revues, films, paintings et al.) were to be inspired through a knowledge of Leonard's work and one group, Sisters of Mercy, even took their name from a Cohen song.

Leonard's next entry on to a French stage was atop a white horse on August 2 in Aix-en-Provence, sunny southern France. Leonard's reduced 11-song set (with just two new songs: 'Joan Of Arc' and 'Diamonds In The Mine') was broadcast on French AM radio. This was a week after a set at a Folk Festival at Forest Hills, New York, and a month before his Isle Of Wight Festival performance, famous for many reasons other than his participation.

The third (and last) Isle Of Wight Festival took place on

43

East Afton Farm, Freshwater, over four days from Friday, August 28 to Monday, August 31. It has been described, among other things, as "the British Woodstock" and "the last great festival". It certainly boasted a sensational line-up: The Doors, The Moody Blues, The Who, Chicago, Joni Mitchell, Kris Kristofferson, Joan Baez, Donovan, Procol Harum, Miles Davis, Free, Ralph McTell, Emerson, Lake and Palmer, Jethro Tull and Jimi Hendrix (his last UK gig before his death on September 18).

Leonard and The Army, hardened concert-veterans by now, sang most of what could be called their normal programme: 14 songs with three Cohen poems – in concert order: 'Dead Song', 'They Locked Up A Man' (from the as yet unpublished 1972 collection *The Energy Of Slaves*) and 'A Person Who Eats Meat'. Quite what Leonard was expecting from his four-in-the-morning audience of hundreds of thousands of wet, tired and sleepy people is anybody's guess: he probably didn't know either; Leonard told *Sounds* magazine: ". . . the whole thing was delayed so we all flaked out in this trailer. They woke us up and we got up there in this kind of daze . . .". *Rolling Stone* reported that "[he] tonelessly soothed the flaked-out multitudes". The three official tracks released on three different albums ('Sing Another Song, Boys' on 'Songs Of Love And Hate', released in 1971, 'Tonight Will Be Fine' on 'Live Songs' in 1973, and 'Suzanne' released in 1995 (as part of a 25th Anniversary Festival compilation on two CDs) were scarcely representative of his 80-minute set, which also featured some between-song improvisations and ended with 'Seems So Long Ago, Nancy'. A slightly longer version of 'Tonight Will Be Fine' was later included on a CBS triple-album with tracks from this Isle of Wight and the Atlanta Pop Festival in July.

Murray Lerner (whose earlier documentary on the Newport Jazz Festival was widely acclaimed) filmed most of the on-stage action as well as the goings-on elsewhere. His raw 'rock doc' lay unseen for the best part of the next 25 years until he assembled a two-hour cut from more than 60 hours footage, subtitled *Message To Love*, which was first broadcast on

BBC2 Television in August 1995, and which has since been released on video and laserdisc. A tired and drawn 'Suzanne' is included. As for Leonard, it did some good, and it did some harm. And just about enough of both to lure him back to Europe 18 months later for an extensive tour of 20 cities, itself turned into a notable film by Tony Palmer called *Bird On A Wire.*

IV

Between The Darkness And The Stage

Leonard returned to the US and to Columbia Recording Studio A in Nashville, where he continued work with 'The Army' and producer Bob Johnston. 'Songs Of Love And Hate' (working title – 'Leonard Cohen: Army') was more or less ready by the following November and due for release at Christmas. In December, Leonard and his Army played some concerts, mostly in Canada: Ottawa, Toronto – where the *Globe and Mail* announced him "Entertainer Of The Year" – and Quebec, plus at least one in Berkeley, California, as reported by Jack Hafferkamp for *Rolling Stone* and reprinted in the introductory pages to the 'Songs Of Love And Hate' songbook, trying out the new songs a few more times. As a result, the album's release was delayed. Jacques Vassal informed us of a couple of reasons: firstly, Leonard flew back to London to work with Paul Buckmaster, a well-known and respected strings arranger who had previously worked with David Bowie and Elton John. They added string and horn dubs to several tracks. "Children's Voices [from] The Corona Academy in London" (to quote from the album's little booklet) were also added on two tracks – 'Dress Rehearsal Rag' and 'Last Year's Man' – Leonard refers to his pleasure on hearing them in this latter song in his sleeve-notes on 'Greatest Hits'. Secondly, a late decision was made to replace the Nashville studio recording of 'Sing Another Song, Boys' with that from the Isle Of Wight.

The title of this third album, eventually released in April 1971, is a misnomer. 'Songs Of Hate And Love' would be more accurate since they follow each other in that order. Other elements are also evident: earth in 'Avalanche', 'Diamonds In The Mine' and 'Famous Blue Raincoat'; fire in 'Joan Of Arc'; air in 'Love Calls You By Your Name' and water in 'Last Year's Man', 'Dress Rehearsal Rag' and 'Sing Another Song, Boys'. It was the longest Cohen album so far at almost 45 minutes with the least number of songs: eight, of which seven are studio recordings and one live. These are mostly long songs: three over five minutes in length and three more over six. In contrast to the tautness of the 'Room' songs, the mood here is expansive. So the record company couldn't really have expected that much success from the single releases – 'Joan Of Arc' c/w 'Diamonds In The Mine' (CBS 7292) and 'Dress Rehearsal Rag' c/w 'Avalanche' (Columbia 4-2991).

The basic tone is set with the grimness of 'Avalanche', from a text originally published in *Parasites Of Heaven*. Clean and rapid fingerwork contrasts with Cohen's slightly stretched and slurred vocals. Leonard: "There is something in the voice that is really wiped out . . . it's a disturbing voice . . . there is anxiety there." Indeed. I'm not so sure that he really wanted to conquer the pain of the rejection and dejection anyway. Those added strings enhance the forbidding F minor opening, over which Leonard's vocals sound very weary. But the change from minor to major tonality at the end of each first line (on 'avalanche' in verse one and 'pedestal' in verse three) lifts it a little and prevents it all getting *too* morose. Leonard gets away with it because we are now accustomed to his style. (Nick Cave should be ashamed of himself for his travesty of the song on the 1991 tribute album 'I'm Your Fan'.) As a concert solo, this is a familiar post-intermission 'opener', often with lyric changes in verse five (line four: "I who rule the Seven Seas" instead of "I who have no need") and in more recent years with verse six often omitted altogether. The last two lines of the song, where he stretches "beloved" and "wear", are powerful . . . like he's surfing the note. The final discord on the strings confirm the shadow, the shadow of his wound.

'Last Year's Man' is a wordy song, full of both evocative and provocative imagery, with several familiar Cohen themes evident, including the 'Military' (soldiers/army/fighting) and the 'Religious' (Bethlehem, Jesus, Cain). Joan Of Arc is introduced in verse one.The song also has a fine sense of musical style and structure yet suffers from being highly underestimated. Leonard: "The song had too many verses and it took about five years to sort out the right ones." That being the case, he started the song around 1966. Which is interesting because he turned out to be Next Year's Man in 1967 with his début album!

The only known live performance (and better it is too!) of the album's third song 'Dress Rehearsal Rag', whose title or lyric may come from 'Avalanche's final verse, was in the 1968 BBC television show. Leonard prefaced that performance with these words: "There's a song in . . . Czechoslovakia called 'Gloomy Sunday' that was forbidden to play because every time it would play people would leap out of windows . . . It was a tragic song . . . I have one of those songs that I have banned for myself – I sing it only on extremely joyous occasions when I know that the landscape can support the despair that I'm about to project into it . . ."

So, Scott Joplin it ain't. It's another six-minute Song Of Hate. Leonard's voice enlivens the unpleasant and distressing images with references to drugs ("the veins stand out like highways all along your wrists") and razor blades with music (1967 copyright) that is savage. In the repeated last line of the 'chorus', the shadows lift. But only momentarily. *Melody Maker* critic Roy Hollingworth's preview got it spot on: " 'Dress Rehearsal Rag' . . . was certainly very depressing, with the use of incredibly screwed-up images. Cohen's voice was its usual melancholic self . . . The overall quality of the track was brilliant." The reference to the Rosicrucians and the line "they will give you back your hope" seems to be an extension of the advert for Rosary Beads containing water from Lourdes in 'Beautiful Losers'.

Disconsolate . . . depressing . . . distressing – it's just one low after another on this record; and it inversely peaks, bottoms out, you might say, with 'Diamonds In The Mine'. Discrepant title too, since the lyrics insist "There are no diamonds in the mine." (The 1991 'Leonard Cohen Anthology' made a valiant attempt with its '(No) Diamonds In The Mine' title.) Jacques Vassal compared it to Dylan's 'Like A Rolling Stone'– but 'Ballad Of A Thin Man' or 'Positively 4th Street' would be nearer the mark. Neither of these Dylan songs (or any other, for that matter) comes within reach of this subterranean seam of condemnatory disgust at no friends, no letters, no grapes, no chocolates, no diamonds and, ultimately, no comfort.

Cohen's most distressed vocal of all (evident also in 'Leaving Green Sleeves' in 1974) spits, groans and croaks over some fervent country picking and rhythm from Charlie Daniels and crew, with some nifty cymbal and hi-hat work (uncredited). Corlynn Hanney and Susan Mussmano join on the chorus. At just four minutes, it's the shortest song on the album.

And so to some Love Songs. The first, 'Love Calls You By Your Name', is not unlike 'Last Year's Man' with its graphically detailed imagery – going nowhere, but well crafted nevertheless. Not every song tells a story, as Rod Stewart might have said. This relentless five-verse song moves through a combination of subtle chord changes and string overdubs (there's too much swelling in verse three) with a series of "between the . . ." lyric lines, most of which are cleverly constructed (e.g. "between the dancer and his cane"), though a couple are puzzling (eg. "between the sundial [not "sundown" as printed in the songbook] and the chain"). The delayed concord of melody line and accompaniment on the title words at the end of each verse is splendid but the horns in the final verse are irrelevant. Apart from Leonard's wrongly-pitched second line "love" in verse four, it is a song well sung. That said, it was included on only two tours: 1974 in Europe (Leonard: ". . . a song about the place between the beginning and end of things where you summon yourself", Paris, October 19) and 1975 in Canada and USA – played far too fast, but kept together by Leonard's inspired lead with many a lyric alteration. Stephen Scobie dismissed the song for being too elaborate. Dorman and Rawlins were more perceptive in seeing some kind of rekindled hope in the ashes of a former relationship.

This is close to what 'Famous Blue Raincoat', another classic and well deserving a pedestal all its own in the Cohen Hall Of Fame, may purport to portray. Leonard sings a letter from his hotel room in New York to a friend "deep in the desert". So far so good . . . unravelling the complexities of the rest of it, with such contradictions as "my brother, my killer" makes the lyric a good long, deep read.

Leonard appears to have forgotten the exact scenario in which he found himself when he wrote this song. I would say it goes something like this: Leonard's friend is a man with whom he has "shared" Jane, now sleeping in Leonard's place which is either on or near Clinton Street, New York. Jane has recently left this man who's busy with his new life in the desert where Leonard hopes he's keeping a diary of events. The man was set "to go clear" – a multiplicity of innuendo here: perhaps it's drug-slang for quitting; or maybe it's just simple-speak for going away. 'Clear' is also a term used by scientologists, so Leonard may be referring to some state of consciousness here. Whichever, the singer cares enough to enquire as to what happened. 'Lili Marlene' is perhaps a coded nickname for another woman in whom the man was interested and when she fails to arrive at the station, he looks after Jane (who was 'with' Leonard at the time, but had gone away for some reason – was she his 'Winter Lady'?), so eloquently succinct in the marvellous "flake of your life" line. When Jane returns to Leonard (where had she been?) she had become "nobody's wife" – Leonard belittles himself in acknowledging Jane's new-found status . . . at which point in the story he realises that Jane has actually left his apartment . . . and Leonard nonchalantly passes on to his correspondent her best wishes. The singer advises his friend that he holds no grudge against him for the time he spent with Jane, though should he ever come to visit them in New York, Jane may not be there since she is now free. He concludes the letter by thanking his friend for helping Jane with a problem that he himself didn't even try to solve.

The complexities and nuances of the relationships between the singer, Jane and the Other Man, past and present, invite many interpretations. Familiar themes pertain in the lyrics – 'the loser' is particularly evident here. After a *real* introduction lasting almost 25 seconds on acoustic guitar, with some gentle bells-cum-windchimes in the background, Leonard's vocal line is steady and secure, backed at first by some ethereally muted "da daa"s. The range of the vocal is narrow with the tune moving up and down in simple steps, usually by one tone, sometimes by two, and the song peaks around its final three lines and the first couple of the second chorus.

The spell is completely shattered by the rather disagreeable 'Sing Another Song, Boys' which follows. It would have been better to have shifted out of 'Famous Blue Raincoat's final A minor and segued into the strong G major of the final track 'Joan Of Arc'. Jacques Vassal says the studio recording of this song was rejected in favour of this 1970 Isle Of Wight performance. There is passion here, well brought out by all concerned – great keyboard work in particular – and an infectious stompy 6/8 rhythm; but it's less a Song Of Love, more of Non-Love ("let's leave these lovers wondering/ why they cannot have each other"), a series of aimless and confusing images culminating in his extended 'la la la' cop-out, lasting almost two minutes, or so one might think. In Frankfurt Leonard explained: ". . . the song pertains to dissect the intimate connections in the ordinary relationship. Coming to no satisfactory conclusions, the author of the melody abandons it and begins another song – hence the title 'Let's Sing Another Song, Boys' . . .". So that explains it. But there's more – Leonard continued: ". . . at which point in the author's mind he envisaged the audience rising to its feet, their throats burning and singing the new song which speaks of the ends of all the tyrannies that we place upon each other in the living room, and the song is completed in a great triumphal march on The Bastille."

It comes as no surprise to those who were at Leonard's 1970 concerts to hear 'Sing Another Song, Boys' following 'Famous

Blue Raincoat' on this record, since they were performed in that order in many of those shows. 'Live Songs', however, should have accommodated this song, track nine I'd suggest, and thus that album could have finished more appropriately with 'Tonight Will Be Fine', rather than the moribund 'Queen Victoria'.

As if to reinforce the point made at Frankfurt, Leonard finally abandons his song in order to start another, in this case, 'Joan Of Arc', the final, and at almost six and a half minutes, the longest track. It's an absolute gem; and, as if to emphasise an earlier point, he certainly shows again he knows how to use his 'la la's.

In the mid-Sixties, in New York, Leonard had met former Velvet Underground musicians Lou Reed and John Cale. Then he saw Nico, the Cologne-born former model who appeared in Andy Warhol's movie *Chelsea Girls*. Leonard developed an unrequited crush on her. "I had been writing a lot of poems to Nico with no discernible response on her part," he told *Melody Maker*'s Allan Jones in June, 1974. "She was a sight to behold. I suppose the most beautiful woman I'd ever seen up to that moment . . . I started writing songs for her then." His song 'Joan Of Arc', he later admitted "came through her." (Paris, October, 1974.) In fact, he also stated that 'Joan Of Arc', who was first introduced in 'I Met You' (*New Poems* 1968), again in 'Last Year's Man', then later in 'The Energy Of Slaves' (No 24, page 32), ". . . was written for a German girl I used to know, she is a great singer, I love her songs . . ." (Paris, again.) The lyrics are in the form of a conversation between the Maid Of Orléans and the flames of the fire which eventually consumed her at the stake in Rouen. It's an ideal duet – and one which has not been surpassed either before or since Leonard and Julie Christensen's performances in 1988 and 1993. On the album-take, Leonard sings everything, at first with some backing echo of his own voice reciting the first four lines, and again (a neat stylistic touch this) for the final four lines, over gentle acoustic picking, with his female support. It's a fine four-verse lyric (the chill of the opening 'Avalanche' finally dissipates in the embrace of fire and flame), with good delineations of both protagonists, containing several points of Cohen-reference to matters sexual, religious, social and historical.

Released as a 7" single (CBS 7292) in several European countries, each with a different picture-sleeve (c/w 'Diamonds In The Mine') it was singled out for praise in many an album review: "... more effective than anything I've ever heard him do" wrote Roy Hollingworth in Melody Maker, January 2, 1971. "The other highlight is 'Joan Of Arc' ..." wrote Arthur Schmidt in *Rolling Stone*, September 2, 1971. So how come it was left off 'Greatest Hits'?

Film director Robert (M*A*S*H) Altman included three Cohen songs in his new movie *McCabe & Mrs Miller*, shot in 1969 but not released until 1971, starring Warren Beatty and Julie Christie. 'The Stranger Song', 'Winter Lady' and 'Sisters Of Mercy' were chosen to highlight the story of life and new enterprise in a snowy American northwestern boom town, around the turn of the century, with new arrival Beatty endeavouring to set up a bordello in the Church, duly managed by Christie, while managing the gambling set-up in the saloon and keeping the townsfolk guessing as to his real identity – all in the face of some dangerous opposition from local mining operators. The film was praised as much for the acting as for the scenery, camera work and attention to detail, and Leonard's music was also mentioned in dispatches. Its re-release in 1990 and subsequent availability on commercial video prompted the *Guardian* to remind us of the power of this "wonderfully rich and resonant piece of film-making." It is beyond the remit of this book to evaluate the use of Leonard's music in subsequent movies, but there have been quite a few since *McCabe & Mrs Miller*, though not all of such stunning calibre, but catch if you can: *The Second Coming Of Suzanne* (1972), *The Wedding* (1978), *Love At Large* (1988), *Pump Up The Volume* and *Bird On A Wire* (both 1990), *Life According To Agfa* (1992), *Caro Diario*, *Exotica* and *Natural Born Killers* (all 1994.)

Meanwhile, miles away from Tinsel Town and in an altogether different reality, Cohen was the recipient of an honorary degree of Doctor Of Laws from Dalhousie University in Halifax, Nova Scotia. The following year, the University of Toronto bought his manuscripts.

Leonard's tour of Europe in March and April 1972 certainly gave the lie to the opening line "I have no talent left" in poem No 102 in *The Energy Of Slaves* published later that same year. Tony Wilson wrote: "it was a total success" in his review of the opening show in Dublin for *Sounds*, March 25. Although the tour was relatively small-scale (everything is relative, after all), he ended up playing 21 concerts to audiences in 20 cities with first-ever gigs in Ireland, Scotland, Scandinavia, Switzerland, Belgium, Netherlands and Israel – all of which he would subsequently return to in future tours – in just over a month. Bob Johnston and Ron Cornelius were the only 'Army' survivors to play in the new band, now comprising David O'Connor (guitar), Peter Marshall (double-bass), and blonde vocalists Donna Washburn and Jennifer Warnes (who spelt her name "Warren" at that time.)

A total of 28 Cohen-sung songs were then available on record. Leonard chose to present 17: six from his first album, seven from his second and four from 'Love and Hate'. Roy Hollingworth commented that "he sang everything he is rightly adored for" in *Melody Maker* on April 1. Half-a-dozen other selections made up the repertoire: the standard 'As Time Goes By', 'Banks Of Marble', 'Kevin Barry' (an Irish rebel song), 'We Shall Not Be Moved' (the American Labour song), 'Passing Thru' (the Richard Blakeslee song "arranged" by Leonard) and the original version of 'Chelsea Hotel'. In addition, Leonard was often wont to improvise to keep the energy of the concert flowing, to keep the Muse in tow; in their splendid collection of Cohen song lists, Gerhard Schinzel and Michael Lohse identified almost 20 'ad libs', with titles such as 'I'll mind your coughing, baby' (London), 'If there's anything that doesn't please you tonight', 'There's a forest of microphones' and 'I always wanted to sing for naked people' (all in Amsterdam). Tony Palmer, former music critic for the *Observer*, co-director of Frank Zappa's *200 Motels* in 1971 and several other 'rock-docs', was interviewed and appointed to make a film of the tour.

Each venue became Leonard's Room and his songs, averaging around 17 per night, came over "like a meditation". Even when his P.A. played up in some shows, he just played it cool. Repartee and rapport were in abundance throughout, from the Dublin audience who "burst into song on the first chorus of 'So Long, Marianne' . . . and needed no other encouragement to join in when they felt like it" (*Sounds*, March 25) to the rapt "you could have heard an unused tissue drop" silence in London the following week (*Melody Maker*, April 1), and the tears in Tel Aviv and Jerusalem at tour-end.

CBS released five songs and two improvisations from the tour on 'Live Songs' in 1973, and most of the Cohen songs performed were included in *Bird On A Wire*, the subsequent 85-minute film, which was premièred in 1974. When Robert Christgau wrote in *Esquire* magazine that Leonard's voice ". . . has been called monotonous but it is also the most miraculous vehicle for intimacy that the new pop has yet produced", he managed to anticipate much of what became evident on this 1972 tour and the film. One particular highlight was Leonard's original 'Chelsea Hotel', different in lyric ("I remember you well in the Chelsea Hotel/ In the winter of 67/ My friends of that year were all trying to go queer/ And me I was just getting even") and form (extended chorus) but not in reverential temperament to the later #2 on 'New Skin For The Old Ceremony'.

The filming technique used on *Bird On A Wire* draws on D.A. Pennebaker's celebrated *Don't Look Back* documentary of Bob Dylan's 1965 UK tour. In Cohen's case, the cameras pan the stand-up songman in fine mesmeric form on 'Bird On The Wire', 'Seems So Long Ago, Nancy' and 'Famous Blue Raincoat', a bouncy 'Passing Thru' – filmed in mid-grapple with the Tel Aviv security guards who objected to Leonard's request to his faraway audience to come sit nearer the front– and many more 'favourites', with backstage 'shit and chat', airport and hotel arrivals and departures and the final denouement in Jerusalem with Leonard's initial embarrassment there (his "home town") ultimately turned to climactic triumph with 'Hey, That's No Way To Say Goodbye' and 'So Long, Marianne' and hardly a dry eye in the house.

Tony Palmer explained in 1991 that most of the concert-footage was filmed at the Belle Vue in Manchester as it seemed pointless and far too expensive to film the same songs every night of the tour. The edit premièred in London at the Rainbow Theatre on July 5, 1974, was the *second* version – produced from some 90 hours of film – because Leonard, who came to London to supervise the new version, was not happy with the first. Tony Palmer told me that he would be appalled at the release of a video of the second version as it was "a bowdlerisation of some wonderful material" and "did not represent the best" of what he and Leonard had done. He doesn't have a copy of his original cut. Pity.

'The Energy Of Slaves', Leonard's next poetry collection, was issued in 1972 though several poems date from 1967, with one each from 1961 – written in Havana – 1965 and 1966. It is a difficult read at times: there is a *lot* of negativity right from the outset in No 1 with the lines "There is a war on/ but I'll try to make you comfortable" to the last, No 116: "We'd like to write more often/ but we are busy . . ." The poetic tone, clearly continued in song on 'New Skin For The Old Ceremony, is uncompromising, terse, hurtful (almost gleefully so in some poems – "There is no one/ to show these poems to"), strident and cruel, while some seem genuinely tender ("I try to keep in touch wherever I am") and maybe just a little frail ("O darling [as we used to say]"). It was hardly bedtime story material for his and Suzanne's first child, a son, born in September, and named Adam Nathan.

The collection is a sea-change from the style and grace of *Parasites Of Heaven,* six years earlier. It was to be another six years before Leonard appeared in print again with *Death Of A Lady's Man.* Ira Nadel eloquently described Leonard's progress from "the mythology and lyricism" of *Let Us Compare Mythologies* and *The Spice-Box Of Earth,* through "the historical realities in 'Flowers For Hitler' and 'Parasites Of Heaven'" into "the inferno of self and self-hatred in 'The Energy Of Slaves'." The reader might well have been justified in asking the question: "Well now, Golden Boy, where is your famous golden touch?" after ploughing through these 116 texts. Ira Nadel again: "He then rose toward purgatory in 'Death Of A Lady's Man' before approaching paradise in 'Book Of Mercy'." Even though in the interim we had to be bruised and soothed and bruised and soothed again with 'New Skin For The Old Ceremony', 'Greatest Hits', 'Death Of A Ladies' Man' and 'Recent Songs' respectively.

The book is not without humour, however. Or the 'con'. As Stephen Scobie points out, Leonard "has too good an ear not to be aware of the prosaic sound of some of the poems and the crassness of others." But the notion of self-disgust *is* pervasive. It's difficult for him to dodge his self-inflicted fists-in-the face – these are not shadows of wounds, he's not wiping away the jam: this guy's in deep shit, and he's determined to tell everyone about it.

But then everyone heard that Leonard had retired; or had wanted to disappear; or that the 1972 tour was his 'swan song'; or something about him quitting and not coming back. These were just rumours, however, brought about by a misunderstanding on the part of *Melody Maker* writer Roy Hollingworth, printed in February 1973, and compounded a couple of weeks later by Alastair Pirrie's interview in *Sounds* in March. 'Live Songs' released in April helped to convince the public that Leonard was still around.

V

Wounded In The Line Of Duty

'Live Songs' is a motley collection of nine songs and one
instrumental; two were taken from two different (and how!)
1970 concerts, London and the Isle Of Wight; and seven others
from four venues in 1972: London, Berlin, Brussels and Paris.
The final track was recorded in Leonard's rented farmhouse in
Franklin, Tennessee. If the commercial notion was to provide
some kind of musical memento of the 30 or so concerts in
Europe in 1970 and 1972, the issue of this 49-minute disc (and
its two link 7″ singles) smacked of poor judgement. The first
album track was improvisation, not a real song; and the track
marked 'Improvisation' was a rambling instrumental of 'You
Know Who I Am'. And as for 'Queen Victoria', whose words were
originally printed eight years earlier in *Flowers For Hitler*, it
scarcely met either criterion of the album's title, though it
'looks' good as a printed 'song' (in 'Greatest Hits' songbook,
1978) with its repeated E minor to C chords.

Alternatively, the album could be heard as a cleverly chosen
programme highlighting Cohen's development as a performing artist, with elements of improvisation, high emotion, great
ensemble playing – and a finely judged sense of 'giving' the
song to the audience – on which specific level the album is
a splendid showcase. The introduction in French on 'Bird
On The Wire' in Paris ("comme un oiseau sur la branche/
comme un ivrogne dans la choeur de la nuit/ j'ai cherché ma
liberté"), the sombre 'expliqué' to 'Story Of Isaac' in Berlin
and the "deep in your velvet seats" remarks in London are
good examples of this.

Daphne Richardson committed suicide by jumping off the roof of Bush House, the BBC Radio building, in London, before this album was released. She was obsessed with Leonard and had written to him many times. He told *Zig-Zag* interviewer Robin Pike he was "struck by the power of her communications." They had met briefly in London in 1972 and agreed that her illustrations would be included in *The Energy Of Slaves*. But her mental health was unstable and doctors and nurses didn't believe that she was in communication with Leonard. When Leonard did try to contact her from the States in reply to obviously desperate telegrams, he was too late. One of her writings, 'Transfiguration', adorns the back cover of 'Live Songs', with a multi-coloured drawing that focuses your attention on the word 'INTENSITY' in the middle of her piece (page three of a longer document, it would seem). It is an intense album, preaching its way through 'Passing Thru', infecting 'Nancy' with resignation ("the morning had not come/ Nancy was alone") and cranking up 'Tonight Will Be Fine', with its extra (unpublished) verses, into a bellow-along revivalist finale – before the becalming tenth track encore.

Vocally, Cohen is in great shape. The support from The Army in 1970 was live and kicking; in 1972, as seen in the *Bird On A Wire* documentary, there was more tightness and intimacy. 'Sing Another Song, Boys' (from 1970) should have been included instead of intruding on 'Songs Of Love And Hate'. But it was to be twenty or more years before another official live album was released and even that was criticised for not being a double-album. CBS did release a couple of singles: one for the European market (CBS 1544) with 'Passing Through' c/w 'Nancy', both from the London concert; while in the UK (on CBS 2494), record-buyers were treated to 'Bird On The Wire' (Paris) and 'Tonight Will Be Fine' (Isle of Wight 1970).

One song surprisingly not included on the 'live' album was 'Sisters Of Mercy'. In the meantime, it lent its title to an off-Broadway "cabaret evening", a collection of Cohen writings and songs presented in cabaret style. It centred on Leonard's close encounters with the female kind, and was presented at the Theatre de Lys in New York, produced by Leonard's manager Marty Machat and directed by Gene Lesser, from September 25 onwards after its summer première in Niagra-On-The-Lake. Nicholas Surovy, Gale Garrett and Emily Bindinger were among the cast, and Cohen was present at some of the rehearsals for the show. Emily would later sing backup vocals on Leonard's 1974 and late 1975 tours. There were 15 performances up to closure on October 7. By then Leonard was deep in the Sinai desert, entertaining front-line Israeli troops as they engaged their Egyptian opponents in what developed into the Yom Kippur War. It was, he later recounted, just a matter of getting into a jeep, with a guitar and a machine gun, and driving out to the soldiers to play for them while they shone flashlights for him. In another interview he said he also wanted to sing in Cairo. Clever. Proof, if such were needed, that in addition to his many and various recording and concert experiences he was not so much continuing to age as continuing to sage.

And continuing to write, of course – songs, poems, prose. The former would surface on his next album in 1974; the latter not so immediately. Leonard withdrew his completed manuscript, possibly called *Notes For The Clean Life*, from his publishers a couple of years later. Its revised version probably became *The Woman Being Born* before finally emerging in 1978 as *Death Of A Lady's Man*. Working titles were and continued to be an integral component of Leonard's working practices. 'The Return Of The Broken Down Nightingale' is a good example! This was one working title for what became 'New Skin For The Old Ceremony'. It's a paraphrase of what Leonard said to one audience early on the 1972 tour in an attempt to explain his inability to keep singing amid dreadful PA problems. *Crawdaddy* reported that the new album sold a quarter of a million copies in Europe in the first six weeks after release.

The average playing time for each of these 11 songs (the

largest number on a Cohen disc until 1994's 'Live In Concert' with 13) is less than three-and-a-half minutes; in sharp contrast to the five and six-minuters of 'Love And Hate'. Each packs a punch like a two-finger measure of Jack Daniels, neat, in the early hours. Producer John Lissauer takes much credit for the 'sound' on the album – sparse, clean edges, hard edges (unlike all those curvy bits of the explicit *coniunctio spirituum* on the front cover of the Dutch release; buyers in the UK and USA had less carnality to confront). It was also Leonard's first full colour cover; the first without his face on it; and it enjoyed the long and singular distinction (until 1988) of having every song performed live in concert, which it then shared with 'I'm Your Man'. Stephen Scobie hailed it "Cohen's masterpiece of the seventies"; Bob Woffinden in *NME* opined "It's not a great album . . . but it will certainly do." With the benefit of hindsight, of course, there were many treasures to appreciate here – 'classics' like 'Chelsea Hotel #2', 'There Is A War', 'Who By Fire' and 'Lover Lover Lover' (written in the Sinai desert), which have scarcely left Leonard's live reper-toire since. This last song was chosen as the first single in Europe (backed by 'Who By Fire', CBS 2699) with at least four different picture-sleeve covers. 'Take This Longing' and 'Why Don't You Try' were released as B-sides in 1976 (for 'Suzanne' and 'Tonight Will Be Fine' respectively, to promote the late 1975 'Greatest Hits' compilation). The songbook was particularly interesting – helpful too with all songs in the same key – in prefacing the music with several pages of reviews (two from *Rolling Stone* one each from *Crawdaddy* and *New York Times*) and, best of all, a long interview with *Crawdaddy*'s Paul Williams. Plenty of Cohen-speak to plough through in that one.

Despite the album title, Leonard had still not yet shaken off his old subservient self, since the 'chorus' of the opening song was actually taken from poem 31 in 'The Energy Of Slaves'. It acted as the serious flip-side to the rather tongue-in-cheek first two verses; the final double quatrain reversed the positions and 'loser Cohen' wailed his own defiant integrity, all delivered in uncharacteristic stop-start-stop phrasing, but accompanied by a fine ensemble of sax, bass, drums and piano (John Lissauer) with Emily Bindinger and Erin Dickens on backup vocals.

'Chelsea Hotel #2' is a compressed revision of the song first heard in some of the 1972 concerts, and so vividly captured in *Bird On A Wire.* (The rewrite was also filmed – as a concept-video in his 1983 project *I Am A Hotel.*) It is his Three Minute Elegy For A Fellow Worker In Song, whom we now know to be Janis Joplin, though at the time it wasn't made clear. Leonard himself revealed her identity in his later Seventies shows but later blamed himself for having admitted as much. Whereas the much longer original song meanders and wallows, '#2' is concise. It has a simple acoustic broken-chord accompaniment, with a subtle hint of trombone on the chorus, and a sombre but tender vocal line.

The song is an amalgam of the graphic, the melancholy and the sentimental (isn't that true of many Cohen songs!) with candid lines like "we were running for the money and the flesh", "clenching your fist . . . you fixed yourself" and "you said . . . we are ugly but we have the music". Leonard may well not have spent much time in retrospective thought about Janis: "I can't keep track of each fallen robin" – but he did write a great song about her and his attempted disclaimer in the final line is unflattering to both his and her memory.

Cohen relocated the action from a house to a hotel room for the second song, and other locations followed: the human body in 'Lover Lover Lover', written for the soldiers in the Sinai desert during his visit there in 1973; the 'other battlefield' – i.e. the metaphysical kind – in 'Field Commander Cohen' and 'There Is A War'; and the courtroom in 'A Singer Must Die'. They are all surrogates for the real location – the lover's bedroom – as in 'Why Don't You Try', 'I Tried To Leave You', 'Take This Longing' and 'Leaving Green Sleeves' in which Cohen offers his observations on the feelings between a man and a woman. All these songs have a musical resonance which is both authoritative and reassuring.

'A Singer Must Die' marks the end of Cohen's main exposé of the war between the man and the woman; he has seemingly exhausted his supply of verbal ammunition, and must resort to "la la la"s to conclude his own defence. There's a high ceiling in this song's courtroom and Leonard's voice seems to bounce off it, and his self-confessed guilt is compounded with his own double-tracked line in the third chorus. His concert performances of this song included an extra verse which happily is included in 'Stranger Music'.

The final four songs are each in turn concerned with loving, leaving, longing and ultimately, losing. 'I Tried To Leave You' (one of the shortest songs on the album, in later years it would develop into one of his most extended when used as a vehicle to highlight and introduce his support musicians) is the most succinct of love songs despite Leonard's lazy, almost uninterested vocal. 'Who By Fire' is "based on a prayer recited on the Day of Atonement" and simply lists various ways of dying, sung with Erin and Emily over guitar, intermittent strings and tuned percussion including bells. This take sounds like a demo recording; the 'real' song would finally emerge *summa cum laude* on the 1988 tour (though 1979 performances were pretty good too) with an intro that really allowed the song to sing. 'Take This Longing', like 'Chelsea Hotel #2', was a revised version of an earlier song, 'The Bells', which Buffy Sainte-Marie had recorded on her 1971 album 'She Used To Wanna Be A Ballerina'. The differences are mainly in the lyrics; the 1967 original had no hint of "Take this longing from my tongue . . ." as the chorus, though a few verse-lines are somewhat familiar. Leonard wrote 'Take This Longing' with Nico in mind. In a previous song, 'I Tried To Leave You', Leonard's arms were open wide for his lover on their narrow bed; in this song, he is still waiting for her embrace – "everything depends upon/ how near you sleep to me", but he sings this song more tenderly, with more conviction. The arrangement – girls, guitar, saxophone – is simply ravishing.

Not content to let the ashes of the furnace into which we have ventured cool down, Leonard offers one final angry rake-over in 'Leaving Green Sleeves'. His vocal line is edgy and rough – completely at odds with the graceful elegance of the accompaniment in which the real 'Greensleeves' seems to be lurking, aching to break free. The descending chords A minor, G, F and E in the verse contrast with the up-and-down progression of C, G, A minor and E minor in the chorus. There is bitter and passionate recrimination at the end: "I reached for you but you were gone/ So lady I'm going too" thereby bringing the chorus of 'Is This What You Wanted' into even sharper focus, and thus the album concludes, Leonard's final painful chorus ringing in our ears, on a unifying note of what Stephen Scobie called "Cohen's anti-romantic discord."

In his long and detailed *Goldmine* piece in February, 1993, William Ruhlmann wrote that after 'New Skin's release, Leonard and John Lissauer worked together on more songs, quoting Leonard thus: "We did, I'd say, a side and a half . . . six or seven songs . . ." Titles mentioned were 'Came So Far For Beauty', 'Guerrero' and 'Anthem' (Leonard: "no relation to [The Future's] 'Anthem'").

It had not previously been the policy of CBS to release a new Cohen album in high summer. They did just that in 1974 with 'New Skin For The Old Ceremony'. The world première of the 1972 tour documentary *Bird On A Wire* had taken place in London in July – so the 'Suits' must have seen their big chance. Leonard was also in town to promote the film but he seemed more interested in boosting the PR campaign for his friend Irving Layton's *Collected Poems*.

Suzanne and Leonard's second child, a daughter they named Lorca Sarah, was born in September. That same month, his earlier 'film promo' visit was trumped by an even more remarkable marketing 'coup' – Leonard sang some of his new songs at the CBS Convention in the Grand Hotel in Eastbourne, a rather sedate seaside town on the south coast of England, on September 5 and 6. The previous week he'd 'opened' his 1974 campaign with a full-length concert at the

Ancienne Belgique in Belgium. But the tour proper opened in
Paris. If the press reviews are to be believed, the words "funky"
and "up beat" would best summarise the 34 performances in
50 days in 27 cities. After Paris, there were ten shows in
England and Scotland, then via Copenhagen to 17 more in
five different countries though by now it was clear that most of
Cohen's audiences were in Germany. The final two shows at
the Olympia in Paris were remarkable, the second in particular, commencing at 1 a.m. with 31 songs.

Leonard's new three-man band comprised Jeff Layton
(various guitars, mandolin, banjo, cello – the *sine qua non* in
'Love Calls You By Your Name'), John Lissauer (his co-
producer on 'New Skin' – various keyboards, mellotron
included) and Johnny Miller (bass), with backup from Emily
Bindinger (spotted in *Sisters Of Mercy*, the 1973 off-Broadway
show) and Erin Dickens. All had worked on 'New Skin For The
Old Ceremony' and would play again with Leonard on later
tours and albums. Compared to the rather lean offering of less
than 20 songs per night in 1972, the average in 1974 rose to
about 28, with many shows therefore lasting well over two
hours. A typical set-list comes from Brighton, September 16:

1. Bird On The Wire
2. So Long, Marianne (the two usual 1972 openers re-
   appear; and would again in 1976)
3. Love Calls You By Your Name – début on this tour
4. One Of Us Cannot Be Wrong
5. Diamonds In The Mine – not played in 1972; later moved
   to last song before intermission
6. Why Don't You Try – the first 'New Skin' song (of nine)
   this evening
7. Joan Of Arc
8. Who By Fire
9. Lady Midnight – disrupting a three-in-a-row group from
   'New Skin'
10. There Is A War
11. Hey, That's No Way To Say Goodbye

Intermission

12. solo – Chelsea Hotel #2 – briefest of intros, no Janis story tonight
13. solo – The Stranger Song – preceded by a little improvisation tonight
14. solo – A Singer Must Die
15. solo – You Know Who I Am – not unusual to have four solos together
16. The Partisan
17. Story Of Isaac
18. Famous Blue Raincoat
19. I Tried To Leave You
20. Sisters Of Mercy
21. Lover Lover Lover – later repeated as final song
22. Take This Longing
23. Is This What You Wanted – the second group of three-in-a-row from 'New Skin'
24. Suzanne
25. Tonight Will Be Fine

Encores:
26. Seems So Long Ago, Nancy
27. The Butcher
28. Bird On The Wire – usually the signal to get ready to go home
29. So Long, Marianne – again
30. Lover Lover Lover – and again!

More than anything else, this tour introduced Leonard's practice of set-structure which he would maintain right up to his last tour in North America in 1993, i.e. a bunch of songs (the number can vary from about eight or nine to about 12) played by him and his band comprise the concert's first half; after the intermission, Leonard alone on guitar for between two and four songs (in the Eighties and Nineties he also played keyboard and relied on support from his female backups); then the full band came back and played out the rest of the show, with encores.

Leonard introduced most songs with a brief rap. The tapes confirm a momentum to these 1974 shows (even more evident in 1976) unlike 1988 and 1993, when the emphasis was on control and elegance. There was an energy and an impulse in the faster songs. 'Diamonds In The Mine' and 'Tonight Will Be Fine' were two good examples, which threatened to completely usurp his clichéd "gloomy poet cum downbeat singer" image. He knew that. And worked on it too.

So, a good concert, like a fine wine or well-written letter to a friend, had to have form, line and shape. And style. He worked on that too. Stripped down to the minimal backing of piano, bass and guitar, Leonard's acoustic carried the music along: 'Love Calls You By Your Name', 'One Of Us Cannot Be Wrong' and 'Famous Blue Raincoat' for example, were a little quicker than on record – and in this context, better. They underwent different treatments on later tours, of course, though it's a shame 'Love Calls You By Your Name' didn't make it into the 1979 set: Raffi Hakopian and John Bilezikjian could have really made something out of that.

Whatever Leonard's motives were in jazzing up 'The Butcher', which at the best of times was an uncomfortable song about slaughter and torture, needles and drugs, blood and ice, into what he might have hoped was a less unpleasant experience, the resultant funky arrangement made for a bewildering four minutes. Some nights (e.g. Brighton, Munich, Paris) Johnny Miller slapped away on bass, John Lissauer's clarinet wailed and writhed over and under Leonard's vocal which was at least a couple of miles down range from Mission Control. Erin and Emily were busy with their own voice-and-tambourine combo too. Perhaps Leonard was trying it out in advance of the 1976 'treatment'.

Unfortunately, of all Cohen's tours in Europe, 1974 was the least well-served by radio and television broadcasts; but the real music journalists did not let him down – and I don't just mean for the London concert (reviewed by Michael Watts in *Melody Maker*, Steve Turner in *NME* and Robin Denselow in *The Guardian*); sub-editors sent out their reviewers to the 'smaller' venues too including Edinburgh, Bristol and Sheffield.

Bob Johnston asked Cohen to sing on an album to celebrate the music of ace country banjo player Earl Scruggs, who also joined in on many of the ten tracks issued on 'The Earl Scruggs Revue – Anniversary Special, Volume 1'. Leonard had already 'arranged' the Richard Blakeslee song 'Passing Through' and sung it on both 1972 and 1974 tours. The recording starts promisingly enough: Billy Joel's piano intro-duction, Joan Baez's straight first verse and chorus, with Leonard in for the second; they're together for the next chorus; after that, it's just bedlam – Baez imitates Dylan, the band imitates A(ny) Band, and any country bounce in the music that we'd maybe gotten used to is riffed and pumped out of all recognition.

Cohen and his own band were back onstage in New York for a three-night residency, two shows a night, at The Bottom Line Club from November 29 to December 1. On December 4, still in New York, he was interviewed by Kathleen Kendal (later broadcast on WBAI Radio): "I don't feel any compulsion just to stand under the spotlight night after night, or year after year ... unless I have something to say or something new to disclose about my own work ..." CBC broadcast a two-hour documentary on December 8.

Shortly afterwards, Leonard flew across the continent for half-a-dozen shows at The Troubadour Club in Los Angeles. Several names dropped by to see a set or two, including Phil Spector. The March 1975 issue of *Crawdaddy* reported that Leonard "was very pleased and encouraged by the enthusiastic reception" he had received in New York and LA. After the Christmas break, they were all off again for a tour through Canada and some US cities. Leonard had last toured in North America in 1970 and naturally expressed much concern that his 'return' should go well. With a CV that boasted five albums, the experience of having performed more than 60 concerts and just as many songs in his repertoire, it augured favourably. A similar concert-structure and set-list as in Europe prevailed. Leonard even slipped in a poem or two: 'The Music Crept By Us' for example in New York and Boston and responded to a request in Philadelphia to sing a song about his grandfather with 'Un As Der Rebbe Singt' and 'As Der Rebbe Elimelech', a couple of old Hebrew chants.

Cohen returned to Hydra, and Suzanne, Adam and Lorca. Away from the intrusion of microphones and speakers, Leonard busied himself with family life. And blackening more pages. Living with a woman and two children must have made him kinda nervous as many lines in his 1978 book *Death Of A Lady's Man* suggest quite graphically. This was an uncomfortable period in his life. It was, as we know, only to get worse.

Some well-attended early winter shows with a new band occupied him for a while. New songs were played: 'Came So Far For Beauty', 'The Traitor Song' and 'I Guess It's Time' – these later reappeared in different versions on 'Recent Songs', as were 'Guerrero' (transformed into 'Iodine' on 'Death Of A Ladies' Man') and 'Don't Go Home With Your Hard-On' (also on the 1977 album), slotted in between his greatest hits. But unlike the trio from 1979 which bore some similarity to their earlier versions, both 'Guerrero' and 'Don't Go Home' were completely different as all the music on that album was written by Phil Spector. Leonard's was calypso-style, loose and swingy (the lyrics were printed in *Intensity*, volume 2, No 4, the Dutch Leonard Cohen Newsletter, edited by Yvonne Hakze and Bea De Koning), whereas 'Iodine' became formal and mannered. 'Hard-On's contrasts were even greater: in 1975, the song limped along at about 65 beats per minute; Spector zapped it up to almost twice that tempo.

Though the live concert mixture of different styles (jazz, rock, acoustic) appealed to both audience and critics, it was not enough to convince Leonard that he had a real following in North America. Maybe he just timed it wrong. Bob Dylan was knockin' on everybody's door end of October to early December from Plymouth, Massachusetts to New York on his Rolling Thunder Revue. Larry Sloman described a visit (along with Joni Mitchell and Roger McGuinn, without Dylan) to

Leonard, Suzanne and their two children at the time during which Leonard recited the lyrics of both 'Guerrero' and 'I Guess It's Time' (in *On The Road With Bob Dylan*, Bantam, 1978). At the Montreal Forum on December 4, Bob Dylan dedicated 'Isis' thus: "This one's for Leonard . . . if he's still here." Leonard's own mini-tour preceded the eventual release in February 1976 in the USA and Canada of 'The Best Of Leonard Cohen' which had already been issued – as 'Greatest Hits' – in that same November in Europe, where audiences there had to wait until April to hear him play again.

VI

I Stand In Ruins

After just four studio albums, and 39 songs, the record company decided it was time for a 'Greatest Hits' package. Perhaps they thought it was the best (or maybe the only) way to boost Leonard's record sales in North America since his early 1975 tour there had had little effect. This collection of 12 tracks, called 'The Best Of Leonard Cohen' in North America and Japan, was compiled with Leonard's co-operation and he contributed sleeve-notes.

The tracks were: 'Suzanne', 'Sisters Of Mercy', 'So Long, Marianne', 'Bird On The Wire', 'Lady Midnight', 'The Partisan', 'Hey, That's No Way To Say Goodbye', 'Famous Blue Raincoat', 'Last Year's Man', 'Chelsea Hotel #2', 'Who By Fire' and 'Take This Longing'.

In 1982, Amiga Records (a then East German CBS concern) released an identically front-covered but different, more representative and more generous, 14-track 'Greatest Hits' compilation, with notes to each song by Manfred Wagenbreth, thus: 'Suzanne', 'So Long, Marianne', 'Sisters Of Mercy', 'Winter Lady', 'Take This Longing', 'Lady Midnight', 'Our Lady Of Solitude', 'Bird On The Wire', 'Lover Lover Lover', 'Chelsea Hotel' (sic), 'Diamonds In The Mine', 'The Partisan', 'Seems So Long Ago, Nancy' and 'Passing Thru'. Several more Cohen 'Hits' albums have been released in the past 20 years or so; none bear 'Volume 2' or 'More' in their titles, although a 1990 German CBS cassette did sneak through with 'The Very Best Of Leonard Cohen' as its sub-logo.

Judy Collins sang with Leonard on her US TV show

Soundstage (simulcast on WBAI FM) in February 1976: "I was looking through a journal just recently and I realised with a shock that it was exactly ten years ago this month, 1966, when I first met through a friend from Canada a great songwriter, poet, novelist and friend . . . Leonard Cohen." They duetted firstly on 'Hey, That's No Way To Say Goodbye' – Leonard fairly solid on the melody while Judy wove her harmonies above and below; Julie Felix had been far less distracting in her 1967 TV duet. Leonard: "There was one person in New York City that listened to my songs and that was Judy Collins . . . I think anything that happened to me subsequently was because of the interest she took in my songs . . ." He then did his solo 'Stranger Song' – easy, cosy. 'Suzanne', naturally, completed the little set – and it's certainly the best performance of all. (Other television appearances were in Europe during the early summer tour.)

Cohen visited Japan in early 1976. His chat with Toru Mitsui (of Sony/CBS company) was published in the March issue of *New Music Magazine* with a photograph of him standing on his head.

His 1976 tour – surely an attempt to turn his clichéd 'dour 'n' dismal' image on its head – began in Berlin on April 22. This was by far his most adventurous outing, touting a back catalogue of 27 songs in 56 concerts in 78 days in 12 countries (44 cities). In Germany there were 17 shows, and English audiences were treated to 14. Such was the energetic and lengthy presentation of his greatest 'loved' and lovesongs this time round (his average on-stage show lasted about two and a half hours for 30 songs) the new tour, though similar in style and format to the 1974 roadshow, was now revving a couple of gears higher. This was no doubt in part due to the presence of a drum-kit on stage, in the capable sticks of Luther Rix, Dylan's drummer on the Rolling Thunder Revue in 1975, and also to the vocals of Laura Branigan, who later became a solo artist in her own right.

Two 1966 songs were heard for the first time: 'The Store

Room' and 'Everybody's Child'. Their lyrics were published in separate editions of *Intensity* (volume 3, No 1 and volume 4, No 3 respectively) while Manzano (in volume 2 of his Cohen lyrics collection) also offers a transcription of the former and of another 'new' song, 'Do I Have To Dance All Night' which CBS released as a single (CBS 4431, c/w a butchered 'The Butcher' – cf. 1974 tour review), not using the Munich Musiclands Studio recording, but preferring the 'live' concert version from Paris, June 6. Leonard dropped it after this tour and it only received a few more lively performances in 1980. This same Paris concert was broadcast (incomplete) on French Radio. The Casino de Montreux concert fared much better with a complete (and superb FM) airing. Some 15 songs were later issued on a 'non official' CD – 'Live In Montreux, June 25, 1976'.

Leonard's habit of singing non-Cohen songs continued with 'Die Gedanken Sind Frei', an old German traditional tune which translates as 'Our Thoughts Are Free', and the rather jolly 'You Are My Sunshine', which had been a US hit for Leonard's oft-cited "hero" Ray Charles back in December 1962. Leonard sang a much less familiar song, 'A Singer Must Die', for broadcast in May on German (ZDF) TV. It was an interesting choice because it was never sung in concert that year. A few weeks later he appeared on A2 in France singing 'Suzanne', 'Lover Lover Lover' and 'Bird On The Wire' accompanied by his band.

'Leonard Cohen – The Poet Of Rock And Roll' proclaimed the posters outside many a concert hall, and evidence of all three pursuits was clearly on display within. Meanwhile, The Rolling Stones were also on tour in Europe – they played Munster, for example, two days after Leonard. They, more than any other movers and shakers, had no lessons to learn from a 41-year old Canadian wielding an acoustic guitar. Leonard, on the other hand, was about to learn a few lessons himself from an altogether different musical revolutionary, none other than the wildly eccentric record producer Phil Spector.

Despite repeated contrasts in his work, nothing could have prepared Cohen's audience for the shock to its aural sensibilities when the stylus hit the vinyl of 'Death Of A Ladies' Man' in November 1977. It was originally released by Warner Brothers (Spector's home-label) in the USA, though CBS stuck by it in Europe.

There are probably more words in print devoted to this album (which reached No. 35 in the UK – no show in the USA) and to his collaboration with Phil "Wall Of Sound" Spector than reviews of all previous discs put together. Leonard himself has indeed launched, not to mention lunched on, many a story about the bullet-filled hamburgers and pistol-packing guards in the various recording studios in Los Angeles. Spector and Cohen were introduced by Marty Machat, their mutual manager-cum-lawyer, after Leonard's three-night stint at the Troubadour Club, in Los Angeles in December 1974.

Of course, as is often the case 'chez Cohen', these were not all new songs anyway: 'Iodine' and 'Don't Go Home With Your Hard-On' were *Cohen* songs (the former then called 'Guerrero') on the late 1975 tour but bore no relation to their 1977 Spectral visions! Nor were all Leonard's lyrics poured fresh from his mid-Seventies decanter: 'True Love Leaves No Traces' used two verses from 'As the Mist Leaves No Scar', published in 1961; 'I Left A Woman Waiting' used two verses from No 27 in *The Energy Of Slaves* in 1972; and 'Fingerprints' used almost all the verses (2, 3, 4 and 5) from 'Give Me Back My Fingerprints' in 1966.

So, in this collaborative deal, Leonard supplied *all* the lyrics. Phil Spector, who had recently worked with Harry Nilsson, Cher, Dion & The Belmonts and John Lennon, wrote all the music. Leonard recorded what he later called "just scratch vocals"; but Phil then took over, literally, keeping all the tapes (as he had also done with Lennon's masters) mixing them in secret, excluding Leonard to the point where he later admitted: "I had the option of hiring my own private army and fighting it out with him on Sunset

Boulevard or letting it [the record] go . . ." (*Philadelphia Inquirer,* April 30, 1985.)

But they *are* all highly musical, each and every one: the introductions (percussion and bendy bass on 'Iodine', the magical little flute on 'I Left A Woman Waiting'), the melodies (lazy and hazy in 'True Love Leaves No Traces') and the arrangements (the cool cool vocals at the end of 'Paper-Thin Hotel', and the country'n'western blitz in 'Fingerprints', up-tempo ancestor of Leonard's own 1992 'Closing Time'). Nothing less should have been expected from Phil Spector. But, the question is: are the music and lyrics compatible? There are indeed many grunts of unity here and the album has much going for it but Leonard's voice is too often too far back in the mix and from that point of view the album is a disaster – people buy Leonard Cohen records to hear Leonard Cohen singing, not swamped by an army of instrumentalists and backup vocalists – 46 are credited, not all playing and singing at the same time, even if it sometimes sounds like it, including Ronee Blakley, Barry Goldberg, Jim Keltner, Bob Dylan, Alan Ginsberg, Steve Douglas and 'Sneaky Pete' Kleinow. Leonard's vocals aside, there were still some fine moments during the album: his 'duet' with Ronee Blakley on the opening song, Steve Douglas' rasping sax solo on 'Memories' and the pensive nature of the title track itself, a long, intricate and demanding original text (and at 9'20″, Leonard's longest studio recording of all). It also contains many personal Cohen details: Stephen Scobie picked out the "blonde madonna" and "monastery wine" (presumably Marianne and Mount Baldy respectively), while Ira Nadel threw some light on the "St. Francis" lines: Leonard was to have written the music for a film about St. Francis of Assisi, directed by Franco Zeffirelli, but his involvement was cut short after Leonard's suggestion that everyone worked for nothing. Donovan later wrote the songs for 'Brother Sun Sister Moon'.

The final verse of this last song could well be construed as Leonard's clever double-edged swipe at both his failed relationship with Suzanne (Barbara Amiel's article in *Maclean's* magazine, September 18, would leave little doubt of this) and with Phil Spector (could he really have written something as barbed as that *during* his collaboration with Spector?). As a Cohen record, 'Death Of A Ladies' Man' ranks bottom of many a list. Many reviewers took delight in rubbishing the whole venture. Harvey Kubernik, on the other hand, wrote a perceptive piece in *Melody Maker* which described the sometimes manic action in the Gold Star studios during some of the early-morning-to-late-night recording sessions yet also managed to convey something of the true grit of these unlikely artistic partners. Ray Neapolitan, now Joe Cocker's personal manager, who was part of Spector's in-house rhythm section at that time and played bass on many sessions over several months, provided his own insight: ". . . when you work for Phil, it's a Phil record, and Leonard was incidental and I think he felt that . . . he'd just come in . . . then he would do a live vocal y'know, but he would pretty much stay out of the fray . . . there was 40 guys in there and Phil would just, Phil was 'on' . . . it was like theatre . . ."

'Memories' is the album's best known song, and one for which I believe Leonard retained a strong liking since he sang it almost every night on the 1979, 1980 and 1985 tours. It was released as a single, (CBS 5882) backed by 'Don't Go Home With Your Hard-On', with Dylan and Ginsberg, who'd been invited back to the studio late one night after dining out with Ronee Blakley and were 'persuaded' to join in on the shout-along-chorus. Leonard was not there at the time. In some European countries, both tracks were edited by a couple of minutes in an attempt to gain air-play. A second, gentler, single followed: 'True Love Leaves No Traces'/ 'I Left A Woman Waiting' (CBS 6095), though even its A-side lost almost half a minute. In the US, 'True Love Leaves No Traces' was relegated to the B-side with 'Iodine' fronting the release, possibly because it was already familiar (by name if not by melody) to some audiences from the 1975 North American tour. No concerts followed the release of this album.

* * *

As we now know, Leonard's personal life was taking a battering on all sides well before the release of 'Death Of A Ladies' Man'. His troubled relationship with Suzanne was coming to an end as inexorably as the life of his beloved mother, suffering from leukemia. Masha Cohen died in February 1978. Both the album and the book served to exorcise his states of panic and loss; the vinyl was totally outclassed by the book in terms of intent and motivation, process and product, yet by some curious twist of inverted critical snobbery, the songs are more often shot down than the book is raised aloft.

Many judgements and opinions were passed on the significance of the plurality of 'Ladies' Man' in the record's title as opposed to the singular *Lady's Man* of the book which followed. There was plenty of discussion too on the unsmiling, double-appearance of Suzanne on the sepia gatefold sleeve-cover – not the Suzanne of the song, but the other Suzanne: mother of Adam and Lorca, though she had been publicly acknowledged previously, for the front-cover photograph of Leonard on 'Live Songs'. The book's title referred to himself and to the 'divorce' from his lady Suzanne, even though they had never gone through an official marriage ceremony. A startlingly frank interview with Leonard appeared in *Maclean's* magazine in September of 1978, shortly before publication of 'Death Of A Lady's Man'. Alongside photos of Leonard, his mother, Marianne and Suzanne appeared sad details surrounding the split-up between Leonard and Suzanne. The split was geographical, too: Suzanne took the children to live and be educated in Paris.

Death Of A Lady's Man had undergone several revisions before reaching its final published form. It began as *A Woman Being Born* which was reminiscent of the lines: "he was trying hard to get/ a woman's education/ but he's not a woman yet" from the album's title-track. It then became *My Life In Art* which is taken from a line in one of the poems, 'The Photograph', as well as a long prose piece. Unlike Leonard's albums, which with their credits, timings and other 'trimmings', were presented so professionally, this new book was confused and confusing. Its tone was unpleasant, yet pathetic too; the language uncompromisingly graphic, bristling with autobiographical innuendo and detail. It may even be pretentious. But, and this is important, there is a passion in the writing that is missing from many of his recorded songs, with the possible exception of 'Please Don't Pass Me By'.

Poetry and prose with diary entries and commentaries on the poems and journal extracts themselves made up this volume, dedicated by Leonard to the memory of his mother. A hint of this style – text followed by a 'commentary' – had first been seen in 'Flowers For Hitler', 14 years earlier, with 'The Pure List and the Commentary'. The front cover shows a reverse image of the *coniunctio spirituum* on 'New Skin For The Old Ceremony' in 1974 (also on the songbook), without the extra Wing of Modesty. Lyrics of two recorded songs: 'Death Of A Ladies' Man' and (most of) 'Our Lady Of Solitude' (on the next album 'Recent Songs') were in there too. One of the longest original texts, as opposed to a commentary, called 'My Life In Art', appears towards the end of the book. It mentions Lili Marlene, a monk on Mt. Baldy, Los Angeles and Sunset Boulevard, as well as Leonard's own creation 'Red Needle', a drink he invented in Needles, California, in the summer of 1975. More than 15 years later, this drink would re-appear during recording sessions for the 1992 album 'The Future' to assist Leonard and his musicians in their endeavours! And in December 1992, while schlepping around Europe to promote this album, Leonard actually made a couple of these 'Red Needles' on camera, for himself and his interviewer Jarl-Friis Mikkelsen, during a Danish television programme, *Talkshowet.*

Leonard's previous book of prose had been *Beautiful Losers* in 1966. It was prefaced with a line from the song 'Ol' Man River' from Gershwin's opera *Porgy and Bess.* I was strongly reminded of two other songs from that opera while reading through this disparate, and at times desperate, mid-Seventies collection of material – amply, yet contradictorily encapsulated in 'Bess You Is My Woman Now' and 'My Man's Gone Now'.

There is no better place to locate Leonard's various positions throughout his disintegrating 'marriage' to Suzanne, his former relationships with Lilith, Monica et al., than in the 212 pages of this book, full of sacrifice and suffering. It had become a full Act Of Confession.

Leonard had long since given up poetry readings, but it was his custom in the mid-Seventies to include some poems in his concerts. 'The Transmission' (2nd commentary) from *Death Of A Lady's Man* was one such humorous favourite, and back in December 1974, on WBAI Radio in interview with Kathleen Kendal, he had read out a much longer passage from an earlier version of 'The Unclean Start'.

In just the same way as *The Energy Of Slaves* was continued in 'New Skin For The Old Ceremony', so too *Death Of A Lady's Man* segued into his next album 'Recent Songs', which more than proved the notion that the 'Ladies' Man' was far from dead. By then, the age of punk, though still very much alive with albums by Blondie, Buzzcocks and Ian Dury & The Blockheads in the charts, was giving way to disco and the likes of Donna Summer and the *Saturday Night Fever* soundtrack, and then to new wave. Leonard came through with his own, and best, reaction: back to basics.

VII

Daily I Renew My Idle Duty

This meant that after the tumult of 'Death Of A Ladies' Man', and all its shenanigans, Leonard was keener to work with a smaller set-up in the studio. It was to mark his true return to form, though it would take the best part of a decade, and three more albums, to convince others that he had done so. Recording began in the spring of 1979 and the resulting album 'Recent Songs' was dedicated to Leonard's friend Irving Layton. They are not all recent songs by any means. Early versions of three had been played in concerts back in late 1975, and one song here not written by Leonard actually dates from 1842.

The album was recorded in the A&M Studios in Los Angeles; Leonard shared production (only his second venture in this area) with Henry Lewy, Joni Mitchell's then producer, and at about 53 minutes in length, it is the second-longest of all his studio albums ('The Future' comes in at just over 59 minutes.) Leonard acknowledged his mother as a major influence in the album's 'sound'; referring to a conversation with her a week before she died, he said she urged him to write songs like those the Cohen family used to sing, i.e. with a violin.

The front cover is a slightly bigger-than-life-size contemporary portrait of Leonard by Dianne Lawrence, copied from a Columbia publicity photograph, and a tiny humming-bird is featured hovering above his right shoulder. (It hovered again, thirteen years later, in splendid colour on the 1992 album 'The Future'.) The European CD booklet contained all the lyrics, musicians and track timings. Incredibly, all this

83

information was omitted from the North American CD issue, despite being included with its vinyl release.

Leonard had first heard Raffi Hakopian playing in a bar and asked him to come along and play on some songs; John Bilezikjian had been recommended and agreed to join Leonard in the recording studio. The credits also inform us that Steve Meador, Charles Roscoe Beck, Bill Ginn, Mitch Watkins and Paul Ostermayer were members of the band Passenger, from Austin, Texas, introduced to Leonard by producer Lewy after a showcase performance they gave in Los Angeles in February that year. Some of the other musicians were, of course, familiar: Jennifer Warnes sang back-up-vocals on his 1972 tour (and would sing on all of Leonard's subsequent albums; in 1987 her own record of Cohen covers would be released); John Lissauer arranged, co-produced and played on 'New Skin For The Old Ceremony' and had toured with Leonard in 1974 and 75; Johnny Miller had also played on 'New Skin' and toured in 1974, 75 and 76; Garth Hudson was a member of The Band. In later years, on various other albums and tours, members of Passenger would re-appear.

In an interview published during the early part of the 1979 tour, Leonard admitted to being a fairly good guitar player but he described the Passenger guys as incredible. Only a few musicians actually play on each track, from just two (bass and piano on 'Came So Far For Beauty') to six ('The Window', 'Our Lady Of Solitude') and apart from 'The Lost Canadian', the overall and lasting effect is private and intense. On 'Recent Songs' Leonard embraced the intimate world of chamber music. Back in his home territory the vocal line is dominant with basically acoustic support. The Debussy mood he had so earnestly sought from Phil Spector on 'Death Of A Ladies' Man' album – an intimate, lush, almost impressionistic rapture – was successfully captured here.

Unique in Leonard's album catalogue, it only delivered one single release – 'The Guests', c/w 'The Lost Canadian' (CBS 7938). After 'Ladies' Man', which spawned at least three singles, a more concerted attempt to re-establish Leonard's position and status in the market-place ought to have been a priority for his record company. That priority was clearly unrecognised. A song book was published in 1980 (arrangements by Frank Booth) with all the songs in the same keys as on the album although the order in which they are printed is bizarre.

The album's opening song, 'The Guests', begins with Leonard's solo acoustic guitar, in E minor, joined just before he sings by Abraham Laboriel on bass, and then by Raffi Hakopian's 'gypsy violin' (as described in several reviews) at the end of line two. Intimacy is established, with oud, violin and organ weaving in and out, contributing fills, sometimes in twos, or individually, or as a trio. There's an aptly stuttering bass in verse six too.

'The Guests' is not just about losers; Dorman and Rawlins saw it as "a song of the rich textures of life in an abundant world and the final summing-up that all face; a song about the haves and the have-nots, the lucky and the unfortunate." Leonard refers to them as the "open-hearted many" and "the broken-hearted few." But irrespective of their social or emotional status, Leonard sees them all, as Guests, stumbling as they enter into the 'house' of . . . whom? Their host is identified simply as "a Voice". Is it God? One clue may lie in Leonard's introductory words to a 1979 performance of the song: "a new soul comes into the world . . . completely separated from everything . . . the great author of this dismal catastrophe, this vale of tears, holds each of these souls into the feast and into the banquet . . ."

The darkness and gloom are dispatched when torches are lit, a door opens and the meal begins; but their very participation in the meal seems only to hasten the guests' dismissal from the banquet, leaving the 'haves' ("the open-hearted") in good spirits, dancing again; while the 'have-nots' ("the broken-hearted", "those who weep") are still without; and those who are lost really are lost. So that by the end of the last verse, Leonard has transformed the initially "broken-hearted few" into "many", and the "open-hearted many" have become the "few". A bleak outlook for an opener. The song was released as a 7″ vinyl picture-sleeve single in various European countries (B-side: 'The Lost Canadian'), in September 1979 – the only single from the album.

'Humbled In Love' retains the key of E minor, the melody being restrained as Cohen is accompanied by 'doo-wop' vocals from five backing singers. Bitterness, despair and anxiety only develop into a hope of sorts as man and woman are brought close to one another in the sixth verse.

The mood lifts at the opening of 'The Window' as violin, now in A major, over sustained organ chords, thin guitar picking and tremolo oud, plays an introductory phrase twice, leading straight to Leonard's vocals. Completing the instrumental sextet are Abraham Laboriel on bass and Ed Lustgarden on cello, his only appearance on the entire album. A missed opportunity here, as the cello could well have contributed to other tracks, adding further resonance and underpinning the violin. This is a genuine three-in-the-bar, slow waltz using just three major chords: A, E and D; the verse-verse-chorus pattern of the previous song is repeated.

The first two verses are hardly optimistic despite the 'bright' opening bars. We hear 'abandoned', 'lost', 'rages', 'remorse', 'sickness' leading into the chorus where opposites such as 'chosen love' and 'frozen love', 'angels' and 'demons' and 'saints' are conjured up. These words are framed in metaphor, symbolism, imagery, giving them life, breath, and they move the song along on a simple, easy melody, where notes rise or fall to the next by a tone or semitone.

There is much to admire in this passionate song: an uncomplicated (hummable) melody, basic chord structure, and well-balanced instrumentation, again with Jennifer's golden vocals; there are some neat stylistic touches too, such as the little ritardando on the final words of each chorus, the 'uncertain' bass line in the final verse (as in the first song's 'stuttering' bass); and the violin, an inspirational highlight of this song. It is perhaps on this, the third track into the album, that we begin to savour its 'Eastern flavour' (as heralded in the 1979 tour programme).

As one song ends on a guitar arpeggio, so the next, 'Came So Far For Beauty', begins on John Lissauer's piano. He co-wrote the song with Leonard and is joined only by Johnny Miller on bass, though there is sustained brass on the chorus. Leonard's voice ("hopeless voice", verse two) has an air of resignation to suit "I left so much behind". With so few players, the texture is sparse; it's the loneliest song on the album. It's a descriptive piece, cataloguing a series of actions – some subtle, some quite drastic – in order to win his lady, but all to no avail. (Certain similarities here with the 1988 song 'I'm Your Man'.) His grief, so overtly confessed in the opening is repeated in the closing words – this time, it is *he* who has been 'humbled in love'.

This official recording is not unlike its earlier version played at concerts in late 1975 when 'The Smokey Life' and 'The Traitor Song' were also tried out. Back then the musicians were Johnny Miller and John Lissauer, joined by Steve Burgh (guitar), Carter C.C. Collins (percussion), and backing vocalists Erin Dickins and Lorri Zimmerman. (Erin had been on tour with Leonard in 1974 and later sang on 'Various Positions'.) The speed of the original melody (itself similar to its 1979 version) was noticeably quicker. The lyrics were slightly different too: [words in italics are the original 1975 version] in verse one, Leonard came so far for *her* beauty, leaving so *very* much behind . . . his patience and *baby* (it was 'family' later on); in verse two, his choice was *very useless* (later it was 'lonely'), but his voice, just *hopeless* then, later became 'very hopeless'. And curiously, in the final verse, the *baby* he had left behind (as in verse one) now becomes his 'family', which is how it appears in the later lyrics. One can only imagine how Leonard would have performed his later, preferred, arrangement, since 'Came So Far For Beauty' was never included on the 1979 or any subsequent tour.

'The Lost Canadian' (*Un Canadian Errant*), another descriptive song, is completely different in character to 'Came So Far For Beauty'. It interrupts the slow flow of ideas and perspectives on Leonard's themes of love, God and women.

The credits inform us that Leonard has Nancy Bacal to thank for its inclusion – she rescued it from the out-takes. It's a pity she didn't plump for the other known out-take from the recording sessions, 'Misty Blue' (yes! – *that* 'Misty Blue') since it was much more in keeping with the mood and tone of the album. In fact, a report in the August 1979 issue of *Acoustic Music & Folk News* relates that Leonard wanted 'Misty Blue' released as a free single (B-side: 'Do I Have To Dance All Night', a live version of which had been released in 1976), but CBS were not impressed by the idea.

It's a fairly straightforward, traditional 19th century folk tune, "arranged by Leonard Cohen" (as printed in the song book, with copyright assigned to his Stranger Music company in 1979), set to French words written in 1842 by M.A. Gerin-Lajoie. Leonard sings in French. He sang in French on 'The Partisan', introduced 'Bird On The Wire' on 'Live Songs' in French, and indeed almost the whole song (re-titled 'Je veux vivre tout seul', in Serge Lama's translation) was sung in French in some concert performances in 1975 and 1976. As for the choice of a 'folk' or 'traditional' tune, he's done that before too – remember the Irish 'Kevin Barry' (1972 tour), the Jewish 'Un As Der Rebbe Singt' (1970, 1974, 1975, 1976 and the subsequent 1979 tour), the French 'Chante Rossignol' (also in 1979) and one from closer to home: 'Red River Valley' (American) which he performed in 1975 and 1979. He has never performed 'The Lost Canadian' in concert.

The sense of intimacy established in the previous four songs is completely lost since a nine-piece Mexican band can hardly be expected to be other than, shall we say, enthusiastic. The narrative – about a soldier in exile after the civil strife in 1837 in parts of Canada, and his feelings at being unable to return home – unfolds in four four-line verses, lines three and four repeated. The translation printed on the sleeve is poor; Leonard himself provided a much better one in the film *Song Of Leonard Cohen*, directed by fellow-Canadian Harry Rasky, made before and during the 1979 tour of Europe and broadcast by CBC in 1980. The scene shows Leonard sitting on his balcony, playing a tape of the song to Rasky and speaking the English translation of each French line; incidentally, when asked by Rasky if he feels "like the person in that song? Canadian, walking around, Mariachi music?", Leonard replies "A little bit."

It's back to a chamber quintet for the intimate delivery of 'The Traitor', featuring violin and oud, Randy Waldman on organ, Abraham Laboriel on bass and Leonard's acoustic six-string. There is also a very sympathetic string group in the mix, under Jeremy Lubbock's direction, which highlights the mood of certain phrases and contributes an overall warmth to the piece. In the days of vinyl, this was the opener on side two, and it introduced an idea or two in the lyrics that can be heard in later songs on the same side, such as 'summer' ("All summer long" in 'Our Lady Of Solitude') and the ending of summer/autumn ("autumn leaves" and "waiting for the snow" in 'The Smokey Life'); there are others if you listen out for them.

This song, too, had an original version. It was performed in late 1975 (the sleeve notes Leonard's thanks to John Lissauer for his assistance on that), but it was a completely different song! The melody line, though similar in some parts, now goes off into new configurations of rise and fall, and the rhythm and delivery in verses three and six is completely altered. The tempo in the original 1975 version was cranked up and more instruments joined in than were playing in the verse. Incidentally, half way through listening to the 1975 performance, I was suddenly aware that part of the tune in the third line of each verse sounded similar to Kris Kristofferson's 'Good Christian Soldier' (from his 1971 album 'The Silver Tongued Devil And I'.) One final point – the lyrics in verses one, three and four are different but the single detail common to both performances is Leonard's confident vocal line.

'Our Lady Of Solitude' is one of only two 'happy' songs on the album (the other is 'Ballad Of The Absent Mare'); the sentiments contained in it offer some satisfaction on the singer's part and are thus in stark contrast to the situations and portrayals of (whosoever's) 'unhappy' predicaments in previous songs. Marked "slowly" (but still the shortest track on the album), we remain in the key of A major; Leonard's lower vocal register is predominant throughout the two verses, climbing into a higher range in the three choruses, thereby covering just over an octave. The lyrics are a longer adaptation of an earlier version first published as 'All Summer Long' in *Death Of A Lady's Man*. The accompaniment is provided by percussion (note the hi-hat and snare-drum), piano, Garth Hudson on Yamaha, oboe – as sublime as it is surprising – played by Earle Dumler, bass (Roscoe Beck) and Mitch Watkins on electric guitar; in just over three minutes, they combine to perform a paean to Leonard's 'Queen Of Solitude'.

The woman in this song becomes a musical personification of solitude. Thus the singer enjoys the intimacy of her touch because he has now made her 'real'. And when he thanks her with all his heart in verse two, you know he really means it since he was safe in her embrace, removed from everybody else. The intimate language (e.g. "I knew her face to face") is charming, delicate even (in contrast to the earlier, more graphic, lingering on thighs and kissing an open mouth), and the musical arrangement (despite Leonard's deep[er] notes) reflects this more muted approach – oboe (its sole contribution on the album, but how evocative, particularly in the second of its two main entries – could it be the 'voice' of his 'Lady'?) and mellow Yamaha-chords being mainly responsible here . . . they don't play many notes, but enough to make a difference. It's a great song.

And from one great song to 'The Gypsy's Wife', possibly one of Cohen's greatest ever. Unlike others on the album which are narrative or confessional in tone, this song does not just simply ask the question "Where is my Gypsy Wife?" ('where' repeated three times in the first line, and a total of fifteen times in the whole song), but *begs* for an answer. Cohen has said that he wrote the song quite quickly. "My own marriage was breaking up and in a sense it was written for *my* Gypsy wife . . . but in another way it's just a song about the way men and women have lost one another . . . and become gypsies to each other." The soulful lyrics, persuasive rhythm, intimate instrumentation (only five players, *and* that violin solo) and Leonard's voice freeze a moment of time, or an *experience* in time, to which we have been granted privileged access.

Many of Leonard's concerts in 1979 and 1980 included 'The Gypsy's Wife'; and again in 1985, but without Raffi Hakopian the performances were simply mediocre. I know of only a handful of performances on the 1988 tours (including Zurich, Paris and London – *with* violin: honours going to Bob Furgo); but none at all in the 1993 shows. Pity.

'The Smokey Life' attempts to soothe us into knowing that there *can* be degrees of trust and compatibility, even when a relationship is disintegrating. Leonard's vocal delivery matches the resignation in the lyrics but there are still the 'happy' memories of former times, and still something tender enough between them which allows him to offer her advice and help – and a final conciliatory gesture "to come on back if the moment lends." After the anguished portrayal of losing his gypsy wife, the singer is reconciled to his loss and grief, and does so through lighter (than normal) characterisation.

Bill Ginn's electric piano is the dominant feature of the introduction, and there's some interesting 'brush' work on drums too by Steve Meador; also in on this are bass (Roscoe Beck) and acoustic guitar (Leonard); there's a 'lazy' 4-in-the-bar swing to it, so it is slightly unsettled— until Leonard and Jennifer ('vocal duet' in the credits) calm us all down; strings are back also, sweeping across in the chorus with a feel of 'surround-a-sound'; and just as in 'The Window' and 'Our Lady Of Solitude' where cello and oboe respectively added texture and colour, so too here the cor anglais in verse two. There's something less 'piercing' about a cor anglais than an oboe – it's a more plangent instrument, and with those chorus-strings, this is a more 'comforting' song. The language is confident and friendly – and yet, all the while, these lovers are parting! Major chords are used to accompany language which is actually melancholy and forlorn (and better suited to minor tonalities). It is the skill, art and craft of this songwriter who has successfully married these two opposing notions.

Leonard follows a verse-chorus-verse-chorus-coda format in this penultimate song; after a brief introduction he and Jennifer sing over the basic quartet of drums, bass, piano and guitar, with those later additions of strings and cor anglais. There was an earlier version of this song, performed in those late 1975 shows; musically it shares that somewhat lazy, hazy, smoke-filled-bar jazz-like mood, though played slower with a few changes to the lyrics. In both versions, Leonard sounds tired, *appropriately* so.

The final track, 'Ballad Of The Absent Mare' is long (12 verses, no chorus) and an allegory for almost all that's gone before: somebody (a guest at a banquet, perhaps) tells the story of a cowboy who has lost his horse, describing his panic, his loss, his breaking heart. He finds her and they are together at last and then she's free again; but in an almost surreal final twist, the whole enterprise turns out to have been the invention of a musing, imaginative singer/songwriter, in the company of his own lover, looking at the cloud formations in the sunset. The song provides a release and relief from the four 'heavy' preceding tracks and brings the album to a gentle close. The song can also be appreciated on another level, as a more romantically sexual *jeu de mots*. Leonard: "The poem derives from an ancient Chinese poem . . . I worked on it with my old teacher, Sasaki Roshi . . . and his wife gave me the Japanese translation . . ." In fact, the original star was a lost ox.

With the Mariachi band accompaniment now less raucous, Leonard and his acoustic guitar get it just right. There's lots of interesting instrumental colouring, and the long instrumental play-out (including a cowboy's joyous 'yeeahoooo') conjures up images of the closing faraway scene at the end of a long, long western movie. And at nearly 53 minutes it has been a long, long Cohen album.

VIII

Lost In The Rages Of Fragrance

Shortly after the release of 'Recent Songs', Leonard toured Europe with Passenger, plus Raffi Hakopian (not as easy on the eye as Scarlet Rivera in Dylan's 'Rolling Thunder Revue' in 1975 but easily bow-to-bow in musical prowess) and John Bilezikjian. Jennifer Warnes and Sharon Robinson sang back-up. After final rehearsals in London, they played 52 concerts, opening in Gothenburg, Sweden, on October 13 and ending just over two months later in Brighton, England, on December 15. It was more than three years since Leonard had been on tour; no concerts followed the release of 'Death Of A Ladies' Man' in 1977, and the song-repertoire was the most extensive of all his tours, before or since. In 1976, he sang 34 songs. Back on the road again in 1979, an impressive total of 45 songs were included in the set-lists with six from 'Recent Songs'. Harry Rasky, the Canadian director, filmed several concerts, including Antwerp, Paris and Frankfurt, and included footage in his documentary *The Song Of Leonard Cohen*, produced by CBC and first broadcast in 1980. A couple of other shorter, but no less fascinating, television programmes were also filmed during the tour: the first, in Stockholm (recorded by Austrian Television on the second stop of the tour) includes some 'on-the-bus-from-Gothenburg' footage with an amusing 'a capella' version of 'Memories', back-stage preparations showing Leonard and Raffi warming up with their short and wordless-with-violin version of the Russian folksong 'Kalinka' and concert performances of 'Bird On The Wire', 'The Partisan', 'Chelsea Hotel #2' and 'Passing Thru'. In

93

addition, 'Suzanne' was broadcast a few years later on Austrian radio. Excerpts from the post-concert interview with Leonard were interspersed throughout. The second, and more musically interesting, programme was recorded in Munich, on October 31, in the television studios of ZDF-TV, in front of a seated, young audience (*very* polite too, since they refrained from spoiling the beginnings and ends of each song with their applause). Nine songs were performed: 'Bird On The Wire', 'The Guests', 'So Long, Marianne', 'The Window', 'Famous Blue Raincoat', 'Passing Thru', 'Memories', 'The Guests' (again) and 'Suzanne', and it's the best visual evidence there is of a 'Recent Songs' 'concert' (even though it's only just about one-third of its usual duration). German Radio (Station WDR2) was in on the act too, broadcasting Cohen's final concert in the country, at Bonn on December 3.

There is no complete list of every song in every show so it's a little difficult to be absolutely precise, but from the information that is available we can tell that on average, Leonard and the band played about 25 songs per concert, from a core-group of about 30; at individual shows along the way, they included 'extra' (almost one-off) songs like 'Ballad Of The Absent Mare', 'Take This Longing', 'Is This What You Wanted' and 'Lady Midnight'; some songs included in the early shows were later dropped, e.g. 'Iodine', and others not in the early shows were brought in as the tour progressed, e.g. 'Diamonds In The Mine'. Two songs, 'Suzanne' and 'Sisters Of Mercy', were performed as solo acoustic numbers by Leonard on a few occasions and elsewhere by Leonard and the band. Several non-Cohen songs were performed including 'Red River Valley' and even 'Silent Night' (in Brighton; a week or so before Christmas), and a jazzy new song called 'Billy Sunday' which was composed during the last few days of the tour and performed at the final UK shows. Leonard and Jennifer Warnes co-wrote another song during the tour called 'Song Of Bernadette' which she later released on her 'Famous Blue Raincoat' album of Cohen covers in 1987.

The 1979 performances showed Cohen to be in good voice throughout and the band were right there in tight support. In a previously unpublished piece, Paul Ostermayer has written: "We were young and energetic, mustering every ounce of taste and good judgement not to lay waste to the exquisite sub-tleties of Leonard's work . . . it was wonderful how the virtuoso talents of John and Raffi, while providing the ethnic colorings so crucial to the tapestry of Leonard's music, also served as a link between Passenger and Leonard, simultaneously hooking up with our energy and serving the spirit of his music . . ."

Every night's concert differed. My recollections of his first London show that year (December 4) match pretty well the evidence on tapes of earlier shows, weeks before, in Munich (October 31) and Hanover (November 11), for example. The structure followed the by-now familiar pattern: Leonard plus band played eight or nine songs together; after the interval, Leonard alone, on acoustic guitar, sang three or four songs ('The Stranger Song', 'Chelsea Hotel #2', 'A Singer Must Die', 'Avalanche' – this last song introduced from about halfway through the tour), and then the band came back for another 12 to 14 songs, including encores. As usual too, Leonard played his guitar all night – except for 'Memories', when he adopted the hold-the-mike-in-the-hand-technique necess-ary for his rock and roll performance of this particular song. I have written elsewhere (in *take this waltz* – A Celebration Of Leonard Cohen, edited by Michael Fournier & Ken Norris, Quebec, 1994) about the visual and musical impact of this rollicking number and it still stands out as one of the high-lights of these shows. Harry Rasky included one such perfor-mance in his film – marvellous.

The concert in Frankfurt, November 1, exemplifies pretty well the song-choice and musical performances of the tour in general:

1. 'Bird On The Wire' – still the opening song; 'standard' arrangement with more lyric changes than on previous tours; electric guitar solo follows the first chorus.

95

2. 'Who By Fire' – *long* introduction by John Bilezikjian on oud, real 'Eastern' – Greek/Mediterranean/Arabic feel, very atmospheric.
3. 'Hey, That's No Way To Say Goodbye' – gentle arrangement, with some nice piano and flute playing, and a ravishing violin solo before the final verse.
4. 'Field Commander Cohen' – the only tour to include this 1974 song; quite similar to the original 'New Skin' arrangement but sounding dramatic (violin and backing vocals), and altogether more 'military' (drums).
5. 'The Window' – song from the new album, introduced into the set-list after about a dozen shows; sounds just like the album version.
6. 'Passing Thru' – introduced, briefly, by Leonard on harmonica, followed by an all-vocal harmonised chorus over sustained organ chords, and then the song takes off; country rhythm, happy mood, with plenty of little instrumental 'fills'; an electric guitar solo is followed by Leonard's 'hands' solo (on this occasion it was on harmonica; on others e.g. Munich, December 1, he simply 'blew' through his cupped hands). The song concluded with vocal harmonies and organ chords. (A new verse, about Billie Holliday and her songs, was included in some other performances.)
7. 'One Of Us Cannot Be Wrong' – 'standard' arrangement, plus wonderful flute and violin duetting before and after final verse.

(Leonard then introduced his musicians)

8. 'Iodine' – *very* rare concert outing; a boisterous rock and roller, providing a very up-beat close to the first set and the only other song from the 1977 Cohen/Spector project ever to be performed. Some altered lyrics towards the end with Leonard improvising a different order of the repeated 'Iodine' lines. 'So Long, Marianne' was adopted soon after as the regular choice to close the first set.

Intermission

9. solo: 'Stranger Song' – most often the first of the solo
   acoustic group; 'standard' performance.

10. solo: 'Chelsea Hotel #2' – introduced by Leonard with
    yet another variation on how he came to write the song;
    this time it's about having written it a long time ago for
    "a very great American singer"; he went on, somewhat
    amusingly, to mention how all singers are destined to be
    remembered, and forgotten, and it not really mattering
    which ones are remembered and which ones are for-
    gotten; and then came the punchline: "this one was
    a great one, her name was Janis Joplin." One or two
    subtle lyric changes e.g. 'handsome men'(v.2) becomes
    'younger men', and 'ugly' (ditto) becomes 'not pretty'.
    Lovely guitar picking, as usual. I don't believe that he has
    ever given a bad performance of this song.

11. solo: 'A Singer Must Die' – the last of the three nightly
    solos; a completely rewritten third verse, focusing on the
    artist's 'self-prostitution'. It is less graphic, more tender
    than the original version. Both versions are printed in
    the 1992 'Stranger Music' selection. Incidentally, the
    grave-price requested by Leonard tonight is $30; in other
    performances on the tour he goes down to $20 or up to
    $40. (And in 'Stranger Music' he asks for just the $12
    option!)

12. 'The Partisan' – the band returns; violin and 'accordion'
    feature early, and the flute and girls in the later French
    verses add colour to a fairly 'relaxed' performance.

13. 'Our Lady Of Solitude' – one of its few (and final)
    live performances, ever. Second 'Recent Songs' inclu-
    sion of the evening. Jennifer and Sharon feature more
    prominently than the album version, but it sounds flat
    and unengaging.

14. 'The Guests' – another from 'Recent Songs'; Leonard
    expressed his surprise to the audience at its 'reception'
    in Germany. (In the ZDF-TV programme he'd attributed

its popularity to the playing of Raffi Hakopian and John Bilezikjian.) He prefaced this performance with an explanation of the song's meaning. Verse five is omitted (and in all other performances too as far as one can tell) which is interesting because *that's* the verse about the "sweet repast" to which 'The Guests' have been invited. The song's 'sound' is as on the new album though it comes across with more animation, especially Raffi's contributions in the penultimate verse and chorus and Paul Ostermayer on flute adding delicate trills and fills here and there. The closing passage on violin is very passionate and might have been extended.

15. 'Famous Blue Raincoat' – lovely intimate feel to start with on this: low-register flute and piano combine to great effect. The mood is broken midway with a rasping, jazzy saxophone solo, which goes on to accompany Leonard through to the end. It's a different arrangement, there-fore, from earlier tours, and not one that brings out the best in the song.

16. 'The Gypsy's Wife' – the last of the four 'Recent Songs' in this show. And a real highlight, too, sounding even better than on the album. It's that violin solo, soaring, sliding and spiralling. Leonard's vocals sound less urgent, more resigned, this time and his musical support is equally sym-pathetic. Great song. Great performance.

17. 'Lover Lover Lover' – another long introduction on oud and drums too, new lyrics all over the place and that shift from the 'minor' verse into the 'major' chorus comes off really well. Rather touching oud fade-out-ending.

18. 'Why Don't You Try' – after a straightforward 'run through', there's a lovely clarinet solo on this, more extensive than the 1974 original, followed immediately by Mitch Watkin's electric guitar solo. Not many repeat efforts of this song on the tour, and none ever since.

19. 'Tonight Will Be Fine' – the audience clap along in time to this; some slight lyric changes (e.g. the walls "must be white" and the floor "must be bare"); a country stomp,

essentially, with Leonard still in good voice (he's been singing for well over 90 minutes by now), another guitar solo, some keyboard, saxophone breaks with a few powerful phrases, Leonard sings verse 3 again, and then he's gone . . . but only briefly – the applause continues and he's back for encores:

20. 'Suzanne' – 'standard' arrangement, with flute added in verse two, and the flute-violin duet brings the song to a close. Very warmly appreciated by the audience – I suppose the one they've been waiting for all night. Before the applause died down Leonard thanked them – "not just for tonight but for your attention to my songs for all these years, I appreciate it very much."

21. 'Memories' – ROCK AND ROLL!! – and such an absolutely fantastic contrast to the previous song. This has got to be the most 'un-Cohen-like' song-performance you could expect. The Phil Spector 'sound' is successfully recaptured on stage and Leonard sings with great gusto. Thousands-upon-thousands of fans witnessed all this during the 1979, 1980 and 1985 tours, it's on the ZDF television show and Harry Rasky's film has preserved another performance. Marvellous memories indeed.

22. 'Sisters Of Mercy' – and in complete contrast, again, to the preceding number. Flute and backing vocalists combine well in the early stages; violin solo at the end but I don't think it fits this time.

23. 'So Long, Marianne' – another favourite, sung with real energy and passion but I think Leonard's voice sounds somewhat strained now. Violin and saxophone team up for a rousing verse and chorus, midway; by the end, however, he has left the stage again. He returns firstly to acknowledge each musician and singer (and his sound engineer) by name to the audience, and then for the final two songs:

24. 'I Tried To Leave You' – as before, an oft-misunderstood title – and again tonight it's greeted with laughter and applause. 'Standard' *vocal* arrangement to the last line,

and then the new 'arrangement' unfolds: a sort of improvised 'solo' performed first by Sharon Robinson, then by saxophone and concluded on electric guitar. (And one of only a few songs on which oud and violin play no part.) Another, longer arrangement would make its appearance in 1985.

25. 'Bird On The Wire' – again, and as before, and bringing the two-and-a-half hour concert to a gratifying conclusion.

Leonard recited some of his poetry in a few concerts, including London (December 6), Manchester and Edinburgh. A new, though somewhat unsteady, song, performed in the final London concert called 'Thirsty For The Kiss' would later resurface, restyled and retitled 'Heart With No Companion', on Leonard's next album, over five years later, in 1985. First though, it was home to Montreal for a rest.

The tour was resumed less than three months later, with a series of seven concerts in Australia. It was the first time Cohen had performed in the country and the audiences received him with great warmth and enthusiasm. The press were complimentary, with rave reviews in each of the three cities. CBS released a four-album boxed-set: 'Leonard Cohen: Songs & Poems' (S4BP 220602) containing 'Songs Of Leonard Cohen', 'Songs From A Room', 'Songs Of Love And Hate' and 'New Skin For The Old Ceremony' (the last with a different front cover, as per the non-controversial USA issue in 1974) and a booklet containing all the lyrics to celebrate the event. Bafflingly, the sleeve-notes credit Janis Ian and Gail Kantor for vocals – they are uncredited on all other issues of this album!

The same material as the 1979 European tour was performed again, averaging about 23 songs per night. 'Recent Songs' was fairly well represented with five songs. Nothing too adventurous in the way of non-album or non-Cohen material was included, though the third Melbourne concert did begin (twice, it seems) with an almost spontaneous, and very good-hearted, 'Another Saturday Night', followed by the 'early' version of 'Heart With No Companion'; and one of the encores was a particularly raucous 'Billy Sunday'. Leonard sang both these latter songs with great confidence, in contrast to their earlier tentative outings (London, December 1979), and he continued his penchant for reciting a few of his poems (e.g. 'The Music Crept By Us'), usually at a most unexpected moment – in one case, immediately after the opening song in the second Melbourne show. On stage, Leonard was in confident mood, in good voice and on good, sometimes chatty, terms with his audiences; his Automat saga about apple pies, round peas and flat pancakes, followed later by the 'spotlight' dialogue, in the March 8 show in Melbourne during his acoustic set, are amusing examples of a relaxed stage presence. The band was as before, though Jennifer Warnes had left, occupied with the promotion of her own new 1979 album 'Shot Through The Heart', and she has not toured with Leonard since. Jennifer did sing with Leonard later in the year, in the first week of October, at the Bread And Roses Festival in Berkeley, California. The *Oakland Tribune* described the performance in the Greek Theatre as a "lark".

Three weeks later, Leonard was back in Europe with the same band (again without Jennifer who had been recording with Bob Dylan in late September), for a month-long tour, visiting many places he had been unable to include in his 1979 itinerary, while others saw him for the second, third and even fourth, time in the space of just a year.

There were 29 concerts on this late 1980 tour; the first in Besancon, France, on October 24, and the last in Tel Aviv, Israel, a month later. Leonard had not played in Israel since the final shows of the 1972 tour, as graphically captured in Tony Palmer's documentary *Bird On A Wire*. To all intents and purposes it was a belated continuation of the 1979 'Recent Songs' tour. As in North America in the early months of 1975, they occasionally played two concerts in one night.

The band, as in Australia, continued to support Leonard in their own individual and collective ways. In another revealing extract from Paul Ostermayer's piece, he explained how they worked with Leonard: "With him we learned how to take a more humble approach to music . . . Leonard's music demanded a dedication to finding the emotional core of each song . . . Another challenge was to focus our playing *through* Leonard. There was to be no going *around* Leonard to impress the audience . . ."

The songs and their arrangements were familiar from the previous couple of tours. Dutch Radio broadcast most of the Amsterdam concert on October 30 (somehow managing to exclude 'Bird on the Wire'), the finest audio evidence we have of these shows. It included a suitably drum-driven 'There Is A War' with a fine 'heavy' electric guitar solo from Mitch Watkins which offered yet another example of the varied scope of Cohen's 'arrangements', which were often miles away from the clichéd 'solo guitar and voice' promoted, and disparagingly too, in the press and elsewhere. They had obviously still not heard the 1976 single B-side, 'The Butcher'; or 'Diamonds In The Mine', 'Storeroom' or 'Do I Have To Dance All Night' for that matter, also from 1976.

IX

I'm Tied To The Threads Of Some Prayer

In an interview with Steve Lake, just minutes after the end of the Frankfurt concert (November 7, published in *Melody Maker*, November 22, 1980), Leonard indicated that after the European tour, he was heading back for more shows in Canada and the USA, then down to Australia, over to France for a week at the Olympia in Paris, and some final concerts in England. None of this ever came to pass; after the second of the two shows in Tel Aviv (November 24), everyone packed up and just went back home. Leonard returned to Hydra for a holiday there with his two children Adam and Lorca. In fact, his next appearance on a concert stage was to be more than four years later in Mannheim, Germany on the last day of January, 1985.

During these non-touring-behind-an-album years, CBS took advantage of the 'gap' in the Cohen market and in some European countries issued several different compilation albums. 'More Greatest Hits' was totally inappropriate since each already contained a good few from the original 1975 collection. In 1980 CBS Germany issued 'Liebesträume' – translation: 'Love's Dreams' – with the subtitle: "Leonard Cohen singt seine schönsten Lieder" – 'LC sings his most beautiful songs' – with a very generous 16 tracks culled from all previous albums, eight of which were on 'Greatest Hits'. In France, Germany and Holland CBS released a series of albums called 'Top Artists Of Pop Music' in 1982, including one on Leonard which presented 12 tracks, five from 'Greatest Hits', including 'Teachers' and 'Leaving Green Sleeves'. Re-issued in 1985 under the 'Golden Highlights' banner, this collection was later reissued on CD in 1990 by Pickwick in Australia. Meanwhile, in 1983 in the UK, Pickwick International, who licensed from CBS, released a real curio: a 7″ EP (also on cassette) in their 'Scoop' series with six tracks: 'Bird On The Wire', 'Lady Midnight', 'Joan Of Arc', 'Suzanne', 'Hey, That's No Way To Say Goodbye' and 'Paper Thin Hotel'. Perhaps the best of all these reissues was in the 'Starsound Collection' from CBS Germany, also in 1983 – a Half Speed Mastered disc – a technique resulting in far superior sound quality – with 12 tracks, 11 of which were on 'Liebesträume', representing the first four studio albums. Decent sleeve-notes too. This compilation was repackaged and reissued in 1989 as 'So Long, Marianne'. Other 'Hits' albums (though again not so-labelled) would continue to appear elsewhere in later years even after 'Various Positions' and 'I'm Your Man'. In 1992 in the USA, prior to 'The Future', Sony Music let loose a ten-track CD and cassette called 'Leonard Cohen Takes Manhattan' with (in order): 'Bird On The Wire', 'Avalanche', 'Take This Longing', 'Tonight Will Be Fine', 'The Guests', 'Seems So Long Ago, Nancy', 'Ballad Of The Absent Mare', 'Hey, That's No Way To Say Goodbye', 'Suzanne' and 'First We Take Manhattan'.

Two Views And Seven Poems, a book commissioned by Leonard's publishers McClelland and Stewart, with seven of his poems alongside the illustrative lithographs of Gigino Falconi, was published in 1980. No new Cohen material here: 'My Lady Can Sleep' from *The Spice-Box Of The Earth* (1961), 'This Morning I Was Dressed By The Wind' from *Parasites Of Heaven* (1966), and the other five from *Death Of A Lady's Man* (1978): 'Slowly I Married Her', 'The Absence Of Monica', 'Snow Is Falling', 'Traditional Training And Service' and 'Another Man's Woman'. Another poem-and-picture book would appear in 1985, just after 'Various Positions', with visuals from the German artist-singer Jurgen Jaensch; and again in 1995 when the text of 'Dance Me To The End Of Love' accompanied paintings by Henri Matisse.

'Fragments From A Journal' was a short piece published in

1980 in *Zero* magazine which listed Cohen as an Advisory Editor at the time. It began: "I lit a stick of incense. I sat down on a small cushion, crossing my legs in full Lotus" and continued with a description of how he came to write a metaphysical song with four eight-line stanzas. One such verse is quoted in full. His friend Anthony replied with a humorous five-line improvisation and the piece ended with Leonard approaching a pretty young woman in an endeavour "to let her know I had been touched by Grace". It almost made her cry. Leonard's friend Steve Sanfield contributed to the same issue.

Leonard was involved in several projects at this time: a rock-opera-cum-musical, song videos, a book, writing and recording the songs for his next album. In addition to his own work, Leonard also found time to look in on rehearsals for *Bird On The Wire*, an off-Broadway production directed by Stefan Rudnicki which used 18 of his songs and poems, and dance-routines, to examine "the integrity of the individual in contemporary society", as explained by the director. Contrary to the many assertions found in a myriad of reference books, press articles and summaries of his career, the five-year period following 'Recent Songs' was not a fallow one.

Leonard collaborated on 'Night Magic' – aka 'Merry-Go Man', 'Angel Eyes' and others before settling on the final version – from 1981 onwards with his fellow Canadian Lewis Furey, viola player on 'New Skin For The Old Ceremony', now turned composer and film director. Chronologically speaking, it was Leonard's next work after 'Recent Songs'. Its categorisation has varied, ranging from pop opera to rock opera to musical to fantasy movie, but Leonard's role was straightforward: he wrote all the words, incorporating Spenserian stanzas. Leonard's 18 songs have the following titles: 'I've Counted What I Have'; 'Wishing Window', 'The Throne Of Desire', 'Throne Variations'; 'Angel Eyes', 'The Law', 'The Promise', 'The Marriage March', 'The Third Invention', 'Clap! Clap!', 'Hunter's Lullaby', 'We Told You So', 'Fire', 'Song Of Destruction', 'The Walls', 'Coming Back', 'Song To My Assassin' and 'The Bells' and Furey set them all to music. In the story, an impatient 35-year-old singer/composer who wants love, money and success, is visited one night by three angels, one of whom falls in love with him . . . and the rest deals with the consequences of their relationship.

Because the main focus of this book is to concentrate on Leonard's *musical* performances I won't dwell long on this particular collection since he does not sing, but there are several points of interest here. Firstly, some of those titles would soon be familiar: 'The Law', 'Hunter's Lullaby' and 'The Bells'. Perhaps we should also include 'Coming Back'. 'The Bells' was the original title of a song, recorded under that name by Buffy Sainte-Marie in 1971, that later became 'Take This Longing' on the 1974 'New Skin For The Old Ceremony' album. Word-wise, 'Hunter's Lullaby' remained pretty well intact on 'Various Positions', but 'The Law' was to have completely new lyrics. 'Coming Back' had nothing in common with the later 'Coming Back To You', though it did have some phrases which were incorporated into another song, 'Dance Me To The End Of Love', also on 'Various Positions'. And 'The Bells' was an early version of 'Anthem' which would appear on the 1992 album 'The Future'.

An 80-minute double-vinyl album of 'Night Magic', labelled as a 'musical', was issued by RCA in Europe in 1985. The credits include Erin Dickens as one of the Angels and Ian Terry, engineer on 'I'm Your Man' and 'The Future', is credited for the vocal recording. *Night Magic*, the 90 minute film with extra dialogue not on the album, starring Carole Laure and Nick Mancuso, was presented at the Cannes International Film Festival on May 17 that year and at the Montreal World Film Festival in August. The reviews which appeared in Variety and the *Montreal Gazette*, among others, were mixed. In any event, both Cohen and Furey won a Juno Award for Best Movie Score. A video-release from Alliance/MCA Canada followed in 1988.

I Am A Hotel features five linked song-videos concerning the goings-on in a hotel, from its ballroom to its bedrooms. Leonard, himself the hotel guest *par excellence* if ever there was one, described it thus: "I sketched out an idea . . . a series of interconnecting vignettes based on some of my songs." The songs in question were 'The Guests', 'Memories', 'The Gypsy's Wife', 'Chelsea Hotel #2', and 'Suzanne'. Mark Shekter then developed the story and the five songs are brought to life on the screen, using Leonard's album versions (to which he lip-syncs, quite successfully too if you watch real close) as the soundtrack. He also appears on screen, dressed of course in grey and black, playing the part of the hotel's resident spirit, an ageless guest providing the link into each of the stories as they unfold. His performance is thus minimal but it does make the 25-minute show more interesting. Leonard: "I'm the catalyst who moves the story gently from one tale to another." These tales revolve around various couples in the hotel: the two young lovers, the hotel porter and the chambermaid, the hotel manager and his long lost wife, the once-famous opera singer and the retired admiral, and the 'hotel spirit' himself, in search of his own true love.

Getting the project off the ground and onto the screen ran into severe problems when the original backers, C Channel Pay-TV, went bust six days before shooting began. CBC came to the rescue and the rest is graphic imagery. The stars were Toller Cranston, the skater, in his first acting role and Anne Ditchburn who was also responsible for the choreography. It was set in the luxurious Victorian splendour of the King Edward Hotel in Toronto. Guests there over the years have included Candice Bergen, Rudolph Valentino, The Beatles, Mark Twain, Rudyard Kipling and Luciano Pavarotti. Filming lasted two weeks in May 1983 under the direction of Allan Nicholls, an associate of Robert Altman, with additional scenes directed by Don Allan. The producers were Leonard's long-time friends Barrie Wexler and Moses Znaimer, and it was the first production by their new Blue Memorial Video company, so-called in honour of Leonard's late musician friend David Blue (born Cohen, no relation), who had died the previous year and to whose memory the film is dedicated. Incidentally, Leonard worked with Francine Hershorn to organise David

Blue's last demo recording session after he had been dropped by Asylum Records. David had covered 'Lover Lover Lover' back in 1975 on his album 'Comin' Back For More'.

A second project, inspired by the making of this hotel saga, the filming of Leonard's first novel *The Favourite Game*, did not materialise. Something which did, however, was the First Prize, a Golden Rose awarded to *I Am A Hotel* at the 1984 Montreux International Television Festival.

I Am A Hotel was Leonard's his first ever experience in video and it certainly influenced, perhaps even prompted, the making of his own next video venture 'Dance Me To The End Of Love', to promote 'Various Positions'. Before that, however, came his 1984 *Book Of Mercy*. Leonard: "The book is the result of my devotion to my God and to a religious tradition. It came about out of what I had been doing, out of a need within me." He was 50 that year, and the book, dedicated to Leonard's Zen teacher, Joshu Sasaki ('Roshi'), contains this same number of what Leonard called prayers, others called them psalms, prose poems or meditations. After its publication in the autumn of 1984, with a Cohen-designed front cover showing two interlocked hearts in the shape of the Star of David, he undertook a promotional tour, travelling around from city to city, signing books and doing interviews. Listeners to the New York radio station WNEW-FM may well have heard him recite No 8, *In the eyes of men he falls*, on the Pete Fornatel show *Mixed Bag* on Sunday, April 28, 1985, a couple of days before playing his first US shows in more than a decade. The following month, the Canadian Authors' Association chose it for their Literature Award in the Poetry category; a nice touch, coming just over a week after Leonard's five shows in his native country, his first concerts in Canada for over ten years.

There was a newspaper interview with Steve Venright, printed in mid-1984, which stated that after the completion of filming *I Am A Hotel* Leonard was still in the midst of recording some of the *Book Of Mercy* texts to an accompaniment of string and woodwind quartet music conducted by Jeremy Lubbock, but this has not yet surfaced. Another recording project mentioned in that article, however, *did* materialise, eventually: 'Various Positions', his 9th album, and in the eyes and ears of many it confirmed Leonard's continuing comeback from Spectorian oblivion to the forefront of his own musical landscape, 'Recent Songs' and *I Am A Hotel* being, of course, his main and valiant precursors on this journey. There was, unfortunately, one player in the piece who remained unconvinced, sceptical even, of Leonard's creative ability; and he saw to it that Columbia refused to issue this new album in the USA.

X

The Holy Books Are Open Wide

Picture the scene: Walter Yetnikoff's office, Columbia HQ, New York, some time in 1984; Leonard himself has just, literally, brought in the tape of his new album to play to the president of his record company. After the first track 'Dance Me To The End Of Love', Mr Yetnikoff complains that he doesn't like the mix. Leonard suggests that Mr Yetnikoff himself should remix it; and later in the same session, Yetnikoff tells Leonard that "they know he's great but just don't know if he's any good".

This account comes from Leonard's own lips, and it is as much as we know, so far, about the circumstances leading up to the non-release of 'Various Positions' by Columbia in the USA. Put another way, Leonard's record company dropped him! This album, therefore, enjoyed the singular distinction of being released by CBS in Canada, Japan and Europe only. It was eventually released in the USA by Passport Records on the Jem label, though not, despite its potential market, in any great numbers. And today it is only available in the USA, on CD, as an import.

There are nine songs on this ninth album. The front cover is a self-shot, very close-up polaroid photo, slightly out of focus. The songs confirm a certain ill-definition of opinion on various themes – thus, Leonard's various positions. Recorded at Quadrasonic Sound Studios, New York, and at just over 35 minutes playing-time, 'Various Positions' is the shortest album in the Cohen catalogue. The compensations, however, are considerable: it's the first all-Cohen-song album

111

since 'New Skin For The Old Ceremony' (1974); Jennifer Warnes' gorgeous voice is on several tracks; *all* the song lyrics are included for the first time ever on a Cohen disc, a practice that was repeated in 1988 and 1992. John Lissauer is back as arranger and producer; and most importantly, of course, there are some great songs. Three other familiar names are in the credits: Erin Dickins on vocals (as on 'New Skin For The Old Ceremony' and the 1974 and 75 tours); Sid McGinnes on guitar, who played on the 1976 tour in Europe; and Leanne Ungar who recorded and mixed the album (she too had previously worked on 'New Skin For The Old Ceremony') and has since become Leonard's main engineer and mixer.

After the sparse, chamber intimacy of most of 'Recent Songs', there is a brighter and broader sound to 'Various Positions', accommodating both the larger number of players and the 'feel' of most of the new songs, while still maintaining the glow and rapport we expect from Leonard's vocals. The almost breathless 'If It Be Your Will' is a case in point.

A black & white video was made for the opening song, a fine example of a 50-year old artist being in touch with what has since become 'de rigueur'. Several singles were issued in various countries; seven of the nine songs were performed during the five 1985 mini-tours, and, in fact, both 'Dance Me To The End Of Love' and 'Hallelujah' have been sung in almost every single concert since then. When 'Live In Concert' was issued in 1994, with tracks from the 1988 and 1993 tours, a new, colour video of 'Dance Me To The End Of Love' was chosen to promote it.

In an interview published in *The Malahat Review* in December 1986, Leonard admitted that when songs are finished and collected together "they generally fall around a certain position: and this position (i.e. that of this new album) seemed to me like walking, like walking around the circumference of the circle. It's the same area looked at from different positions . . ." No change there then – Cohen, an English-speaking Jew in French Catholic Montreal, the 'Yank' in Greece and a decidedly non-Zen Buddhist in residence on Mount Baldy, was merely shuffling along his familiar path. The only difference this time round was that it had been almost six years since his last bout of open-soul searching and we had become accustomed to a two year gap between albums since 1967.

It must have been with much relief, therefore, when Cohen fans *finally* did get their hands on 'Various Positions'. There may perhaps have been an even greater sense of disbelief, however, when they played the first track 'Dance Me To The End Of Love' with its electronic keyboards, up-tempo dance rhythms (marked at 126 beats-per-minute), and a mixed vocal 'la-la' chorus lasting a full thirty-three seconds, before Leonard was heard. The new technology signalled a new direction for Cohen's music which he has continued to pursue ever since. Cohen's voice is strong, employing a wide range of notes, including an octave drop at the end of each verse. The Middle-Eastern melodic lilt is harmonised by Jennifer Warnes and there's a lovely violin solo after the second and fourth verses. There is purpose and verve here, the word 'dance' occurring twenty times. There are Biblical references too, naturally, but it's not a religious song. This is music from a Nazi concentration camp – Leonard has called it "a chilling scenario" – and about the struggle, and joy, of survival. Ultimately, the message, the 'position', is positive and up-beat. 'Dance Me To The End Of Love', the album's longest song was also its lead single, coupled with 'Coming Back To You', one of the shortest (on CBS 4895), and it also became Cohen's first ever album-promoting video (shot in black&white inside a hospital). Since mid-tour 1988 it has opened practically every single concert, displacing 'Bird On The Wire' from its familiar spot in set-lists.

Maybe the second song, 'Coming Back To You', was Leonard's subtle way of underlining the notion that he had finally made his comeback. In the guise of a love-ballad, piano, guitar and a lazy two-beat on the drum with brushed hi-hat lead into the first of four tender 8-line verses, which can all be read as four two-line phrases, with Leonard singing alone until

113

joined by backing vocals on each final couplet. Sid McGinnes on guitar weaves in and around the melody adding that good ol' country twang.

I'm not sure whereabouts on the circle Leonard had moved to when he positioned himself for the sentiments expressed in 'The Law' but his voice sounds tired, further back in the mix than in 'Coming Back To You', though it just seems to be a continuation of that same conversation. The musical accompaniment is brighter – Leonard has backing vocals throughout and the syncopated drum and bass rhythms move the song along. Leonard often brought more life to this song in concert when it sounded dynamic and pulsating and, as we have seen before and since in other songs, he included extra lyrics.

After these draining conversational confrontations, Leonard sought comfort from his mother; in 'The Night Comes On' her words are sung by Jennifer Warnes in her second significant contribution on the album. A straight five-verse narrative, with autobiographical references aplenty, this is probably the only Cohen song in which his mother, father, son, daughter, lover and friends all get a mention. Gentle percussion with bass and acoustic guitars provide the song's heart-beat, along with Jennifer's sensual harmonies and a short instrumental which brings the song to a muted close.

Occasionally some of Cohen's songs sound like demos, as if he's trying them out in the studio in preparation for their ultimate destination: live, on stage. A case in point is 'Hallelujah'. Good though it is on the album – full of melody, rhythm, rhyme, accentuated bass-line, and a surprising dead-stop just before the final fading repeated Hallelujahs – Leonard's line seems dry throughout. In concert, however, it comes to life, with Cohen in full vocal command, while keyboard, drums, backing vocals and a satisfying solo for electric guitar not featured on the album add passionate support. Leonard: "I've always had a live show that was somewhat more driving, more rhythmic than my records have been." CBS released 'Hallelujah' as the follow-up single (c/w 'The Law' CBS 4918) to 'Dance Me To The End Of Love' in several European countries, including Spain, Germany and Holland.

'The Captain' is yet another conversation piece, this time between an Army recruit and his dying commander, in the somewhat incongruous form of a toe-tapping, finger-clicking, country and western stomp, complete with scratching fiddle and honky tonk piano. It's simple and direct reportage with the usual Cohen mix of religious and military references. Leonard's voice is often double tracked. This song has never been sung live, though Cohen did recite it as an encore a few times on the US leg of the 1985 tour.

'Hunter's Lullaby' is that rare Cohen composition in which the title line does not feature anywhere in the main lyric: 'One Of Us Cannot Be Wrong', 'Memories', 'Death Of A Ladies' Man' are the others. Rare too was the 7″ vinyl issued by CBS Australia (CBS 3295) with the song on the B-side of 'Dance Me To The End Of Love'. It is also the shortest track on the album. A simple, rather slight song, it turns on the mother's position of informing her child that the 'pater-familias' is absent from the home, on a mission. Leonard's delivery is as unremarkable as the understated accompaniment. These same lyrics (and an additional verse not sung by Leonard in his version) were also set to music by Lewis Furey for the movie *Night Magic*, where a higher degree of musical sophistication and satisfaction awaits the listener.

As if to corroborate its own insubstantiality, 'Hunter's Lullaby' is followed by another lightweight song, 'Heart With No Companion', thereby providing a neat juxtaposition with the two meatier dialogues, 'Coming Back To You' and 'The Law'. Leonard's vocal is strong in this easy four-to-the-bar number, with gentle acoustic guitar ostinato, a rock-steady rhythm section, plus violin and harmonica fills and supporting vocals in the middle verses. It's undemanding listening, really, compounded by unconvincing lyrics.

'Various Positions' closes with a masterpiece: 'If It Be Your Will', the most serene love-hymn to God that Leonard has ever written. Nothing else, either in print or on disc, comes close to this offer of total surrender. Whereas in 1972's 'Minute Prologue', with his youthful arrogance and inexperience, Leonard dared to heal and soothe all wounds with a song, now, not much more than a decade later, he's not so sure of himself and seeks assurance and reassurance from God in order to raise his voice in song. Jennifer adds her own gorgeous harmonies. In Japan, Sony/CBS released this song as the B-side to 'Dance Me To The End Of Love' (07SP 873) – a fitting coupling, with a superb, full-colour illustration by Akio Maruichi, based on a short scene in the promo-video for the A-side song.

Lagging far behind chart topping Bruce Springsteen's 'Born In The USA', whose re-released lead-single 'Dancing In The Dark' was then enjoying renewed success, 'Various Positions' received mixed reviews, peaking at No 52 in the UK. Among its more perceptive listeners in the US was Joe Saafy whose clever review in *The Washington Post* of May 22, 1985, seemed to identify the very essence of Leonard's entire songwriting oeuvre: "While Cohen's songs range from the confessional to the allegorical, they ceaselessly portray love as a harrowing inevitability, both a necessity and a kind of wilful imprisonment". So, after these nine songs, it's not so much a case of coming full circle as one of spiralling into the centre-maelstrom of passion, melancholy and spirituality. Our aural Cohen-trip may only have lasted 35 minutes or so; ahead, for Leonard and his band, lay six months of touring. 'Various Positions' is still the only album without an accompanying songbook; two songs, however, 'Hallelujah' and 'If It Be Your Will' were printed in the Polish music magazine *Alleluja!* in 1986, transcribed, moreover, in the correct keys.

In 1985, from the last day in January to almost the last week in July, Leonard and the band performed 77 concerts in five short tours that visited Europe (twice), North America (twice) and Australia. As in 1980, plans to perform in Japan came to nothing. With five supporting players, Richard Crooks, John Crowder, Ron Getman and Anjani Thomas, all of whom played on 'Various Positions', and Mitch Watkins, who toured with Leonard in 1979 and 1980, it was Leonard's smallest group since 1974. On these tours Ron Getman substituted his harmonica for guitars and Anjani played keyboards.

With almost indecent haste, the first tour of 1985 began before 'Various Positions' had been released in some countries. The itinerary, 42 concerts in 35 cities in 53 days, included familiar venues such as London's Hammersmith Odeon and the National Stadium in Dublin, and some new locations including his first ever concerts in Portugal and Poland. The final concerts on March 24 in Milan were his first ever performances in Italy, too, and also the last of the two shows-in-an-evening scheduling for 1985. New venues in familiar cities such as Madrid and Munich also figured on this tour. On the other hand, however, Frankfurt missed out despite successful concerts there in the Jahrhunderthalle throughout the Seventies and in 1980; Amsterdam was passed over too, where the Concertgebouw audiences on four previous tours had received him well.

Leonard and his band were welcomed wherever they went and coverage of the concerts was unprecedented. Some of the January rehearsals in New York had been filmed and were included in a 30-minute documentary (in the *Personen-beschreibung* series) first broadcast on German (ZDF) television on September 9, 1985, directed by Georg Stefan Troller. He also interviewed Leonard on camera in New York, Berlin and Paris, part of which featured him reciting 'new' lyrics to his song 'Hallelujah' that would later be incorporated into 1988 and 1993 performances. Leonard was certainly much more involved with pre- and post-gig interviews and in news programmes than before. Some television stations featured actual concert material while others included soundcheck and rehearsal footage in their reports. Danish TV chose to broadcast the last six songs from the Copenhagen concert: 'Sisters of Mercy', 'Memories', 'So Long, Marianne', 'The Night Comes On', 'Passin' Thru' and 'Bird On The Wire'.

Uniquely among all the radio broadcasts over the years,

the Polish Akademickie Radio Pomorze in Szczecin saw fit to issue two 60-minute cassette-tapes containing most of the Warsaw concert complete with English lyrics, Polish translations and transcriptions of some of Leonard's comments to his audience between some of the 21 songs. Leonard was asked by a Solidarity official to invite Lech Walesa, their leader, to his Warsaw concert, thus challenging the Polish Authorities who were holding him under 'town confinement' in the northern city of Gdansk. Reluctant to get embroiled in national politics, Leonard declined. In Wroclaw, the first half of the show did not go well. Leonard was extremely nervous and appeared not to be himself. The People's Hall had hosted Third Reich rallies and only after the interval when Leonard referred to this and to himself being a better singer than Hitler did the atmosphere become more relaxed. This snippet of information can be found in the large-format, 16-page booklet with the splendid title *Alleluja!* containing 12 songs with melody and chords score, including 'Suzanne' and 'The Guests', as well as the only known printed music versions of 'Passin' Thru', 'Hallelujah' and 'If It Be Your Will'. English and Polish translations appear side-by-side with photographs, discography and some biographical material which celebrated the visit. An annual Cohen Festival continues in Krakow.

These concerts were structured in a similar manner to previous tours, with nine to 11 songs performed with the band in the first half, followed by an interval, then Leonard solo for three acoustic songs ('Avalanche', 'Chelsea Hotel #2', 'The Stranger Song'), then the band joined him again for another 10 to 12 songs, thus averaging about 24 per night from a basic core of about 30, mainly from the first and fifth albums and strong representation from 'Various Positions'. Exceptions to the basic format occurred in Madrid, where there were no solo songs, Paris and the first London show. In Manchester the audience heard 19 songs before the acoustic set; and in Linz they only heard one solo song all evening ('Chelsea Hotel #2'). There were no intervals in the 'two-in-an-evening' schedule in Dublin, though a couple of acoustic numbers did feature almost at the end in both. As in 1979, 'Sisters of Mercy' and 'Suzanne' received both 'solo' and 'band' treatments. All concerts opened with 'Bird On The Wire' and about half of them closed with a second rendition, though it did get a third (albeit incomplete) performance in Munich. Seven songs from 'Various Positions' were tried out: 'The Law', 'Coming Back To You', 'Night Comes On', 'Dance Me To The End Of Love', 'Hallelujah', 'Heart With No Companion' and 'If It Be Your Will', with five included in most concerts though 'Heart' received only one known performance on the opening night in Mannheim. Only Leonard knows why: the Mannheim performance was just fine – maybe *that's* what was wrong! It was to reappear six months later as a fairly regular number during the second European Tour. Three songs 'The Partisan', 'Tennessee Waltz' (not written by Cohen, but he added a second verse) and 'If It Be Your Will' were all brought in as pretty regular inclusions after the initial 15 or so shows, taking the place of 'There Is A War', 'Night Comes On' and 'Story Of Isaac'. 'The Guests' was dropped after a couple of early performances (Mannheim, Wiesbaden) and 'Joan Of Arc' was played in well under 50% of these concerts. But as recorded earlier, he can't play everything every night. And when a rarity like 'Joan Of Arc' (in an obvious duet with Anjani) did appear, it was to be enjoyed all the more.

Of course, with a new band, there was a new sound to the songs and with no violin or oud players this time round, the musical textures, subtleties and colourings were provided in many instances by additional vocal harmonies.

After Europe, they all enjoyed a break for a month before Leonard's first concert-tour in the USA and Canada for over a decade, including his home-town of Montreal. But it wasn't all rest. Leonard took part in New York's Carnival Of The Spoken Word (held during the months March, April and May) with public readings of his own work spread over three days. There were media interviews, press conferences and other promotional rigmarole to endure. Mind you, ten years was a long time to be absent from New York so these duties were hardly unexpected.

119

They included a radio interview on the programme *Mixed Bag*, hosted by Pete Fornatel, in the WNEW-FM studios in New York, on April 28, in the course of which Leonard, accompanied by Mitch Watkins, Ron Getman and John Crowder, sang an all-acoustic, slightly slower than the album version of 'Night Comes On'. For a 10.45 am performance on a Sunday morning, it's very good. The 25-minute interview concluded with Leonard reading a text, which he called "a small prayer" from his 1984 *Book Of Mercy* (No 8 – *In the eyes of men he falls*). A few days later he was interviewed on US television by Richard Belzer on *Hot Properties* in the course of which he spoke some words which really do encapsulate his own view (his 'position') on matters personal: ". . . we all live the life of the heart . . . nobody ever masters the heart . . . it keeps on cooking like shish-kebab in everybody's breast . . . and I think it's only concerned with loving and losing and wanting and having . . . most songs affirm that life of the heart and I think they always will . . ."

Articles, ticket adverts, photographs, previews, interviews and reviews filled pages in, among others, the *Philadelphia Inquirer*, the *Mercury*, the *Boston Globe*, *Variety*, the *New York Times*, the *Ottawa Citizen*, the *Montreal Gazette*, the *Toronto Star*, the *Winnipeg Sun*, the *Winnipeg Free Press* (where the accuracy of some song titles was often wayward, e.g. 'Come Back To Me', 'Back To The War') and the *Georgia Straight* (Vancouver's Entertainment Guide). Leonard and his troupe proceeded from the three eastern American cities into Canada to play the last of their nine shows via Winnipeg and, on the far western shores of British Columbia, Vancouver. While it must be said that not each and every newspaper lauded Leonard's perform-ances to the skies, the reception in North America was, for the most part, generous, warm-hearted and sincere. I sometimes wonder if CBS President Walter Yetnikoff ever made it to the Carnegie Hall concert.

As for song-repertoire, the sets were pretty much as in Europe, slightly longer in fact, averaging about twenty-seven per night. 'A Singer Must Die', with new lyrics for verse three, replaced 'Chelsea Hotel #2' and in Boston and New York, on the 10th anniversary of the end of the Vietnam War, Leonard recited 'The Captain'.

'Night Comes On' was played significantly slower than on disc with more guitar backing and though Anjani's harmonies blended well, I wished, and not for the first time, that it was Jennifer Warnes up there. The Boston audience was informed by Leonard that 'The Partisan' had become an anthem for Solidarity prisoners in their internment camps in Poland. "It is to acknowledge their suffering and our undeserved grace that I sing this song," he said. With Richard Crooks keeping the whole thing together, the high 'chill factor' in this song's troubled landscape was indeed registered during these North American performances. Less than a week after Vancouver, they stepped on to another stage over 7,000 miles away, for a series of concerts in Australia.

The Australian programme indicated a second Adelaide show, on June 3, but this did not take place. Coming after the much-heralded return to North America, these performances, as well as those in Europe in late June and July, sounded more relaxed. Some of the songs, 'Dance Me To The End Of Love' is a good example, seem to have broadened out, and without losing any of their inherent energy were less urgent, less precipitous in their delivery; maybe that's what happens when you play a song more than 50 times in about four months.

The song-lists indicate an average of about 26 songs per night (Sydney, May 24, heard a very generous 30) with the usual five or six from 'Various Positions', four solos, (Sydney heard five, the extra an extremely rare acoustic performance of 'One Of Us Cannot Be Wrong') and the rest culled from the same basic core group as before. In fact, in the case of Sydney again, it was practically every song the band had rehearsed for the entire tour!

Prior to both the Brisbane and Sydney shows, Leonard and the band played live on television, on the *Mike Walsh Show*, May 20, with a performance of 'Dance Me To The End Of Love': smooth and relaxed, and on the *Midday Show*, hosted by Ray Martin, May 24, playing 'Coming Back To You':

country'n'gentle. In both cases, Leonard chatted with the programme hosts, both of whom were equipped with every Cohen-cliché, including the inaccurate ones. Leonard fended them off, attempting to put the record straight. On song-writing he said "It's a deep spiritual quest for the truth"; on 'Dance Me To The End Of Love', he said "If a song comes from a deep place it'll have a wide embrace"; on the song 'Suzanne', "I wrote that song 'Suzanne' before I met the mother of my children"; on drinking before a concert, "I usually drink just about enough to feel the vine."

After the second Perth concert, they returned from the Australian west coast to the USA for a couple of shows in San Francisco and Los Angeles. Joni Mitchell and Bob Dylan both turned up at the Wiltern Theatre on June 9. Press coverage continued to be mostly favourable about Leonard's voice, style and poetry, his themes and their musical treatments on disc and in concert, though the *San Jose Mercury* seemed incapable of using a decent recent photograph of Leonard. Elsewhere there were still the surely by now redundant remarks about his dark shirt and suit. There were no new songs in the set-lists but the 'Chelsea Hotel #2' introductory rap continued, as before, to be an amusing feature of the solo set. Perhaps it was to this that Robert Hilburn's review in the *LA Times* referred when he wrote of Leonard's telling witty and disarming stories. Anyway, in the Australian/American concerts, our hero meets Janis Joplin in the elevator and when, in reply to his question as to what she is looking for, she tells him Kris Kristofferson, Leonard admits to being the very same man! After another short break of just under three weeks, it was time to return to Europe.

A few of the cities were familiar to Leonard and the band from their first visits earlier in the year (Helsinki, Oslo and Vienna), but most locations and venues were new. Some gigs were outdoor festival performances, sharing the bills and audiences with other singers and bands, at Roskilde, for example, with The Cure, The Clash and Style Council. The final 16 concerts in 16 towns in 25 days were either a way of accepting fresh challenges in uncharted territory or a way of playing, and in so doing 'winding down', in less prestigious, somewhat less pressured, circumstances after the accumulated effects of over 60 concerts and almost six months on the road.

'Heart With No Companion' returned as a regular after just one performance in the very first show in Mannheim and apart from the shorter sets played at the various festivals (necessitating the exclusion of Leonard's solo acoustic numbers) about 26 or 27 songs were played each night, still including six or seven from 'Various Positions', so they were still clocking up more than two-and-a-half hours on stage. The *Jerusalem Post* published a fairly lengthy review of the Sultan's Pool concert by David Horovitz who cast doubts on Leonard's sincerity in being able to sing the same songs year after year. Four paragraphs later he described the music as magnificent. Admittedly, Leonard's vocal delivery was sometimes uneven, often strained as if he was trying too hard. This was apparent during some songs at Roskilde (and in many performances of 'Memories' in particular) but the very next night in Helsingborg his voice just sounded settled again and in 'Story of Isaac' there was no strain, no push, no problem. There were FM radio broadcasts from the Kalvøya and Guehenno Festivals and of the entire concert in Montreux, and some songs from the Oslo and Guehenno shows were also televised.

By the time they got to Vienna and beyond, the once 'tight' quintet, previously held in strict professional check, became a little more flexible in performance, resulting in some quite splendid versions of 'So Long, Marianne', 'Passing Thru', 'Lover Lover Lover' and (a still infrequent) 'Joan Of Arc'. The Montreux show (July 9) contained fine versions of nearly all these. Even the still-lengthy 'I Tried To Leave You' sounded that much more accessible. On this occasion Leonard borrowed a phrase from 'Song Of Destruction' in 'Night Magic', altered it slightly and conferred the title of "master of sticks and skin" to introduce drummer Richard Crooks. After Montreux, they crisscrossed Europe from Switzerland to northern Spain, to Brittany, and to Sweden before the final shows in warmer Mediterranean climes, concluding the whole 77-concert-enterprise in St. Jean de Luz, in the south-west corner of France, about 10 miles south of Biarritz.

It surely must have crossed Leonard's mind to issue a live album from his 1985 tour. Following his decision not to, however, somebody else did: a double-vinyl album ("audience recording") from Wiesbaden on February 2, containing 20 of that concert's 24 songs; and there are two 'unofficial' CDs, 'Diamonds In The Minefield' and 'Heart Housed In Thornbush', both taken from the Montreux FM broadcast, each containing a different compilation of 14 songs, which attest to the 'late'-85 style. These latter two are, therefore, unrepresentative of the 1985 tour performances as a whole but are important in providing a reasonable compendium of at least one decent show out of so many.

By tour-end, the audiences had the opportunity to draw breath, reflect upon and enjoy the plethora of multi-media Cohen products on offer within the space of a couple of years: a Cohen-scripted movie and linked double-album, a book, a song video, an extended video-sequence, an all-Cohen-song disc and the memories of almost 80 concerts on three continents. There had never been a time when so many Cohen items were all on the market together, receiving so much attention from critics and consumers alike. But it was as nothing in comparison to the reception his next album, 'I'm Your Man', was to receive less than three years later. By the time it was released, Leonard had completed work on several other interesting projects: a compilation release and linked-video, a film, a top US television programme and Jennifer Warnes' new album. But, first of all, he headed back to base on Hydra.

XI

I'll Bury My Soul In A Scrapbook

Credo, a paperback of Cohen poems with illustrations by the 36-year old German artist and singer Jurgen Jaensch, had originally been published in a limited edition in 1977. Following the success of 'Various Positions' in Europe, the collection was enlarged and reprinted in late 1985. The new edition contained 21 poems and two song lyrics ('The Old Revolution' and 'Hallelujah') in English with German translation alongside on the left with the graphics on the opposite page. One other poem 'My Teacher Is Dying' is printed only in German. The selection includes lines from almost every Cohen poetry book, thus: three each from *Let Us Compare Mythologies, The Spice-Box Of Earth* and *Parasites Of Heaven,* 10 from *Flowers For Hitler,* a couple of the 'New Poems' in the 1968 collection and just one from *The Energy Of Slaves.* Even without the visuals it would still be a stimulating read.

'Poets in New York', 'A Moving Picture', 'Miami Vice' (yes! the NBC series starring Don Johnson) and 'Famous Blue Raincoat' are not often cited as part of Leonard Cohen's *oeuvre*. A separate case can be made for the last mentioned since in the eyes and ears of so many it was that very disc, albeit by another singer, Jennifer Warnes, which was responsible for the dramatic upsurge in interest in his music which not only carried over to the release and reception of his own 1988 album 'I'm Your Man' but well beyond it too. Leonard: "Jennifer helped me enormously . . . in the high smoky rooms of power where these things are determined I think maybe my career and my name underwent some kind of revision." An upsurge must, by its very nature, follow a slump but the years 1980–84 were actually very productive for Leonard. The media thought differently but they judged Jennifer's new album – her first solo effort for more than six years – as much for her singing, the arrangements and the mix, as for Leonard's older songs, almost as if 'Recent Songs' and 'Various Positions' and all the stations on the way had not been given serious consideration at all.

Chronologically, after the 1985 concerts, the next project to hand was 'Take This Waltz'. 'Pequeño vals vienés' ('Little Viennese Waltz'), a poem by Federico Garcia Lorca, was chosen by CBS Spain and offered to Leonard to set to music as his contribution on a compilation album to honour the 50th anniversary of the death of his favourite Spanish poet and playwright. He found the existing English translations incomprehensible *and* unsingable and ended up writing his own. Leonard: "That was a very difficult job. It took me over 150 hours." The recording was done in Paris in a studio in Montmartre and is the opening track on the tribute album. Alberto Manzano described it as Leonard's "exquisite techno-surrealist waltz." The musicians were Jean-Philippe Rykiel on synthesizer, and vocalists Mayel Assouly, Evelyine Hebey and Elisabeth Valletti. It was also released as a single in Spain and Holland (each with a different picture sleeve; identical catalogue number: CBS 650210 7) with a non-Cohen B-side, shared between Angelo Branduardi and Paco & Pepe De Lucia.

'Take This Waltz', was Leonard's title: waltz-time, of course, and marked "moderately bright, with a lilt", we hear three bars of intro on synthesizer and then it's straight into Leonard's vocals. Leonard's translation, as printed in 'Stranger Music', divides into four 8-line verses with a final verse of 12 lines. A four-line 'chorus' comes in after verses two and four. All this bears little resemblance to Lorca's original Spanish text. 'Pequeño vals vienés' comprises four six-line verses, each with a different rhyme-scheme, and each separated by the different exclamatory two-line phrase, with a final verse of eight lines. The first three words of the exclamations "Toma este vals" give the title to Leonard's song. His 'chorus' appears only once in Lorca's original, preceding verse two. Leonard: "I'm not ashamed of the translation before anybody except Lorca. This is closer than most but it doesn't touch the beauty of the poem."

There are two versions of this Rafael Alvero-produced album: one with Spanish liner-notes, CBS 450307 1, and the other in English, CBS 450286 1. There was a 20-minute promotional colour video for the album and one (also in colour) for Leonard's song. It was made in the house near Granada where Lorca was born and described in humorous detail in *The Toronto Star* in October, 1986. Leonard's performance on this is quite surreal. He mimes to the soundtrack throughout (as successfully as on 'I Am A Hotel') and is filmed walking on cobbled streets, smoking, and playing a few notes/chords on Lorca's piano. Interestingly, the track was re-mixed a year or so later, adding vocals from Jennifer Warnes and a violin line played by his old friend Raffi Hakopian, before he returned to his native Russia, and the whole thing was then slotted onto Leonard's next album.

Leonard was interviewed by Terry Gross on her half-hour *Fresh Air* programme for National Public Radio and broadcast on May 2, 1986. It was in connection with the USA release of 'Various Positions' since he referred to performing songs in concert "from the very first record to this one." Pretty familiar ground was covered: Buckskin Boys, meeting John Hammond, writing 'Suzanne', his themes of Montreal, the woman and the Lord, being introduced to Judy Collins and singing at a couple of her concerts, not being able to pay the bills despite the many favourable reviews of his then recent novel *Beautiful Losers*, wanting to head for Nashville but staying in New York, returning from Greece to Canada to raise $1,000 in order to return to Greece, the Phil Spector gun-escapade, and so on. Leonard reminisced quite fervently about the time spent with his fellow writers in Montreal when they would meet to read and discuss and analyse and criticise each other's work. Leonard: ". . . there were no prizes or rewards for any of this,

this was just a devotion to a certain mad idea of what craft and expression was . . . you had to defend every word and it tended to turn you into quite a serious worker in that realm."

A second major radio interview with Leonard was broadcast a few months later, on September 20, 1986. CBC's documentary, *The John Hammond Years*, had reached part 12. Hosted by David Tarno and alternating extensive comments from Leonard with his studio recordings ('Bird On The Wire', 'Stories Of The Street', 'Suzanne' et al.), it was to all intents and purposes 'The 1960s Life and Music of Leonard Cohen'. The same stories were repeated. John Hammond spoke too, of course, recalling how he was briefed about Leonard: "A friend of mine said 'John, there's this poet from Canada, who I think you'd be interested in, he plays pretty good guitar and he's a wonderful songwriter but he doesn't read music and he's sort of very strange. I don't think Columbia would at all be interested in him but you might be.' So I said, well, fine . . ." What comes across in the 55-minute programme from both men is a warm sense of mutual respect and trust, and the notion that Leonard's musical début in the recording studio was indeed handled by a real expert.

Another recording venture, completed earlier in the year, March 1986, at The Complex in Los Angeles, but not released until 1987, was Leonard's duet on 'Joan Of Arc' with Jennifer Warnes on her ground-breaking Cohen-covers album 'Famous Blue Raincoat'. It was also available on the B-side of a UK 12″ single. The 'A' side contained the premier recording of his 'new' song 'First We Take Manhattan' and (the 'old') 'Famous Blue Raincoat', both lyrically altered by Leonard for Jennifer. Her album, the record label's début release, also premièred the issue of 'Ain't No Cure For Love', also re-written by Leonard for her in advance of his own 1988 version on 'I'm Your Man', and 'Song Of Bernadette', co-written with Leonard on the road during the 1979 tour of Europe. Several of her musicians later played on Leonard's next two albums and Jennifer also acknowledged help from Marty Machat, Leonard's lawyer. Vinyl and European CD-sleeve photos show

Jennifer and Leonard in conversation on the set of her promo video for 'First We Take Manhattan', in which Leonard also featured briefly, and the inner-sleeve has a pen-drawing by Leonard showing two hands holding a burning torch, with the title "Jenny Sings Lenny".

So what's to be made of this 8-minute duet? Jennifer: "That was done pretty classically. Actually Leonard suggested it should be done in a medieval style . . ." Evidently, the suggestion wasn't taken up. The song opens with a minute's worth of meandering intro before finally a few 'real' bars usher in Jennifer clean and clear at 1'05". Drums and keyboards are in support throughout, particularly on the 'la la la' chorus. Leonard, as befits the narrative, sings verse three, the second half of verse four, verse six and verse eight, in a pleasant baritone not dissimilar to that on 'Various Positions'. Unfortunately, the lyric inclusions are inaccurate: the third and second-from-last verses are printed in the wrong order and the final verse itself is not printed at all. The concluding two minutes, without Leonard's participation, comprise the oft-repeated 'la la la' chorus over crescendo-ing drums and multi-tracked vocals before the final fade-out. It's good, as good as and maybe even better than many concert performances with Leonard's various partners from earlier tours, but good as it is, it sounded even better in the 1988 and 1993 concerts with Julie Christensen.

To help promote the album in Europe, Jennifer and her band played a showcase concert at the Café Park in Munich on April 15, 1987, performing eight songs including six Cohen titles ('Bird On The Wire', 'Coming Back To You', 'Famous Blue Raincoat', 'Ain't No Cure For Love', 'First We Take Manhattan' and 'Song Of Bernadette'). Leonard, glass of red wine in hand, merely introduced the show. In referring to her 'Famous Blue Raincoat' album Leonard said: "It is, in my opinion, a most brilliant achievement, and in many respects represents the definitive treatment of many of my songs." Next day, at the Sheraton Hotel, he and Jennifer continued the album's promotion with individual and joint press, TV and radio interviews. They spoke of their next possible joint ventures – Jennifer singing his English transla-tions of Edith Piaf's songs; and an evening's entertainment in the theatre ("with exquisite lighting") entitled "Hello, I'm Leonard Cohen." Many articles written about Cohen after 1988 often refer to the Warnes album as having been *the* album which rekindled public interest in his work. Critics who had ignored Leonard's more recent successes or referred to him as "something in the Sixties or Seventies" suddenly rushed to give 'Famous Blue Raincoat' rave reviews and only then did they re-evaluate and re-interpret Leonard Cohen and his songs, poems, and other work. They managed to re-present Leonard Cohen to a whole new audience through another singer and her covers, acknowledging him as being great and, in so doing, managing not to have to apologise for neglecting him and his work for all those years.

Soon after 'Famous Blue Raincoat', Jennifer recorded Leonard's 'Ballad Of The Absent Mare', rewritten for her by him as 'Ballad Of The Runaway Horse' in a duet with bass-player Rob Wasserman, released on 'Duets' in 1988, and in 1993 on CD. She sure knows how to sing a Cohen song. As it happened, around this time, former model turned singer-songwriter Felicity Buirski released her own début album, 'Repairs And Alterations', containing several Cohen-influenced turns of phrase. 'Leonard C' is credited in her sleeve-notes. If she were ever to turn her attention to covering some of Leonard's songs (perhaps 'Nancy' and 'If It Be Your Will'), she could easily look Judy Collins and Jennifer Warnes in the eye and have nothing to fear. Even the Queen of Motown, Diana Ross, has tried one – 'Summertime', actually co-written by Leonard and Sharon Robinson, on her 'Red Hot' album containing several R&B tracks. No other song details were given on the sleeve. The lyrics can be found in Volume II of Alberto Manzano's translation. Interestingly, another Cohen lyric, this time as yet unpublished, 'It Just Feels', was recorded by French singer Sylvie Maréchal on her 1992 album 'Faith Healing', with music by Dave Stewart of Eurythmics.

One of Leonard's most unchacteristic appearances occurred in the US cop show Miami Vice on BBC1 on August 8, 1987. In an episode called 'French Twist' Leonard played a character named Zolan. In two separate scenes, darkly besuited, holding short conversations in French over the telephone, Leonard played the Head of Interpol – Zolan. The first clocked in at about 35 seconds, the second at about 12, though he was only on-screen for four of them. Leonard explained later that his children had urged him to accept the offer to do the show: something to do with maintaining street-credibility (his? theirs?!) among their peers! He also admitted that his 'part' was subsequently given to another actor.

A few days after his 52nd birthday, Leonard was in the audience for "A Black And White Night" concert at the Ambassador Hotel in Los Angeles when Roy Orbison, backed by Bruce Springsteen, Jennifer Warnes, Elvis Costello, k.d.lang and several others sang a selection of his own greatest hits. When Leonard soundchecked in 1993, he often encouraged his band to "Orbisise" the music!

Leonard did appear in another quite different visual document in 1987, a Jurgen Lutz-directed film called *A Moving Picture*. Produced in association with CBC, Société Radio Canada and TVOntario, this 55-minute movie, billed as "a romantic dance fantasy", included in its soundtrack a version of Leonard's yet to be released 'First We Take Manhattan' with some lyrics that were not on the 'I'm Your Man' release in 1988. Leonard is featured in one five-minute scene, about 15 minutes into the film, as a party guest in a dance-gymnasium, adopting a variety of poses: chopping tomatoes, lying on a bed and lip-synching to the soundtrack, standing watching the energetic dance routines, standing chatting to other guests, and dancing – all to the *synthesizer-driven* music of his 'Manhattan'. The camera work is quite energetic, following the dancers, wheeling and spinning around the room among the party guests. There is a short atmospheric coda with Leonard, sitting astride a turned-around high-back-chair surveying the post-party debris around the room which segues into the next scene and on to the rest of the film. Jennifer Warnes' cover of 'Famous Blue Raincoat' comes in over the final credits. Songs and music by Laurie Anderson, Kate Bush, Buffy Sainte-Marie and The Penguin Cafe Orchestra are also in this impressionistic and impressive movie.

XII

I'm Burning Up The Road

Cometh the end of the Eighties, cometh the album 'I'm Your Man'. There are eight songs on this 41-minute disc, Leonard's tenth, most of them recorded in Montreal and Los Angeles where he had by now taken up almost full time residence. Seven are Cohen originals including 'Take This Waltz', originally recorded for the Lorca project in Paris in 1986 and remixed a year later in New York to include Raffi Hakopian's violin contribution, and one co-written with Sharon Robinson. In addition to writing and singing, arranging and producing the songs, Leonard also played piano and keyboards instead of his acoustic guitar for the first time ever on one of his albums. But what the credits don't mention is how much *deeper* his voice had become since 'Various Positions', only three years earlier. Most reviewers mentioned this and Leonard himself attributed it to the vast amounts of cigarettes and red wine consumed in the interim. Cohen listeners were subjected therefore to a double whammie when this disc hit their decks: those way-down lower-register vocals and no guitar.

Themes of social, sexual and sensual concerns predominate now, replacing the religious fervour-cum-angst in *Book Of Mercy* and 'Various Positions'. And, for once, the majority of reviewers were united in their wide-spread acceptance and praise. The reception was *sensational.* The *New York Times*, for example, hailed the album as a 'masterpiece'. 'Gold' status was achieved in Canada, 1,000,000+ sales in Europe (250,000 in its first month of release), No. 1 position

133

in the album charts in several European countries including Spain and Norway (where it occupied the top slot for 17 weeks, thereby achieving 'platinum' status and causing Leonard to quip that every household in the country must have bought it). Later in the year, Columbia Records awarded him their International Crystal Globe for his 5,000,000 "overseas"(!) album-sales. Previous recipients included Bob Dylan and Bruce Springsteen. Leonard had hit the B I G time. Seriously.

So why is he pictured – by Sharon Weisz – on the front cover with a half-eaten banana? It was a casual snap taken as he ate his lunch during the filming of Jennifer Warnes' video for her cover of 'First We Take Manhattan', and Leonard decided it best symbolised his own particular stance vis-à-vis the message of his new record. But just in case anybody missed the point, Leonard would later enclose two dollar bills with a letter to several of his record company's sales reps in order to help them with telephone expenses incurred in promoting his new album. Seriously.

As it turned out, somebody must have taken the hint. Columbia's promotion squads went into top gear; out of the eight songs on the album, *seven* were issued as singles. It is beyond the scope of this study to provide an exhaustive world-wide list of each and every release and we also need to realise that by 1988, most everybody's albums and singles were being issued (indeed, thousands-upon-thousands of most everybody's back-catalogues were also being *re*-issued) on CD, as well as on vinyl, and the 12″ single was going strong too. In Cohen's case, several of the tracks below were released in these additional formats – bonus issues you could call them, to continue to attract the public's attention to his work, or to make up for the lost opportunities and the mess they made with 'Various Positions', 'Recent Songs' and others. The lead single, of course, was 'First We Take Manhattan' c/w 'Take This Waltz' (Spain) and 'Sisters Of Mercy' (in England/ Holland/ Spain, again), followed by 'Ain't No Cure For Love' c/w 'Jazz Police' in the UK and in Canada; in Norway, a promotional single featured 'Ain't No Cure For Love' on the A-side with 'Manhattan' on the B. 'Everybody Knows' c/w 'The Partisan' in Holland and Spain. (In 1992, 'Everybody Knows' was re-released on the B-side of 'Closing Time'.) The title-track, 'I'm Your Man' was issued in Holland and Spain c/w 'Chelsea Hotel #2'. Not forgetting 'I Can't Forget' c/w 'Hey, That's No Way To Say Goodbye' in Holland.

CD-single releases included 'First We Take Manhattan' c/w 'Sisters Of Mercy', 'Bird On The Wire' and 'Suzanne'; 'Ain't No Cure For Love' c/w 'Jazz Police', 'Hey, That's No Way To Say Goodbye' and 'So Long, Marianne' – at around 17 minutes for each. A couple of 12" vinyl-singles also featured these same tracks. There were a couple of 3" CD-singles – 'I'm Your Man' c/w 'Chelsea Hotel #2' and 'Who By Fire' and 'First We Take Manhattan' c/w 'Suzanne' and 'So Long, Marianne', with slightly less playing time. 'Tower Of Song' was not released as a single. Columbia was determined to plug both Cohen's present album and his back catalogue concurrently.

'First We Take Manhattan', was synthesizer-driven. By the end of the Eighties we should have expected that and known better not to be shocked by it but we still were. This was in fact the *third* version of 'First We Take Manhattan' following those in the dance film *A Moving Picture* and on Jennifer Warnes' 'Famous Blue Raincoat'. Arranged and performed by fellow-Montrealer Jeff Fisher (also responsible for 'Jazz Police'), we hear 15 seconds or so of rhythm'n'chords (A minor and D minor, as per the song book), then an overdubbed almost-distant 'trumpet' figure leads to Leonard's vocals at about 0'35. The tone is menacing, sombre – remember, it's been three years since his last record, itself rejected by Columbia in the US. Leonard: "I wanted a kind of Clint Eastwood/ Serge Leone background to this song . . . which has a kind of strong appeal to the gathering of an invisible army to act on the psychic landscape . . ." This florid explanation contrasts neatly with his remarks in Munich, in April 1987, about how limpid he wanted his new lyrics to be.

The original version of the song was called 'In Old Berlin', and concerned itself with "the nature of evil"; some of its earliest material was used for 'Dance Me To The End Of Love'. The opening lines of this final version refer to 'coming back' in order to pay 'them' back (one presumes his record company in the US). The mood of word and music are as one; though quite how Leonard magnifies the time-scale to the 20 years in the first line – bringing it all back to 1967, the very year of his big break, thanks to John Hammond – is still somewhat baffling.

Dominique Isserman, a Paris photographer to whom the album was dedicated, directed the promotional video of this song. In black and white, of course. For this, they travelled to a cold beach in Normandy, and spent many a cold, wind-blown hour walking on the sand. Leonard, unshaven, looks uncomfortable throughout. And very cold.

Leonard's vocal on the second track, 'Ain't No Cure For Love' is as cold leather to Jennifer's lace on her 1987 cover version. The words are different too; Leonard wrote the original song for Jennifer; now, for his own purposes, he rewrote the chorus, and composed new lyrics for verses three and four. Leonard's 'sound' is different: after a rasping saxophone introduction over bass and keyboards, the drums take over the four-in-the-bar stomp, and though it's gentler than 'Manhattan', and with a slight hint of swing, it's not exactly a 'cosy' song. Leonard: ". . . it hasn't worked out well between men and women but nobody can penetrate the need . . . nobody can tolerate the ache of separation . . . everybody makes a continuing negotiation for a changing deal with Love because we need it so much . . ." (cf. final lines of the chorus in 'The Guests'.)

'Everybody Knows' was co-written with Sharon Robinson, his 1979/80 tour back-up singer, with whom another collaboration would appear on 'The Future' in 1992. It's back to D minor and there's an edge to his voice on this track, *really* deep now, that carries along the steady 1-2-3-4 beat and before you know it three verses have been sung. En route, a couple of surprises: 1) first time ever Leonard has played keyboard on disc; 2) in verse 1: John Bilezikjian on oud comes in at 0'33" to colour the 'poor and rich' lines; and he plays on through verse two in a delicate counterpoint which lifts the melody above semi-growled lyrics which are a Cohen critic's dream: some of the most dismally clichéd negativity on the theme of love, ever . . . and yet the 1-2-3-4 beat won't give up. Jennifer Warnes is there on the title line at the end of verse two and throughout verse three. And when the chorus breaks into F at 1'58", it's a sweepingly lyrical 'ménage-à-trois': baritone, soprano, oud; with the omnipresent '1-2-3-4' now joined by strings, it's the most engaging passage on the album thus far.

Three further verses, all with oud and Jennifer's often multi-tracked support, highlight racism, 'the plague' (AIDS, on Leonard's own admission though he broadens it to include the breakdown of our "psychic immune system") and Christ's crucifixion while Leonard rails against corruption, poverty, mendacity, greed and infidelity. But this is a *song*, so we are obliged to incorporate the vocal and instrumental input into our reception of it. Manzano likened its effect to a punch from a velvet glove. *Penthouse* magazine (September 1988) complimented Cohen on making the unthinkable singable. Let's settle for that.

And so to the title song. More Cohen keyboard work opens this 'moderately slow' track (timed at c. 92 beats per minute, so it's not actually *that* slow). Over three verses he lists a dozen ways, many of them blatantly sexual, in which he would serve his lover, including his wearing a mask, taking her hand, examining every inch of her, fathering her child. Very limpid. He's not sick but he is prepared to try any 'cure' for his love, even though he knows he won't ever find one. *Rolling Stone* magazine in June, 1988, saw it all as "conspiratorial friendliness." Indeed, it's a song which comes off especially well in concert.

In one of its earlier versions, Leonard had included, then rejected, some "funny lines" about him not being so happy since the end of World War 2. These were later to be found in 'Waiting For The Miracle' on 'The Future' in 1992. Then it

137

became a song called 'I've Cried Enough For You', but that didn't work out either. After a few more re-writes 'I'm Your Man' finally evolved into its present form. Leonard: "... a perfect little song."

Vinyl copies brought us a dance, 'Take This Waltz', to begin side B. This is the remixed version of the 1986 'Lorca' tribute song, originally included on CBS Spain's 'Poetas En Nueva York' / 'Poets In New York' to celebrate the 50th anniversary of Lorca's death. Leonard's vocal track, recorded in Paris, is untouched. Back in the US, he managed to contact Raffi Hakopian a matter of days before he was due to leave and return to his family in Russia. Leonard flew to New York and recorded Raffi's violin contribution there. Jennifer's vocals were added later. Assuming you'd already bought the tribute album, or the single, and were therefore familiar with the 1986 'Take This Waltz', you might have thought as verse one danced out of your speakers that it was just the same track; but the thought will have vanished in less than a minute when Raffi came in, and less than 30 seconds later, with Jennifer too. With his violin and her aching vocal harmonies, the song just lifts, lilts and sways, ending on a highly *musical*, and sensual, verse five (fragrant too: 'wild hyacinth', 'dew', 'moss'). There's a case for the remix sounding better than the original.

At 3'58", 'Jazz Police' is the shortest track on the album. Leonard: "An interesting failure. I tried to fix that up – it didn't quite work. The song basically allows the composer and singer to embrace the position of delightful irresponsibilities, to be able to play with certain ideas that are held by the listener and just let them disintegrate into a laugh. I wanted to write verses that would start with very serious propositions, against racism, against oppression, against repression, and disintegrate into meaninglessness, but with a smile. So, much of the song is based on that sense of freedom of not having to be responsible for where something is going." In another interview with *Musician* magazine in July 1988, Leonard cited its origins from his time spent with the fusion group Passenger in 1979/80 and how *he* was a kind of musical sentry guarding against their use of certain intervals which are more than evident in this very song. Co-written with fellow-Montrealer, Jeff Fisher, who also arranged 'First We Take Manhattan'.

Of all the introductions on this album, the most personable is for 'I Can't Forget', with its nifty xylophone ostinato from Lenny Castro which also stays in behind the vocals on this hip-swinging, semi-inebriated jaunt down to Phoenix which is just irresistible. The Warnes/Jude Johnstone choral overdubs throughout and particularly in the chorus, are captivating. Leonard had changed the song from an earlier version as a metaphorical epic about the liberation of the soul, related in terms of the Exodus of the Hebrews from Egypt ("too heavy and ponderously theological"). He recited some of the rejected lyrics in a WNEW-FM interview with Pete Fornatel in July 1988.

Leonard's voice, similar to that on 'Ain't No Cure For Love', is less gravelly than on other songs like 'First We Take Manhattan' and 'Everybody Knows'. The melody line uses a wider range of notes and compared to tracks three and six it's an altogether more hummably memorable tune. At around 120 beats to the minute though, it's quicker than the second track and should have lasted much less too – it's that long instrumental which makes it go on so. Mind you, 'Sneaky' Pete Kleinow is on steel guitar (last heard from on the 1977 'Death Of A Ladies' Man' album), so maybe *that's* why it went on so. Perversely, this is the only song on the album not included in the song book.

'Tower Of Song' was the last to be written, and is the final number on the album. Leonard: "I had the luxury of stepping back and reviewing my life up to that moment. The humour is unavoidable. I think it's the best song on this record, there is something about it that is complete . . . something accurate, something true about it." The studio take is arranged, played (on keyboard) and produced by Leonard, though he is, as ever, not entirely on his own since Jennifer's multi-tracked cooing "da do dum dum"s support his closely-miked recitative.

Leonard concluded this enterprise on a valedictory note, as he had also done on 'Various Positions'. But, as we know, in both instances he resisted the lure of the exile's path and offered his services anew, to God in the former and in the latter, to his lover ("But you'll be hearing from me, baby"), and how! Down the track, just four years later, in the future.

More immediately, the new album promo-tour in January and February 1988 took Leonard across Europe to France, Germany, Norway, Sweden, Finland, England, Austria and elsewhere to contend with the barrage of media interviews. Compared to previous tours, the PR machine this time round was firing on all cylinders. He appeared on several TV shows, performing – truth be told, miming – 'First We Take Manhattan' in front of Dutch, German and Swedish studio audiences, in all cases with two gyrating female back-up singers. In Oslo, he chose 'Ain't No Cure For Love' and 'Take This Waltz'. Very often clips of, or in some cases the whole of, the video 'First We Take Manhattan' accompanied television and radio reports. Of particular interest was a 40-minute documentary on Finnish television in February, neatly subtitled so we heard Leonard without the nuisance of the overdub, and we got to see most of the 1985 German TV-video of 'Hallelujah'.

The 'I'm Your Man' tour had originally been scheduled for September/October 1987 through to December in the USA. But Leonard's protracted efforts to complete the songs naturally forced these plans to be cancelled. Finally, a couple of months after the release of what was becoming his biggest-selling-ever album, Leonard, then 53 years old, embarked on the biggest-ever tour of his career. Part one took in Europe – 41 cities, 59 concerts in 89 days, including five (the last ever) of those two-in-an-evening shows, then just four gigs in the USA, two in different venues in New York, and a final couple on the west coast at Berkeley and Los Angeles. Part two visited Canada and the USA – 19 cities (10 in his native country and 12 in the States), 22 concerts in 25 days, thus making a grand total of 85 performances. This compares with 77 on the five mini-'Various Positions' tours in 1985, and is just a few less than the combined tours of 1979 and 1980.

The band numbered eight and included John Bilezikjian,

the only member to have played on 'I'm Your Man', and Steve Meador – both had last been together with Leonard on 'Recent Songs' and the 1979/1980 tours. The others were Tom McMorran, Bob Furgo, Bob Metzger, Steve Zirkel, and back-up vocalists Julie Christensen and Perla Batalla, who got her audition through knowing Julie and was asked to sing 'If It Be Your Will' with Leonard, all of whom were playing with Leonard for the first time. With a bigger band of supporting musicians, many of the songs were 'fuller' in sound, especially the 'I'm Your Man' inclusions, though several retained much of their 1985 character.

The tour was promoting 'I'm Your Man', of course; no surprise, therefore, in finding that seven of the album's eight songs were in the core-repertoire of 33 songs (just as in 1985). 'Jazz Police' was not played in Europe. Some songs from the 1985 tour were dropped: 'Diamonds In The Mine', 'Famous Blue Raincoat', 'Lover Lover Lover', 'Memories', 'Tennessee Waltz', 'The Guests', and 'The Night Comes On'. For the rest then, with a 'Safety First' policy out front, 'Songs Of Leonard Cohen' and 'Various Positions' were represented by half-a-dozen songs each, five from 'New Skin For The Old Ceremony', three from 'Songs From A Room', two from 'Songs Of Love And Hate', and one each from 'Live Songs' ('Passing Thru') and 'Recent Songs' ('The Gypsy's Wife' – quite rare, maybe only six performances in the whole of 1988). 'Death Of A Ladies' Man' was not represented. Most audiences heard six of the new songs: 'Ain't No Cure For Love', 'I'm Your Man', 'First We Take Manhattan', 'Tower Of Song', 'Everybody Knows' and 'Take This Waltz' (in their usual concert order). 'I Can't Forget', surely one of the most accessible of the new songs was played in each of the first seven shows but thereafter received less than that number of performances in the remainder of the tour. Three non-Cohen songs were included, 'The Partisan', 'Passing Thru' and the Elvis standard 'Can't Help Falling In Love' which was performed only once, as far as is known, in the first of the two Oslo shows on May 7.

141

Some other observations: 'Hey, That's No Way To Say Good-bye' was dropped from the set-lists after the double-Lund shows on April 24, never to re-appear; followed a week later by 'The Law' (ditto). 'Story Of Isaac' was performed just once as far as we can tell, in Munich, and then picked up again, more than 40 concerts later, in Rome; and we had to wait until the end of May to hear 'The Partisan', though it remained in the set-lists until tour-end.

A typical set-list, from Milan's Teatro Orfeo on May 17, ran as follows:

1. Dance Me To The End Of Love
2. Ain't No Cure For Love
3. Who By Fire
4. Bird On The Wire
5. I'm Your Man
6. Sisters Of Mercy
7. Coming Back To You
8. First We Take Manhattan

Intermission

9. solo: Avalanche
10. solo: Chelsea Hotel #2
11. solo: Stranger Song
12. Tower Of Song
13. Everybody Knows
14. Joan Of Arc
15. There Is A War
16. Take This Waltz

Encores:

17. Hallelujah
18. So Long, Marianne
19. Suzanne
20. Heart With No Companion
21. I Tried To Leave You
22. Whither Thou Goest (a cappella)

This final song, 'Whither Thou Goest', was an all-band a cappella rendition of some words from the Book Of Ruth (Chapter 1, verse 16) in the Old Testament; it closed almost every show from Helsinki (April 28) onwards, though it had actually been the opener for the previous show in Stockholm. As above in Milan, 22 or 23 songs on average were played per night. This worked out at around two hours twenty minutes on stage. Two longer exceptions were Munich and London (May 31) with 26 songs each, clocking in at over 2½ hours.

For most of those 140 or so minutes, Leonard eschewed his guitar (a six-string Gibson Chet Atkins Special with nylon strings, tuned down by two tones to accommodate his lower vocal register), except of course when he performed his acoustic numbers, and sang full-frontal to his audiences, eyes often closed, both fists cupped to his chest, one holding the microphone and the other its wire, as can be seen in many of the photographs which accompanied newspaper reviews. This contrasted greatly with seeing him having to focus between the darkness and the stage and the buttons on his keyboard through a one-eye-torch-like-contraption. For most of the time, though, he stood pretty still during each song's delivery, swaying from time to time at the end of a line, or between a verse and a chorus, or to make some kind of enraptured movement with his upper torso to give a word or a phrase particular emphasis. He sidled across to Perla and Julie for 'Take This Waltz' and 'Joan of Arc'.

After the wide coverage devoted to Leonard's promotional tour around Europe at the beginning of the year and then to his new album, the 'I'm Your Man' tour attracted much more attention than any previous excursion; more pre-publicity; more air-play for the two singles 'First We Take Manhattan' and 'Ain't No Cure For Love'. As for the actual reviews, as ever they were a mixture of the good and the deeply unimpressed. Some London review headlines read: 'Cohen's touch of class' (*Daily Telegraph*), 'Plumbing the depths' (*Evening Standard*), 'The laughing boy' (the *Independent*), and while one reviewer reported that Leonard's voice had improved in the 18 years since his first performance at the RAH in 1970, another found his voice to be a "lachrymose grunt". They couldn't even agree on Bob Metzger's guitar solo in 'Bird On The Wire': one complained about it being "messy", while another thought it "energetic". In most reviews praise was not in short supply for both Perla and Julie. A few days later, the Dublin papers read: 'Cohen gets the crowd with him' (*Evening Herald*), 'Cohen becomes Laughing Lennie' (*Irish Press*), 'The depression now approaching from the west . . . but the fans still love Lennie' (*Sunday Independent*), and 'Rave, Rave, Rave' (*Sunday World*) – three out of four wasn't that bad after all.

Several concerts were filmed and later broadcast on tele-vision though none in its entirety, some interspersed with a Cohen-interview – including Oslo on May 1 where eight songs were filmed with great colour definition. There was a marvel-lous interview too, during which Leonard showed several pages of sketches and drawings from his notebooks; indeed, the rather grandly titled 'Leonard Cohen Water Colours Portfolio', containing three hand-painted autographed water-colours as silk screen prints in a very limited edition of 200, was currently on sale at $500 (US) from his European promoters' office in Copenhagen. Other visual material would be seen in an interview with Denise Donlon taped and broadcast in North America in mid November and December. Concert footage was also televised from Milan (May 17; four songs), Paris (May 28; nine, maybe ten, songs), London (June 1; 11 songs), London (again, June 5: just the one song performed – 'Tower Of Song', yet even that was edited down when broadcast), San Sebastian (May 20; 20 songs), Athens (June 19; one song in rehearsal, and one from the show), Reykjavik (June 24; nine songs, great backstage material) and Roskilde (July 2; six songs). The London (June 1) and Athens footage was included with some interview material from an earlier BBC programme (broadcast in May but filmed in Paris in February) as part of a much longer and more prestigious BBC documentary, which was first aired just over six weeks later on July 15 in the UK. The following year it was released on an official video entitled 'Songs From The Life Of Leonard Cohen'. The musical items from this video also appeared on an unofficial CD, entitled 'Last Of The Bohemians', issued in 1993, and have also been included in several later documentaries, such as 'Adrienne Clarkson's Summer Festival' in 1989.

Radio broadcasts were not quite so numerous – just Cologne (April 10) and Amsterdam (April 18), though again, both were incomplete recordings (19 songs and 21 songs respectively). TV and radio, and 'private' interviews, on the other hand, were regularly conducted as part of the routine, en route, in Mainz, Stuttgart, Munich, Berlin, Cologne, Mannheim, Hannover, Hamburg, Amsterdam, Helsinki, Aarhus, Oslo, Vienna, Zürich, San Sebastian, Paris, London and Reykjavik as far as our researches indicate. There are probably others.

Leonard's crew taped the Amsterdam (April 19) and San Sebastian (May 20) shows and one track from each show later surfaced on 'Cohen Live' in 1994. From Amsterdam – 'Heart With No Companion', sixth song that evening: no intro, Leonard started the song himself and was then joined by drums, bass, picked electric guitar and his own strummed acoustic during the first verse; the girls were in on the chorus and Bob Furgo lurked here and there on violin. Bob Metzger stabbed away in the bridge, followed by some more violin and then keyboard. 'One Of Us Cannot Be Wrong' from San Sebastian was altogether different. This song, not a regular on this tour after the first half-dozen or so shows, was bound to be warmly received, particularly as it had been omitted in the 1985 tour (apart from one known single acoustic performance in Sydney, May 24); and even in 1980 it was hardly ever heard. This 1988 arrangement was an enticing mix of Hymn and Soul – Leonard's delivery veering from the cantor to the raconteur, with support from Julie and Perla and a catchy arpeggio guitar-riff bringing a mid-verse climax in each of the first three (of four) verses, after which an electric guitar played a verse, dying away to make way for Leonard's final lines. The texture was immediately sparse and lean again before the final triumphant whole-band climax in the last few lines. Or so we thought – there was more. Tom McMorran played some jazzy lines at 4'18" and Leonard repeated the last half of verse four. Keyboard, drums and 'angels' brought it to an end.

Seventeen songs (probably not in concert-order) from the Bergen show (June 28) appeared on an unofficial double vinyl album called 'I'm Your Live Man'; as yet it remains the only Cohen-recording to contain the new song 'Whither Thou Goest'.

One other TV appearance is worthy of mention. On a Swedish TV show called *Jacob's Backstage* in Stockholm at the end of June, Leonard sang two songs 'I'm Your Man' and 'Tower Of Song' playing his Technics keyboard and accompanied by Julie and Perla, on a boat, which doubled as the studio for his interview with host Jacob Dahlin. The chat is somewhat unmemorable but the sight of the 'angels' wrapping themselves around 'their man' during the songs is most definitely not!

Three days after their final European date in Denmark (Roskilde, July 2), in a venue strongly resembling an aircraft hangar, they were on a decidedly plusher stage in New York for the first of just four USA dates. This was just a toe in the water prior to their forthcoming visit to Canada and the USA in the autumn for more than 20 concerts. Same basic song-lists as in Europe: 'I Can't Forget', 'One Of Us Cannot Be Wrong' and 'Passing Thru' were still out, allowing 'Story Of Isaac' and 'If It Be Your Will' back in, as well as 'A Singer Must Die' for its first and only known performance (Carnegie Hall) in the whole of 1988. Leonard was interviewed by Pete Fornatel on WNEW-FM Radio just before his New York concerts. In this conversation Leonard expounded at some length on several topics, including his use of religious symbolism and the notion of 'the ladies' man'.

Leonard kept a low 'between tours' profile in 1988; three broadcasts in September on Irish and German radio stations kept his name and work before the public to some degree. Too late for Europe, of course, but they were fair attempts by this medium to focus on his songs without too much of their customary cliché-cynicism. A two-part Irish Radio documentary (RTE 1, produced in the Religious Department) entitled *How The Heart Approaches What It Yearns*, was broadcast on consecutive Sundays (September 5 & 12). John McKenna spoke at length with Leonard, covering most of the by-now familiar bases but focusing particularly, in the first programme, on Cohen's interest in and attitude to historical figures such as Abraham, Isaac, Joan Of Arc and Bernadette Soubirous; and in the second on 'ordinary people' – stories from the street. Some useful insights into Leonard's lyrics and word-craft were offered but unfortunately precious little on his musical invention; a missed opportunity I'd say. John McKenna later received a Jacobs Radio Award for these and several other such programmes. Later that same week (September 11) on German Radio, the journalist Christof Graf presented a 70-minute insight into Cohen and his work with lengthy extracts from album and concert recordings. In this context, mention should also be made here of a brief television interview with Leonard on CBS News *Nightwatch*, broadcast on November 11, since it shed further light on the Cohen-psyche. After giving his opinions on the blues, country music, prose and poetry writing, and on the hard work needed to bring a song to completion, Leonard was asked which particular *book* he found himself going back to most often. He replied – and in so doing headed off the well-trodden Lorca pathway of conversation – "The King James version of The Bible", praising its language, authority and magnificence of presentation. He went on to say that the Psalms of King David, or the story of King David, was the prototype of every poet, every singer and every writer. Then came the following interchange: "Are you a religious man?" . . . Leonard: "I wouldn't say so, no." "I would think so, but you don't think so?" . . . Leonard: "Well, you wouldn't want to advertise yourself that way on national television . . ." "Because . . .?" . . . Leonard: "You'd never be able to get a date."

On the night that interview was broadcast, Leonard was

performing in Ottawa, the last date in Ontario before completing the 1988 road show with just another five concerts. The second tour of 1988 had kicked off in Edmonton with Leonard's first ever performance in the Jubilee Hall. The following night in Calgary was a 'first' too; and there were to be a few more: Seattle, Portland, Austin, Washington, Ann Arbor and Chicago. Heading down to Phoenix was not on the schedule.

Song-wise, 'So Long, Marianne' was dropped; 'Jazz Police' was brought in for almost every show; there were not too many performances of 'Passing Thru' or 'Coming Back To You'; just a single known performance of 'I Can't Forget', in Portland – a notable concert when all eight songs from 'I'm Your Man' were played; and just the one known 'Stranger Song' – in the final show in New York.

Compared with some of the European notices mentioned above, the early press notices in Canada and the USA were exuberant, for example: "Poetic Cohen delights Q.E. crowd" (*Vancouver Sun*, October 27) and "Cohen voices bold and beautiful songs of love" (*Seattle Post-Intelligencer*, October 29).

The North American shows averaged just over 24 songs per night. Toronto (November 9) was later partly broadcast on a CBC Radio show called *The Entertainers*. Different song-sets from this concert were broadcast on two programmes with two different host presenters though both showcased the same six songs from 'I'm Your Man' and the new a cappella closer. Karen Gordon's programme contained interview material, including some from the 1986 John Hammond tribute, splitting the twelve songs into three mini-sets. Ralph Benmergui's interview with Leonard also broke up his broadcast of thirteen songs into three parts. An unofficial CD, entitled 'Warm Reception', containing these songs except the last one, appeared in 1993. Ralph Benmergui interviewed Leonard again later on Canadian Television in February 1993 on his CBC programme *Friday Night* – one of the better 'head to head's in the Cohen video-archive.

One show in Austin (November 1) was filmed and later

broadcast in 1989 as an *Austin City Limits* TV Special. This US TV full-concert début, at 54 years of age, was in many respects his long belated introduction to American audiences. Unfortunately, only nine songs (but again six from the new album) were broadcast: 'First We Take Manhattan', 'Tower Of Song', 'Everybody Knows', 'Ain't No Cure For Love', 'The Partisan', 'Joan Of Arc', 'Jazz Police', 'If It Be Your Will' and 'Take This Waltz'. The 1994 live album contained one of these, 'If It Be Your Will', and two not broadcast, 'Hallelujah' and 'Who By Fire'.

'If It Be Your Will' received no applause after the first few bars so perhaps the Austin audience failed to recognise it. Played every night, it developed into a highly intimate trio piece, with Leonard on guitar and the two girls, with only occasional subtle keyboards highlighting a phrase here and there. 'Hallelujah' opened with a slow kick-start on drums and guitar arpeggios, similar to 'One Of Us Cannot Be Wrong', but compared to 1985 this arrangement was meditational, even devotional, albeit far from serene. The highlight was Bob Metzger's passionate guitar solo. The final track from Austin was 'Who By Fire'; a good, well balanced performance, though the intro, lasting a mere 40 seconds, was very short. A few days earlier, in Vancouver, Cohen's longer introductionary minor ostinato under oud and violin sounded far more haunting. This performance would have been a better choice than the less persuasive Austin take.

XIII

A Heavy Burden Lifted From My Soul

Jools Holland, ex-Squeeze vocalist and keyboard player turned TV presenter on both sides of the Atlantic, regularly hosted the US TV programme *Sunday Night Live.* His guests on February 13, 1989, included Leonard, Julie and Perla. They performed 'Tower Of Song' and 'Who By Fire'. Leonard, on keyboard in the first song, and acoustic guitar on the second, was vocally secure in both. But it was fellow guest, Sonny Rollins' saxophone playing, particularly on 'Who By Fire's introduction and conclusion, which really lifted both performances. The Was (Not Was) boys were among the instrumental back-up too; perhaps it was this collaboration with Leonard that prompted his later guesting on their 'are you okay?' album in 1990.

CBC continued to champion Cohen with a documentary *An Evening With Leonard Cohen* on March 3 which included interviews with Leonard and live footage from Paris 1988: 'Bird On The Wire', 'Ain't No Cure For Love', 'Suzanne', 'Joan Of Arc', 'So Long, Marianne', 'Hallelujah', 'Tower Of Song', 'I Can't Forget' (perhaps – difficult to pin this down to Paris), 'Sisters Of Mercy' and 'The Partisan', though not all were complete. Among interviewees to shed their little light on Cohen and his work were Jennifer Warnes, film-maker Harry Rasky, Judy Collins and his Montreal friend from way back Moses Znaimer (they had both been students together of Irving Layton), now president of Toronto City TV and founder of the Much Music TV Network. Some snippets from the 1988 BBC documentary (itself released on video later that year) were also included as were clips from *I*

Am A Hotel, 'Dance Me To The End Of Love' and both Leonard's and Jennifer's 'First We Take Manhattan'.

That same month, and next, various TV stations in the USA and Canada broadcast the *Austin City Limits* selection. It was reported in later months that this particular programme became the station's most requested show ever. Which must have pleased BBC and SMV executives who had decided on a May video-release for the 70-minute television documentary first broadcast on BBC in July 1988. Entitled 'Songs From The Life Of Leonard Cohen', the front cover is the familiar 'I'm Your Man' pose, though the banana is now its natural colour. The 15 musical numbers were listed on the back cover, though without dates or locations: 'First We Take Manhattan', 'Suzanne', 'Chelsea Hotel #2', 'Take This Waltz', 'Hallelujah', 'Who By Fire', 'Bird On A [sic] Wire', 'Red River Valley', 'So Long, Marianne', 'Famous Blue Raincoat', 'The Partisan', 'Joan Of Arc', 'Ain't No Cure For Love', 'Tower Of Song' and 'Dance Me To The End Of Love'. The blurb informed that material had been shot on location near Athens and in New York City and combined with "rarely seen footage of Leonard's childhood and early career." True enough; the detail that most of the songs were actually filmed in London's Royal Albert Hall was omitted. The full breakdown was as follows: songs 1 – 7, 9, 12 – 15 are from London, June 1; 8 was blown on harmonica by Leonard, at Perla's insistence, filmed in his house on the Greek island of Hydra (his first visit there since late summer 1985); 10 was sung in the dressing room in Athens (June 19) and 11 was filmed at the Athens concert itself. Essential viewing.

In order to cash in on Cohen's newfound popularity and faced with the prospect of having to wait another three years for another album, CBS Holland released a budget-priced 12-track CD, 'So Long, Marianne', which was a blatantly re-tracked 'Greatest Hits'. This time round, the song-selection was: 'Who By Fire' 'So Long, Marianne', 'Chelsea Hotel #2', 'Lady Midnight', 'Sisters Of Mercy', 'Bird On The Wire', 'Suzanne', 'Lover Lover Lover', 'Winter Lady', 'Tonight Will

Be Fine', 'The Partisan' and 'Diamonds In The Mine'. The first seven are a direct lift from the 1975 'Greatest Hits' compilation and I doubt if many could disagree that they are among his finest work. No sleeve-notes; not even to acknowledge that this particular compilation first appeared on vinyl six years earlier in 1983 from CBS Germany.

Since 1989, this same CD has been re-issued four times, on each occasion with a different sleeve design, but still no sleeve-notes: in 1990 on CBS Collector's Choice; also in 1990, by the way, on cassette by CBS Germany, with four bonus tracks: 'You Know Who I Am', 'Is This What You Wanted', 'I Tried To Leave You' and 'Please Don't Pass Me By (A Disgrace)'. The tape is subtitled 'The Very Best Of Leonard Cohen', whatever that means. Again in 1992, Sony/Columbia in Australia issued the (original) 12-song collection and in 1993 Sony/Columbia UK put it out with a shocking array of inaccurate credits re song-dates on the inner-sleeve; and more recently in 1995, again from Sony/Columbia UK, though with just one accreditation error, this time on the inner-sleeve. It was certainly a missed opportunity not to include some text, perhaps a mini-biography, a justification as to song-choice, or a few Cohen-quotes on his own compositions. An even stranger collection than the 'So Long, Marianne' disc escaped Quality Control (CBS Australia) in 1990: 'Highlights' (at almost 47 minutes) contained: 'Lover Lover Lover', 'Is This What You Wanted', 'Avalanche', 'Hey, That's No Way To Say Goodbye', 'Leaving Green Sleeves', 'So Long, Marianne', 'Suzanne', 'Story Of Isaac', 'Teachers', 'Chelsea Hotel #2', 'Memories' and 'Bird On The Wire', thus making it as much a showcase for the 'New Skin For The Old Ceremony' album (with four songs represented) as the début album (ditto.) No mention was made of the fact that this compilation first appeared on vinyl back in 1982, and again in 1985. Nice sleeve photograph though. This whole re-issue campaign and the motives behind it is interesting since Leonard's original 1975 'Greatest Hits' album had recently been bought up in tens of thousands in the wake of his 1988 concert tours in England – three consecutive sold-out nights at the Royal Albert Hall – and across Europe.

Leonard was 55 on September 21. CBC celebrated with 'Adrienne Clarkson's Summer Festival', in which her conversation with Leonard in his Montreal house at work on his *Collected Poems* was the main focus of the programme. Leonard was also filmed in a variety of informal locations: shopping for olives, inside a supermarket (the same one as in *Ladies and Gentlemen* . . . in 1965), sitting on a bench and talking to the camera in a snowy Parc du Portugal just outside his home, and then inside, at work on his computer, entering the lyrics of 'The Stranger Song', at which point an extract from his first-ever appearance on Canadian TV (*Take 30* hosted by Adrienne Clarkson, on May 23, 1966) singing this very song, was shown. At the end of the 50-minute programme, Adrienne said Leonard was still working on the poems and the book was expected to be out "next fall". That would have meant Autumn 1989. It was another three years before it finally hit the bookshelves.

His friend Moses Znaimer hosted a December 3 CTC TV (Toronto) broadcast (in the *The Originals* series) of a remarkable Cohen interview (with Jim Hanley) during which his opinions on the 'social fabric', parliamentary systems, the war against countries which supply drugs, the power of television, religions and vice were freely given. Leonard: "I feel I'm on the front line of my own life and I don't really have time to develop a description of what I'm doing or where I fit in." It was a welcome change then from the usual songwriting/performing/touring/recording agenda.

1990 was, by contrast, a quieter Cohen year. Robert Altman's wonderful *McCabe & Mrs Miller* was re-released in April, followed soon after on video "in its original aspect ratio . . . special widescreen version." It received more than just a few (UK) reviews in newspapers and magazines, some even mentioning the impact/importance of the Cohen songs.

Also in the newspapers around this time were reviews of 'Kerosene Man', the first solo album from Steve Wynn, former front-figure of rock band Dream Syndicate, which mentioned his "clearly widened musical horizons . . . [moving] into areas typical of Leonard Cohen and Van Morrison", and that he was assisted by Cohen's back-up singer Julie Christensen. *Bird On A Wire*, an action movie, directed by John Badham, whose previous work included *Saturday Night Fever* and *War Games*, starring Goldie Hawn and Mel Gibson, was also released. The Neville Brothers sang a slightly rewritten version of 'Bird On The Wire' as the theme tune, and the single, produced by Dave Stewart from Eurythmics, reached the UK Top Ten. It was also on their album 'Brother's Keeper' which climbed to No 60 in the US charts and, depending on which reference book you consult, to either No 35 or 25 in the UK in mid-August. Cohen-watchers will have spotted Buffy Sainte-Marie guesting on the album too. *Pump Up The Volume*, a teenage-angst movie, directed by Alan Moyle, and starring Christian Slater, was released later in the summer, and it featured two Cohen songs, 'Everybody Knows' and the wonderful 'If It Be Your Will'. Interestingly, bizarrely even, Leonard's album version of the first song was featured in the movie itself but not on the CD-soundtrack; instead, 'Everybody Knows' was covered by Concrete Blonde. We also got to see the album cover of 'Various Positions' on screen as local 'underground' DJ Slater played 'If It Be Your Will' . . . the needle is seen tracking at the beginning of the vinyl yet the song is the album's finale.

And then we heard Leonard's 'new voice' though it was just one song. Credited as 'lead vocal' on David and Don Was' 'Elvis' Rolls Royce' on their new disc 'are you okay?', Leonard recited four 12 line verses, deadpan, more like a slow rap than a song, telling the story of . . . well, of Elvis' Rolls Royce being shipped across the Atlantic from London, England to Graceland, Tennessee. The interesting mismatch of lyrics, funk-rhythms and twee chorus with Leonard's lead bass lasted about three-and-a-half minutes.

A much more fascinating mix could be heard and seen in Newfoundland, at the Stephenville Festival première of *Sincerely*

A Friend, a musical dramatisation of 24 Cohen songs, written by Canadian playwright Bryden MacDonald. (It would later feature in September 1991 in Toronto at The National Festival Of Canadian Theatre.) There were two acts, thus: I – 'The Guests', 'Famous Blue Raincoat', 'Bernadette', 'Sisters Of Mercy', 'Tower Of Song', 'Dance Me To The End Of Love', 'I Came So Far For Beauty', 'So Long, Marianne', 'I'm Your Man', 'Don't Go Home With Your Hard-On', 'Jazz Police' and 'First We Take Manhattan'; II – 'Who By Fire', 'Suzanne', 'Ain't No Cure For Love', 'Take This Waltz', 'Comin' [sic] Back To You', 'Joan Of Arc', 'The Partisan', 'Chelsea Hotel #2', 'Everybody Knows', 'The Law', 'Bird On A [sic] Wire' and 'Hallelujah'. All original albums are thus represented. The show, with a cast of five, scored for keyboards, guitars, bass, woodwind, percussion and cello, "focuses on Cohen's dark side. It's populated by hard, seamy characters – the under-belly of society – in a slum-like setting at night-time." (*Montreal Gazette.*)

Loranne Dorman and Clive Rawlins focussed on a much brighter Leonard Cohen character and his work in their substantial study *Prophet Of The Heart,* published by Omnibus Press in October 1990. The 383-page book investigates, analyses and catalogues Leonard's family history, his poetry, novels, songs, films, videos, dramas and commentaries. The authors acknowledged Leonard's assistance during their research by putting 60 or so hours of his time at their disposal while visiting him at home in Montreal. By far the most comprehensive biography available – with a detailed works list, bibliography and discography but, sadly, no index – it is a finely detailed, occasionally inaccurate, meticulous account of The Man and His Work. Leonard meantime was busy recording songs for his next album; but everything came to a halt when his 18-year old son Adam was seriously injured in a car crash on the island of Guadaloupe in the West Indies. Leonard visited him daily in hospital in North York, Toronto. This hiatus was to last four months. After Adam's recovery he enrolled in the University of Syracuse, New York. Recent reports state that he is writing songs and has performed several gigs with his band in New York.

In March 1991, at the 20th Anniversary Juno Awards in Vancouver, Canada's musical equivalent of the Oscars, Leonard was inducted into the Juno Hall Of Fame, thus joining other luminaries such as Oscar Peterson, Hank Snow, Glen Gould, Neil Young, Joni Mitchell and Maureen Forrester. There was plenty of media coverage for this prestigious event. It was a long afternoon-into-evening session, so timed to allow it to be broadcast live to the East Coast, with stage performances from several bands, singers and rappers, including M C Hammer. Moses Znaimer read Leonard's 'citation' which led to a trio of live musical tributes from Suzanne Vega, Aaron Neville and Jennifer Warnes who sang 'Who By Fire', 'Bird On The Wire' and 'Joan Of Arc' respectively, punctuated by archive material (mostly from Adrienne Clarkson's 1989 programme mentioned above). There was a standing ovation as Leonard walked to the mike to receive his plaque, a few minutes of gracious and humorous words of thanks, saluting by name the previous recipients with the quip: "Two women of genius among all that exuberant masculine prominence. It causes me to reflect it's going to be hard to get a date in the Hall Of Fame." He followed this with an almost complete recitation of his 'Tower Of Song' and then exited briskly stage right to a second standing ovation. The *Edmonton Sun*: "Cohen's magnificent speech... was both eloquent and very funny."; the *Calgary Herald*: "Cohen delivered an acceptance speech full of wit, charm and poetry." Most newspapers carried photos of the two main Juno winners: Celine Dion (Top Female Vocalist) and Colin James (Top Male Vocalist) and a few, including the *Toronto Sun, Georgia Straight* and the *Calgary Herald*, had pictures of a smiling Cohen.

Leonard had something grander to smile about a few months later when he was appointed to the rank of Officer of the Order of Canada, the second insignia. The Order, established in 1967, "recognises outstanding achievements and service in various fields" (The *Montreal Gazette*, June 27.) 72 fellow Canadians were also duly honoured.

Six weeks before the Ottawa Investiture, on September 16,

'I'm Your Fan', by far the most important musical event for Leonard in these between-albums-years was released. It served to bring his music to an even wider public, in this case, a much younger public, than the audiences attracted by Jennifer Warnes' breakthrough 'Famous Blue Raincoat' in 1987 and Leonard's own 'I'm Your Man', which had confirmed his come-back into the main musical arena. His personal involvement in this project was nil.

Here's the background. The whole venture was initiated almost by chance through a conversation between Francis Black (of The Pixies) and Christian Fevret, 27-year-old editor of the French popular music magazine *Les Inrockuptibles*, on a train platform in summer 1990. The result was an album of Cohen covers, as follows: The House Of Love – 'Who By Fire', Ian McCulloch – 'Hey, That's No Way To Say Goodbye', The Pixies – 'I Can't Forget', That Petrol Emotion – 'Stories Of The Street', The Lilac Time – 'Bird On The Wire', Geoffrey Oryema – 'Suzanne', James – 'So Long, Marianne', Jean-Louis Murat – 'Avalanche IV', David McComb & Adam Peters – 'Don't Go Home With Your Hard-On', R.E.M. – 'First We Take Manhattan', Lloyd Cole – 'Chelsea Hotel' [sic], Robert Forster – 'Tower Of Song', Peter Astor – 'Take This Longing', Dead Famous People – 'True Love Leaves No Traces', Bill Pritchard – 'I'm Your Man', Fatima Mansions – 'A Singer Must Die', Nick Cave And The Bad Seeds – 'Tower Of Song' and John Cale – 'Hallelujah'. Vinyl buyers may well have been annoyed since it had neither the lyrics, photos nor musician and production credits which the other formats had.

Issue No 30 (July/August 1991) of *Les Inrockuptibles* published a 20-page interview with Leonard in French, illustrated with a splendid mix of formal and informal black and white photographs. With the magazine came a free 4-track CD, 'Voulez-vous chanter Cohen?' containing two songs from 'I'm Your Fan', namely Bill Pritchard's 'I'm Your Man' and Peter Astor's 'Take This Longing' as well as two out-takes, 'Paper Thin Hotel' by Fatima Mansions and a longer version (by two-and-a-half-minutes, all instrumental) of 'Suzanne' by

Geoffrey Oryema. This in turn was followed by another promotional item, another four-track CD (SAMP CD1546) with three more out-takes, namely 'The Queen And Me' (i.e. 'Queen Victoria') by John Cale, 'There Is A War' by Ian McCulloch, and a four-and-a-half-minute all-instrumental version of 'Suzanne' by Geoffrey Oryema; 'Paperthin Hotel' by Fatima Mansions (as on the previous disc) was also included.

'I'm Your Fan' generated enormous interest on both sides of the Atlantic with reviews covering all shades of negative and positive opinion from, for example, "this collection has little value" (*Puls*) to "one of the very few cover-version compilations worth buying" (*Time Out*). Leonard himself repeated his old adage that his own critical faculties went into "immediate suspension" when he heard anybody else sing his songs but that he was always pleased when it happened since it helped to keep his work before the public.

And it was to happen all over again, and again: in 1993 and 1995.

But he was not the only Canadian poet to receive such public acclaim that autumn. Irving Layton, his long-time mentor and friend, was honoured at the International Festival Of Authors in Toronto in late October and made a rare joint appearance with Leonard on television the following day, interviewed on *Much Music* by Denise Donlon. In the course of their conversation, enlivened by good humour all round, Leonard recited some lyrics from an unfinished song 'If You Could See What's Coming Next', some of which were subsequently incorporated into the next album's title song. Then he broke out with an impromptu 'banana song' at the sight of the 'I'm Your Fan' cassette cover. Irving duly took the cue and they duetted on 'Yes, we have no bananas'.

And then he was off to Ottawa for the Investiture Ceremony on October 30 to be received into The Order Of Canada.

His habit of reciting album lyrics in interviews continued. 'Anthem' was chosen during his conversation with Ernst Buchmuller on a Swiss Radio (DRS III) programme on November 22. A few days later, The *Montreal Gazette* carried a report that

Leonard had written the incidental music for a play called *Everyone Else A Stranger,* by Ted Allen. Intriguing to say the least, for later in the March 1993 issue of *Saturday Night,* Ian Pearson wrote that Leonard had written some "chamber music" for a Ted Allen play called 'Helen's Song' and that it had turned up as 'Tacoma Trailer' on 'The Future'.

Whichever. But there was no doubting that 1992 was the year of Leonard's second 'Second Coming', so to speak: just as 'Famous Blue Raincoat' in 1987 had paved the way for a major Cohen revival-cum-acceptance in 1988, so too did 'I'm Your Fan' in 1991 which heralded 'The Future' the following year. Its November 1992 release, more than four years after 'I'm Your Man' – the second longest gap between Cohen albums – was warmly welcomed and applauded by most reviewers, critics, commentators and fans alike.

Leonard continued to grant interviews and promote the forthcoming album. One such session, broadcast on March 1, was for the French television station Antenne 2. The interview was conducted in Leonard's car as he drove through Los Angeles, playing tracks from the new album on the car-stereo. He said he liked to do that (instead of always just hearing them in the recording studio) because he could imagine other people doing the same after buying his album.

In May, McGill University, Leonard's *alma mater,* conferred on him an Honorary Degree. The following month, Jennifer Warnes released her new album, 'The Hunter', co-produced with Roscoe Beck and Elliot Scheiner, which contained a three-way-collaboration between Leonard, Warnes and Amy LaTelevision called 'Way Down Deep', described by Andy Gill in *The Independent,* as "a gentle chant extolling the rhythm in the heart." At 5'41", it's the longest track on the album. She sings with some big names here – Richard Thompson, David Mansfield, Van Dyke Parks, and some familiar Cohen players too: Mitch Watkins, Roscoe Beck, Bill Ginn, Vinnie Colaiuta, Lenny Castro, Perla Batalla; Jennifer's bass-player Jorge Calderon later featured on 'The Future' and toured with Cohen in 1993.

LaTelevision is certainly a weird surname. 'Weird Nightmare' – a 19-track concept album, released in September in tribute to the memory of jazz-giant Charlie Mingus, conceived and produced by Hal Wilner, contained Leonard's weirdest recording: a recitation of Mingus' poem 'Chill Of Death' over a musical arrangement by Art Barton (who played trombone in Mingus' band and had also worked for Duke Ellington) of Mingus' composition 'Eclipse', with vocals by Diamanda Galas. At 7'15" it is the longest track on the album, though Leonard only comes in at 2'50". His basso profundo is so far back in the mix with such an esoterically eclectic percussion section – clappers, whirly tube, didjeridoo, Tibetan cymbals, Cone Gong, Cloud Chamber Bowls – and extremely agitated bass clarinet and soprano lines to the fore as to make his quasi-ostinato recitation practically redundant after 5'25" or so. Other artists on the disc include Keith Richards, Elvis Costello, Robbie Robertson and Dr. John.

XIV

From This Broken Hill I Will Sing To You

It was a shame that Leonard's next album wasn't called by its working title 'Be For Real', as this would have restored some sort of equilibrium after the Mingus CD. In any event, 'The Future' made it to the top of the pile – for no good reason other than it's also the title of the lead song.

Of these nine tracks, eight are songs with the final item an instrumental, the first such non-vocal inclusion since 'Improvisation' on 'Live Songs' in 1973. Leonard wrote five of these songs, one was co-written, again with Sharon Robinson, and the other two are covers.

Released in late November 1992, it was dedicated to Leonard's companion of several years, the American actress, Rebecca De Mornay of *Risky Business* and *The Hand That Rocks The Cradle* fame. She co-arranged 'Waiting For The Miracle' and 'Anthem' and co-produced this latter song too. Lasting a few seconds under an hour it's the longest studio album in the Cohen catalogue. The front cover shows the 1979 humming-bird in mid-flight over a blue heart, under which lies a pair of open six-link handcuffs. And the cover prints line after line of credits, including Leonard's five co-producers, and there are some familiar musicians too from earlier Cohen albums and tours, some fresh from working with Jennifer Warnes. Again Leonard plays no acoustic guitar. 'The Future' was issued 25 years after 'Songs Of Leonard Cohen', and in the same month as Bob Dylan was honoured at Madison Square Garden to celebrate his 30th (actually his 31st!) anniversary with CBS. And for those counting, the fourth song, 'Closing Time', was Leonard's 100th album track.

His voice is deeper on this album than on 'I'm Your Man' despite having given up smoking around 1990 when even then it was deep ("about 50,000 cigarettes deeper" he was wont to quip at the time). But it's not less tuneful for being in such a register. Melodies still sound like melodies rather than recited monotones – the most persistent of the critics' charges – though the sophisticated mid-Nineties technologies he employed will have played a big part in ensuring this. His vocal range is less adventurous, but Cohen would be the first to say it's not Mozart. It's not bubble-gum either: there's a fair degree of sophistication not previously encountered in Cohen compositions.

For commercial considerations clearly, yet for the first time ever on a Cohen record, the opening song and the album title are identical. Leonard growls the first few lines. The language is stark – there are no ambiguities here – his vision of the future is clear: it's murder. A quaver+crotchet bass-line is the simple rhythmic pulse of the whole song. The structure is more complex. The song was the obvious choice for a single and it appeared on CD in several different 'edits'. A colour video was also made in which Leonard spends much time getting drenched, or standing ankle-up-to-knee-deep in water, indoors.

In an interview with Harold DeMuir in *The Georgia Straight* in June 1993, Leonard explained that he'd begun working on 'Waiting For The Miracle', with Sharon Robinson, in the early Eighties and that complete versions had been ready for release (for 'Various Positions' and 'I'm Your Man'). Jennifer Warnes was reported to have sung it on her June 1987 tour of Canada following the release of 'Famous Blue Raincoat'. In Cohen's apocalyptic future the only thing to live for is a miracle. Twenty years earlier, he'd wanted the future left open (in 'Sing Another Song, Boys'). Anjani Thomas's multi-tracked vocals in the chorus add a 'surround-a-sound' layer not often encountered on recent Cohen songs. With Leonard's languid delivery, although his melody is broader than in the previous song, we're talking 'stone angels' here, as Mark Lepage suggested in the *Montreal Gazette* in November 1992. The CBS press-release described the arrangement as "sinuous" and "slinky".

'Be For Real' was written by Frederick Knight and is copyrighted 1975 thus making it Leonard's most contemporary cover. Although marked 'slow and steady', Leonard's version is 'soul and heady'. For someone who had previously said that he found it difficult to sing the word 'baby' as a term of endearment in song, Leonard sings it here, more than half-a-dozen times, *and* for the third song in succession.

A three-strike drum fill then gentle strings, distant organ and cooing back-up vocalists precede Leonard's entry at 0'19". Verse 1/chorus/verse 2/chorus follow with a short organ link (at 3'08", and he speaks over most of it anyway, though the words are not printed) to the final chorus. The strings outlast the final drum-kick by a few seconds and by the end of this, the shortest, track on the album Cohen was sounding like Barry White. In the *Dallas Morning News* in December, 1992, Tom Maurstad noted a "tactile intensity" to Leonard's delivery. So, here was a song that would have transferred well to the concert hall. As yet, not yet.

Leonard's watercolour with the legend "Paris again . . . the great Mouth Culture . . . oysters and cheese . . . explanations to everyone" (also in the 1988 tour programme) was the front cover of a USA CD-single (CSK 5607) containing 'Be For Real', 'Always' and 'Hallelujah', the first ever Cohen single release to include *two* non-Cohen songs.

It's back to G major for 'Closing Time', a four-square country stomp that maintains a compulsive energy throughout its exhausting six minutes. There's quite an element of 'fun' in this song and the accompanying B&W video, directed by Curtis Wehrfritz, certainly brings this home. The lyrics are graphic and contrast with the rather unimaginative melody line, again arranged in four-bar phrases and this time with a marked anacrostic pattern throughout. But this song does not turn on a tune – it is driven by the twin thrust of an impetuous lyric and the bass-biased accompaniment. It's the only track on the album featuring Julie Christensen and Perla Batalla together.

'Closing Time' was released on a variety of CD-singles; one of the more interesting was a maxi-single (Columbia 659299 2) with 'First We Take Manhattan', 'Famous Blue Raincoat' and 'Winter Lady' in a limited edition-cum-numbered box set containing the four little colour album prints from which each song was extracted; that particular edit ran 40 seconds longer than on the album.

'Anthem', originally titled 'Ring The Bells', was begun in Montreal in 1982 and continued on Hydra. As with 'Waiting For The Miracle', Leonard thought he had it ready for the two preceding albums. Ten years later, he gave the credit to Rebecca De Mornay for co-arranging and producing it to his satisfaction. Paul Zollo (in *SongTalk*, Vol.3, Issue 2) regarded it as the album's "centrepiece" proclaiming "that it is in the breakdown of things that we can find illumination". Leonard: "The heart of this record is the line that goes 'there is a crack in everything; *that's how the light gets in'.*" [my emphasis].

Some have described the song as 'elegiac', others 'sombre'. These words also apply to Leonard's vocals. A little hoarse too. After a short introduction and a couple of verses, he is joined on the chorus by the gathered voices of the LA Mass Choir. In the repeated chorus after verse five, Leonard's thrice-reiterated "that's how the light gets in" leads into a long MOR string-led hummed play-out.

In many an interview before and after 'The Future's release, Leonard spoke of having written almost 80 verses for 'Democracy', from which his final selection of six was used for this recording. Leonard: "Before I can discard an idea, I have to write it. Completely. In all its terms, in all its loyalties to rhyme, rhythm and stanza. I can't eliminate the half-written verse because it is in keeping with the rhythm and the rhyme scheme that the idea manifests itself." (The *Philadelphia Inquirer*, November 26, 1992.) In some 1993 concerts (e.g. Stockholm,

London, Frankfurt, Toronto and Boston) he recited some of the discarded verses before performing the album version.

This is another song about the future but unlike the title track it is not a warning. This time round, and for more than seven minutes, we are offered an up-beat, positive message. Many familiar Cohen scenarios flash past: war (v.1), religion (v.2), stories from the street (v.3) and of domestic strife (v.3) – all employed to illustrate Cohen's belief that it is out of the ashes of these very conflicting scenes that Good will eventually emerge. It is perhaps for this song that Paul Zollo's words (which he applied to 'Anthem') would seem more appropriate. Not that the military drum-roll leitmotif would suggest such, but the chorus (whose lyrics can be traced to the words "Sail on, sail on, O Ship of State", in the sixth section in Book One of *Beautiful Losers*), featuring powerful backup from Jennifer Warnes and Julie Christensen, certainly leaves no doubt of this. To emphasise his geographical target, the three letters *U S A* are each presented (both in the score and in concert) as crotchet beats where most other notes are quavers; *and* the front cover of an American CD-single (Columbia 44K 74778) shows a 'stateless' print of the USA.

With the main thrust and arguments of his political and socio-domestic issues now spent, Leonard concluded the album with a couple of love songs and a long instrumental play-out, none of which as yet has ever been performed in concert. 'Light As The Breeze', an erotic narrative detailing a couple's evening's intimacy through the act of cunnilingus, is a delicious, off-beat waltz with Leonard's close-miked vocal taking us through an initial, almost breathless, sense of anticipation, towards a later desperation but concluding on a final note of consummation. The five-note melody in the verse combines with just three chords to convey this lover's song of love and hate – and love again. The chorus brings in Jennifer Warnes for her first real 'romantic' duet with Leonard since 'If It Be Your Will' on 'Various Positions'.

The notion of Time and the duration of relationships figure consistently throughout this album – from, for example, "waiting night and day" ('Waiting For The Miracle') through "staying home tonight" ('Democracy'), to "for something like a second" ('Light As The Breeze'). It is perhaps in the final (and longest) song, 'Always', that a lover's hopes and anxieties experienced during such times are encapsulated. The healing power of Love: a timeless notion indeed. Willie Nelson, Roberta Flack and Little Richard and many others have had a go at this 1925 Irving Berlin 'classic' in their own inimitable ways. Indeed, Leonard's mother was known to have sung it around the house. Harry Nilsson's 1973 cover has a lot going for it too.

In just the same way as 'Democracy' was pared down from its extensive length for commercial reasons, so too was this eight-minute take chosen from several much longer versions, some lasting more than 20 minutes. Leonard: "We couldn't stop playing it." Paradoxically, with just two verses, it's the shortest lyric on the entire album. His own invention of tequila, cranberry juice, Spritzer and fresh fruit which he called 'Red Needle' – concocted in Needles, California, back in 1975 or so – fuelled the recording sessions. Interviews in *Maclean's* (December 7, 1992) and *Rolling Stone* (January 21, 1993) include this story – and the recipe.

As for the music: it's slow, loud and undiluted R&B. It takes a couple of minutes to heat up, but from c. 2'40" onwards, Leonard, in his lowest register (especially on the third-last word "year" at 7'30", held for a full five seconds) and the girls are really smoking, backed by a great band (which includes an ice rink organ). A Weissenborn guitar solo at 3'35", the brass fills coming through gloriously in the mix and the piano throughout, are but three highlights.

The final track, 'Tacoma Trailer', a six-minute instrumental, was originally composed for a stage-play. It is, to all intents and purposes, a right-handed piano solo over a low synth-strings accompaniment. In D flat; 4/4 time, marked 'moderately slowly', with the added instructions to play 'mp' (translation: medium quietly) and 'cantabile e molto legato' (translation: in a singing style and very smoothly). Many of the songs on this album could be thus inscribed but it might just be the only Cohen song ever to include such detailed Italian instructions.

Leonard does not perform on this piece at all. Bill Ginn takes the honours here. At times it sounds similar to an extended keyboard introduction for 'Dance Me To The End Of Love' but it would sound even better as its coda since, considering most of the material on this album, that would effect a neat thematic juxtaposition.

As had become his custom, Leonard then proceeded from his Los Angeles recording studio to various television and radio studios in Europe to promote his new album. Pete Gzowski, his Toronto friend caught him en route, early on November 18 for *Morningside*; next day it was television's *Canada A.M.* Scandinavia, as usual, claimed his initial attention when he crossed the Atlantic – with appearances on Norwegian, Danish and Swedish programmes. Just as in 1988, he often sang and sometimes mimed his way through a couple of songs for TV audiences, this time round he went for 'Closing Time' and 'The Future'. Although he was not yet 60, several presenters took the opportunity to word-play on his Sixties image and reputation and link it to his next-but-one birthday. French TV (Channel M6) screened a fine documentary in December with concert footage (Paris, of course) from the Seventies and more recent video clips by cover-artists like James ('So Long, Marianne') and John Cale ('Hallelujah'). In the same week Leonard appeared on another French TV channel's chat-show, *Le Cercle De Minuit*, alongside fellow guests Geoffrey Oryema ('Suzanne' on 'I'm Your Fan') and Graheme Allwright. He conversed in French throughout.

Leonard was featured on prime time US television: on the *David Letterman Show* (February 10) he sang 'The Future', live, nervously, self-censoring the first line of verse two to "Give me speed and careless sex" (he would sing this on all his live television appearances) and then made a gaff of the continuity after verse three, but he recovered well and finished on the chorus, without verses 4-6 anyway. Another semi-'Future' was performed on *The Tonight Show*, hosted by Jay Leno on April 16. Leonard: "It was very gracious of you to invite me to chop this song in half." Ralph Benmergui interviewed Leonard on CBC's *Friday Night* (February 12) after a stirring 'Closing Time' and a standing ovation, laughs and plenty of chat. 'The Future' closed the show. He seemed equally at ease as a DJ hosting *In Concert* (on ABC TV) on March 6, introducing music from, among others, Mick Jagger.

Two rather younger rockers, Sebastian Bach (from Skid Row) and G.L. Moore (from Triumph) presented Leonard with his winning Juno award for Male Vocalist Of The Year at the Toronto ceremony on March 21. Neil Young was a losing nominee that year for his 'Harvest Moon' which had been released just weeks before 'The Future'. Leonard's companion Rebecca de Mornay could be seen on the set as Leonard rolled through 'Closing Time'. Leonard's video of this song won a Juno that night also.

With the start of his 1993 tour in Europe just over a month away, Leonard started rehearsals with his band. The only new face was Jorge Calderon though he was well known to Leonard through playing on Jennifer Warnes' last two albums. Perla, Julie, Bobs F and M and Steve had toured with Leonard in 1988; for Bill and Paul, their last gig with Leonard was in Tel Aviv 1980. Bill, of course, had most recently played 'Tacoma Trailer' on 'The Future'. As a warm-up, on the morning of April 18, they performed a pre-tour concert at The Complex (one of several recording studios Leonard had used for 'The Future') in front of a small invited audience. His show was one of the occasional Sunday morning *Columbia Records Radio Hour* broadcasts which (to quote the *Boston Sunday Herald*) "airs several times per year on 85 stations [but] ties itself to no set schedule." Eight songs were later released on a promotional single CD with a legend explaining that the radio programme was broadcast monthly on over 100 stations nationwide. The selection of songs was interesting: 'First We Take Manhattan', 'Ain't No Cure For Love', 'Coming Back To You', 'Dance Me To The End Of Love', 'Democracy', 'Waiting For The Miracle', 'The Future' and 'I'm Your Man'. As would so often be the case in later full-length concerts, most songs (in this case, five out of eight) were prefaced by Leonard's recitation of a line or two. It's a well-balanced 50 minutes with a particularly fervent 'Coming Back To You'. 'The Future' and 'I'm Your Man' are noticeably quicker too. A trio of unofficial CDs later appeared with all these songs, and several others purportedly (but mistakenly so) from the same concert: 'Los Angeles 1993' has the above eight plus four more: 'Bird On A Wire', 'Everybody Knows', 'Avalanche' and 'Suzanne'; 'Above The Soul' has these 12 plus 'Tower Of Song' and 'I Can't Forget'; and 'First We Take L.A. Then We Take Berlin' advertises all 14 but only contains the first dozen. The giveaway is the audience sound from song nine onwards.

After this mini-gig, Leonard and the band took a flight to Scandinavia and prepared for the first concerts of the 1993 tour in Europe which lasted 36 days. They performed 28 concerts in 25 locations, mostly one-nighters. Three extra shows were in Holstebro, Stockholm and London. Holstebro, Odense, Ghent, Bologna, Konstanz, Nimjegen and Koblenz were all firsts, as were several locations in some otherwise familiar towns. A few were outdoor festival performances, sharing, as in 1988, both bills and audiences with other acts (as unlikely as INXS, Robert Plant and Def Leppard) which necessitated shortened set lists. Excluding these from the calculations, an average of about 22 songs was played each night, with an on-stage playing-time of just under two-and-a-half-hours.

A total of 29 songs were played in Europe 1993. Leonard's nightly 'solos' were 'Avalanche' and 'Suzanne'. His other customary acoustic numbers, 'Chelsea Hotel #2', 'If It Be Your Will' and 'A Singer Must Die', together notched up just six known performances. No 'Stranger Song' at all, however, though it had been sung on every tour since 1970. Five songs from 'The Future' were in: 'The Future', 'Anthem', 'Democracy', 'Waiting For The Miracle' and 'Closing Time' (usual concert order). The only unrecorded song to be included was the purely vocalised (*à la* 1988) 'Whither Thou Goest', sung at perhaps just a couple of German shows (Berlin and Frankfurt). The album 'I'm Your Man' was best represented with seven (of its eight) songs although, as before in 1988, 'I Can't Forget' was soon (and just as inexplicably) dropped, on this occasion after the Scandinavian leg of the tour. They played four each from 'Various Positions', 'New Skin' and 'Songs Of Leonard Cohen'; a couple from 'Songs Of Love And Hate'; 'Bird On The Wire', of course; and just 'Passing Thru' from the fourth album, albeit for only the three concerts in Hamburg, Frankfurt and Munich. Having omitted 'Memories' from the set-lists in 1988, it was no surprise therefore to see Leonard exclude it again in 1993. It was a pity he did not choose a 'Recent Song'.

Unlike all previous tours, there wasn't a single non-Cohen song in the repertoire, with the recognised exception of 'Passin' Thru'. However, in the first London show (23 years *to the very day* since his first concert in the very same Royal Albert Hall), Leonard successfully managed to revive the whole folk movement, though perhaps for no more than several nanoseconds, when he briefly gave us a few impromptu bars of 'Banks Of Loch Lomond', 'Rule Britannia' and 'In Days Of Yore' in the midst of some good-natured banter with his highly responsive audience. A couple of days later, Leonard and band played three songs: 'Democracy', 'The Future' and 'Dance Me To The End Of Love' live in a BBC studio on the *Later With Jools Holland* programme. The last time he'd performed in a British television studio was back in the summer of 1968.

Almost every show opened with 'Dance Me To The End Of Love', usually followed by seven, sometimes eight, more to the intermission. The 'guitar' songs after the break sounded world weary, even a bit throaty, but the passion was there and to have an acoustic 'Suzanne' so soon into the proceedings made up for that. Leonard's deliberate slowing down on "golden voice" in 'Tower Of Song' was even more obvious than in 1988. Audiences loved it. 'Closing Time' too – since, paradoxically, it meant the show was 'over', and Leonard would be right back for all the encores.

One 'non-musical' aspect of the shows which deserves a mention was the large glitter-ball, suspended above the stage, which revolved slowly during 'Take This Waltz', bathing the audience in mobile fragmented specks of light – not unlike the silver minnows oft-mentioned in the song's intro, and the lilies of snow in the actual lyrics.

The other encores usually included a rapt confessional 'Sisters Of Mercy' with Leonard leading on acoustic guitar, spoilt by Paul's inappropriate sax solo between the second and third verses; 'Hallelujah', now sounding more the reverential hymn it should be (with a mixture of the 1984 and 1988 lyrics) and that sumptuous Bob Metzger guitar solo; a passionate 'So Long, Marianne' introduced by Perla and Julie harmonising on some new lyrics: "Here comes the morning boat/ Here comes the evening train/ Here comes Marianne now/ To wave goodbye again." The verse-order throughout the tour was certainly inconsistent but the song was not any less enjoyable for that, nor for it being incomplete; nor indeed for it sounding the most valedictory arrangement ever. The May 10 London audience heard the one and only performance in Europe of 'A Singer Must Die' – the first time Leonard had sung it in England since December 1979; he chose 'If It Be Your Will" for the penultimate song of the evening in Paris and Madrid. 'First We Take Manhattan' was encored in both London shows, Madrid and Berlin.

Another extract from the insightful piece by Paul Oster-mayer is relevant here: "(. . . whereas '79 was energetic and reckless) '93 was strong and elegant. Steve and Jorge provided a rock solid foundation, while everyone else, through maturity and familiarity with Leonard's music, created a beautifully crafted accompaniment to his poetry. His songs had never been presented so elegantly . . ."

FM radio broadcasts of Helsinki, Oslo, Gothenburg, Copenhagen and Zurich certainly captured the quality and essence of 'The Future' tour, though only Zurich was complete. For those who missed the Swiss programme, no less than nine different unofficial CDs have since been released with some, or indeed all, of the Kongresshaus show.

Three days after leaving Vienna, Leonard and band were rehearsing in Kitchener, Canada, preparing for what was by far his most extensive North American tour ever, incorporating 38 performances (compared to the 22 in 1988 and almost as many back in 1975). Starting this time in the east, they played half-a-dozen shows in Ontario and Quebec and one in New York, returning to Canada for three consecutive nights at the O'Keefe Centre in Toronto (where the shows were taped and six tracks later included from two of them on the 'live' album) and then headed westwards to the coast, and south through California, following more or less the 1988 itinerary, with several additional venues, all the way back to the Lisner Auditorium in Washington DC. Which is where the tour was originally scheduled to finish. However, such was the acclaim for Leonard's stage-show in 1993 that seven more concerts had to be arranged; and so, along with first-ever gigs in Thunder Bay and Saskatoon, they headed out west again re-playing Toronto, Winnipeg, Calgary, Vancouver and brought the tour to an end in Victoria, just a month after their first visit there, though I'm not so sure Leonard's voice was up to the demands of these extra dates even if 'Back By Public Demand' was cited as justification.

The core-group of songs was reduced from the 29 in Europe to 27: the two songs dropped: 'I Can't Forget' and 'If It Be Your Will'. Incomprehensible. There was an average of 22 per night and in most cases the *same* 22 – thereby forming the most stable set list on any tour I can remember. A typical set, for example, was Toronto, June 16 – as follows:

1. Dance Me To The End Of Love – a smouldering invite to the evening ahead.
2. The Future – the premonitory, yet pacey, 'showpiece'; the girls in good voice. Leonard: "May I affirm our intention to reach the level of your hospitality in our performance . . ."
3. Ain't No Cure For Love – relaxed.
4. Bird On The Wire – even more so; bluesy too with searing sax and those "it's over" lyrics – now *three* minutes longer than the original 'Room' version.
5. Everybody Knows – steady steely 'Futurish' admonition.
6. Anthem – the one that tonight floated up reverentially (fervently other nights) to seek that little crack . . .
7. There Is A War – a comfortable, though under-par vehicle, highlighted by funky guitar, organ and saxophone fills.
8. First We Take Manhattan – up-tempo also, of course, to provide the set's closer.

Intermission

9. solo: Avalanche – unengaging at the start, better as it went on.
10. solo: Suzanne – a little cautious tonight. (And *extremely* unusual for this song to be programmed so early.) But gorgeous, nevertheless.
11. Tower Of Song – predictably humorous reception in all the right places. (Surely the ultimate encore!)
12. Democracy – strong all-band delivery of this futuristic declaration.
13. Waiting For The Miracle – the last of the four 'Future' songs tonight; extended flute plus synth intro leading to very much the album-take.

(Leonard then introduced each of his players)

14. I'm Your Man – a coolish rendition, with his final Kurzweil keyboard contributions of the evening.
15. Joan Of Arc – magnificent duet with Julie.
16. Closing Time – Party-time!

Encores:

17. Sisters Of Mercy – slow, serene (apart from the silly sax after verse two)
18. Passing Thru' – a loose, good-natured, country ramble.
19. Take This Waltz – vocally tender and yearningful.
20. I Tried To Leave You – work-a-day. Each player re-introduced by Leonard.
21. Hallelujah – in 1988 it was good; *this* is great.
22. Whither Thou Goest – linked-arm, voices-only finale, shorter than usual.

As ever 'chez Cohen' was not the same every night. My notes on this first Toronto show differ from those on the next two nights, and again, say, on the San Francisco concert just over a fortnight later despite a 95+% correlation in song-choice at the Warfield, i.e. 21 out of 22 – 'Chelsea Hotel #2' was in while 'Hallelujah' was out. In Europe, writing in *The Guardian*, Adrian Deevoy described Leonard's "twixt-number repartee" as "a pleasure", though Barry Walters, reviewing the San Francisco gig, found some of the intros more entertaining than the songs which followed. "Impeccable band" and "superb backing singers" were oft-cited tributes on both sides of the Atlantic. Only the Austin concert (July 12) was filmed for television, as in 1988, for the popular *Austin City Limits* series; six songs were later broadcast: 'The Future', 'Bird On The Wire', 'First We Take Manhattan', 'Democracy', 'Sisters Of Mercy' and 'There Is A War'. His "intense facial expressions" (*Rolling Stone*), "close cropped gray hair" (*New York Times*), "dark suit and careful haberdashery" (*San Francisco Chronicle*) and his "clenched fists in front of the chest to emphasise whatever meaning his voice left out" (*Montreal Gazette*) were on view for all to see.

Leonard's voice became gradually less persuasive as the North American tour progressed. By the time it reached sunny California, it was sounding shot. His "white man drone and mumble" (*London Free Press*, June 8, 1993) did seem to have dropped even further down the lift shaft of his throat. We had gotten used to that during 1988; now, as then, it was still his main warhead: the lyrics and their meaning (his) and the interpretation (ours) merely the fall-out. The voice could still carry a melody but the pace of some songs was so (soulfully) slow that just eight songs, in 50 minutes or so, constituted the first set, half of which was needed to accustom the ear to both his low(est) vocal register and the 'adagio' arrangements. Adrian Chamberlain described Leonard's voice rather well in his review (in *The Times-Colonist*) of the June 29 show in Victoria as ". . . a limited instrument, but he makes use of its ragged strengths. And he's a clever technician with an artist's sense of phrasing and delivery".

By tour-end, they had performed in 29 different cities in 56 days; which compared to the hectic schedules of more recent years might seem ungenerous; but Leonard was now 58, not 54, nor 50. In truth, they *should* have played even more, another 30 to 40 shows in Europe; but circumstances prevented them from doing so. Leonard explained thus: "Everybody was drinking too much . . . I started with just half a bottle of wine a night and I was up to four or five bottles of wine a night by the end of the concert . . . and very very expensive wine too, because the more you drink the better the wine has to be, so finally we were drinking Chateau Latour 1982 at $250 a bottle! . . ." His final words to the last audience in Victoria in which he thanked them for being ". . . so diligently attentive and so compassionately receptive" coupled with his wish, as expressed in so many previous shows, for them not to catch a summer cold, provided the typically more elegant Cohen 'modus valedicendi'.

XV

Where Do All The Highways Go

We didn't hear much more from Leonard during the rest of 1993 – but he still figured in the headlines every month well into 1994. A third tribute album, subtitled 'If The Moon Had A Sister' was released on his 59th birthday, September 21. (This, by the way, was Leonard's suggested title for his 'Collection' published later that year.) The disc contained 12 songs, all by female singers, thus providing a splendid antidote to the all-male 1991 'I'm Your Fan'. But they were all in Norwegian and not exactly immediately accessible! Nevertheless, as collections of cover versions go, it was an important addition to the Cohen files.

Leonard flew to Oslo to help launch the CD. His lyrics were rewritten, not translated as such, by Norwegian author and friend Håvard Rem. 'COHEN PÅ NORSK' (translation: 'Cohen In Norwegian') contained: 'Dance Me To The End Of Love' (by Somebody's Darling), 'Everybody Knows' (Kari Bremnes), 'Bird On The Wire' (Kirsten Bråten Berg), 'Suzanne' (Kristin Solli), 'Joan Of Arc' (Claudia Scott), 'Sisters Of Mercy' (Sidsel Endresen), 'The Captain' (Somebody's Darling), 'There Is A War' (Claudia Scott), 'Famous Blue Raincoat' (here re-titled "Did You Ever Go Free?", Kari Bremnes), 'Who By Fire' (Kristin Solli), 'So Long, Marianne' ("So long, little friend", Kirsten Bråten Berg) and 'You Know Who I Am' (Sidsel Endresen). It was greeted with much acclaim, staying high in the charts for months. Some 69,000 plus copies were sold within a year – not bad for the small religious Norwegian record company, Kirkelig Kulturverksted, whose previous bestsellers included "The Bethlehem Rose" (34,000 in 1992) and "Silent Night" (51,000 in 1991).

Back home in Montreal, in October, Leonard was one of the six recipients of a Governor-General's Performing Arts Award, for "lifetime achievement and contribution to Canada's cultural life", consisting of a commemorative medallion, a cheque for $10,000 and Special Honoured Guest status at a Gala in their honour in November in Ottawa. His fellow winners included poet Gilles Vigneault (whose 'Gens de pays' had been adopted by Quebec separatists, who narrowly lost the 1995 referendum to gain independence) and Ludmilla Chiriaeff, whom *The Montreal Gazette* described as "Grand Dame of dance and founder of the Grands Ballets Canadiens".

Meanwhile, over 1,800 miles away in Red Deer, Alberta – between Edmonton and Calgary – preparations continued apace for a Leonard Cohen Conference, October 22-24, described in their programme as "an international and interdisciplinary celebration of Cohen's contributions to fiction, drama, poetry, music, dance and performance." Leonard, though invited, declined to attend. The keynote speakers were both Cohen biographers: Drs. Stephen Scobie and Ira Nadel. Other speeches included a detailed *musical* analysis of 'Take This Waltz'. The Conference also featured the world première production of Leonard's *The New Step – A Ballet-Drama in One Act*, first published in *Flowers For Hitler* in 1964. A musical concert rounded off proceedings on the Saturday night and among the performers was Perla who sang four Cohen songs: 'Bird On The Wire', 'The Window', 'If It Be Your Will' and 'Seems So Long Ago, Nancy'. The group finale was a rousing, and lengthy, 'Closing Time'. 'The Proceedings of the Leonard Cohen Conference' were published in a 132-page paperback edition of *Canadian Poetry* (Issue 33 – Fall/Winter 1993).

Two weeks later, in November, Leonard's own 415-page collection *Stranger Music* was finally published, three years later than originally scheduled, with selections from all his poetry books, six passages from 'Beautiful Losers', and most song-lyrics from all albums right up to 'The Future'. The final pages contained 11 'uncollected' poems dating variously from 1978 to 1987. His acknowledgements included Nancy Bacal (of 'Recent Songs' out-take fame) and Rebecca De Mornay. Leonard undertook a promotional tour visiting Toronto, Ottawa and Montreal at the end of November, and then to the American West Coast: Los Angeles, San Francisco and Seattle in the first week of December, though book-signings did not figure in the schedules. Leonard: "I generally try to avoid signings. It's a performance thing I'm not very good at."

But he was still good at reading the stuff. On *Morning Becomes Eclectic* on KCRW, he recited six poems. One of these, "I heard of a man", was later included on a compilation CD of KCRW items 'Rare On Air'. His opinions on self-censorship (i.e. on the use of 'bad language' in his poetry and song) were discussed during the interview. 'Dance Me To The End Of Love' from the April 18 pre-tour show at The Complex in Los Angeles concluded the broadcast. Leonard also read a selection on Toronto radio, *Morningside*, in conversation with Pete Gzowski, and two tracks from the forthcoming live album – 'Bird On The Wire' and 'Everybody Knows' were also aired.

During the Governor-General's Gala in Ottawa on November 27, fronted by actor Donald Sutherland, at which (a severely close-cropped) Leonard was a Guest Of Honour, Perla and Julie sang 'Anthem', backed by the swaying People's Gospel Choir of Montreal. By the time it was broadcast on TV, a duet of an entirely different nature was already in the record shops – Leonard and Elton John together on the 1943 Ted Daffan song 'Born To Lose', yet another (minor) hit for Ray Charles in 1962. Leonard took the first verse, sounding late-July 93-ish, and was joined intermittently by John on verse three. Many Cohen followers must have found it a bizarre (and demanding) four-and-a-half minutes, though I doubt if it took much out of either singer. Other artists duetting in turn with Elton John on his album 'Duets' included Gladys Knight, Bonnie Raitt and Don Henley. Others who had in some other way connected with Leonard in 1993 were Aaron Neville and Linda Ronstadt in their duet on 'Song Of Bernadette', John Cale who continued to perform 'Hallelujah', Laurie Brown in her splendid CBC *Prime Time* television interview and the British Film Institute in London who screened the 1972 tour documentary *Bird On A Wire* at the National Film Theatre during their season of *Rocking And Reeling* rock films in December.

The January 1994 issue of *Shambhala Sun* should have given us a broad hint that Leonard would eventually head for the hills. By the time 'Leonard Cohen – Live In Concert' was released in July 1994, not only had Leonard and Rebecca de Mornay split up ("She got wise to me," he admitted) but he was then living full-time on Mount Baldy where in his little two-roomed wooden cabin he was allowed the luxury of a synthesizer and a Mac. Computer graphics had lately taken his fancy, six of which were included in Massimo Cotto's 1993 book of Italian translations of most of his lyrics from 'Songs Of' to 'The Future'. Leonard has since often mentioned at least one of the songs he has so far completed: 'I Was Never Any Good At Loving You'. Other songs and a book of poetry are also still on the go.

The live album contained eight songs from three Canadian shows on the 1993 tour: 'Dance Me To The End Of Love', 'Bird On The Wire', 'Joan Of Arc', 'There Is A War' and 'I'm Your Man' (Toronto, June 17), 'Sisters Of Mercy' (Toronto, June 18), 'Everybody Knows' and 'Suzanne' (Vancouver, July 29). The other five tracks were from 1988 concerts in Amsterdam, San Sebastian and Austin. At 72 minutes it's the longest Cohen album in his entire catalogue. A new colour video was made for 'Dance Me To The End Of Love', the album's opener. The last song we hear was the first recorded Cohen song we had ever heard: 'Suzanne'. Credit to Sony/Columbia for the booklet with all the lyrics and the 'technical' credits too; the hummingbird/heart/handcuffs motif is on the cover: all now tinted a warmer shade of red. It should have been a double. Reviews on both continents were generally favourable though several bemoaned the lack of Leonard's spoken intros to the songs which were such an integral part of the pace and poise in those concerts.

When interviewed in connection with his 60th birthday, Leonard put on record that it wasn't such a big deal for him as it was for everyone else: "It's nice to get old . . . everybody will be so polite and respectful . . .". A tribute book, *take this waltz – A Celebration of Leonard Cohen*, was published in Quebec in the week of his birthday, containing poems, reminiscences and articles about Leonard contributed by, among others, Jennifer Warnes, Judy Collins and John Simon. That same month, a new biography (the first in English since 1990) by Ira Nadel was also published. Around this time too there was a decent turn-out of retrospective radio and TV programmes in Britain, France, Norway (he had actually visited Oslo for the Live Album campaign), Germany and Canada, and printed articles-cum-interviews aplenty, some with great colour photographs, which certainly recalled those heady début-album days of 1967.

The year ended with Leonard's voice on the soundtrack of a new film, *The Tibetan Book Of The Dead*, in which he narrated (s-l-o-w and g-r-a-v-e) the history of that book and its contemporary usage. An interview with Buddhist spiritual leader Dalai Lama was also featured in the 95-minute two-part film, co-produced between NHK (Japan), Mistral Films (France) and the Canadian NFB. Leonard's involvement with Tibetan texts can be traced back to his Hydra days. One of his friends on the island was Evan Wentze, a translator of *The Tibetan Book Of The Dead*. On July 4, 1963, for example, Leonard wrote a poem with the lines "Last night I dreamed/ you were Buddha's wife/ and I was a historian watching you sleep" ('The House' in *Flowers For Hitler*).

'Leonard Cohen – entre ciel et terre' (translation: 'LC – between Heaven and Earth') proclaimed the first new smaller-size edition of the French rockmag *Les Inrockuptibles* in March 1995 with a stunning colour front-cover showing the unshaven, close-cropped Great Man in Zen black robes and laceless white trainers. Inside, more great pics and Leonard's considered opinions on Life and Death, and everything of any import in between – and all this thirty years after we'd seen him walking out to audiences, dressed in black trousers and leather jacket, in *Ladies and Gentlemen, Mr. Leonard Cohen* to do just that.

In August, *Billboard* magazine reported that two more songs 'My Secret Life' and 'A Thousand Kisses Deep' were nearly finished. Not bad for the former, considering Leonard was reciting some of its lyrics back in 1988. It may be a while before we hear the latter: Leonard was reported – in *The New York Times* in October 11 – reciting a couple of verses during lunch. Nothing as yet, however, has surfaced in connection with Leonard's contribution (if he ever made one) to a special programme about Sweden's 18th century religious writer/poet Carl Michael Bellman, for which Donovan, Joan Baez, The Dubliners and Björk were also reported to have been approached.

September brought the release of a tribute album called 'Tower Of Song' on the A&M label, the brainchild of Leonard's manager Kelley Lynch. She had originally planned it for his 60th, but it just wasn't ready. Canada actually got it first in August and Gold status followed immediately. Kelley's husband Steve Lindsey also co-produced with A&M's boss David Anderle. The line-up (in track- and song-order) was certainly impressive: Don Henley: 'Everybody Knows'; Trisha Yearwood: 'Coming Back To You'; Sting & The Chieftains: 'Sisters Of Mercy'; Bono: 'Hallelujah'; Tori Amos: 'Famous Blue Raincoat' (a highlight of her live shows); Aaron Neville: 'Ain't No Cure For Love'; Elton John: 'I'm Your Man'; Willie Nelson: 'Bird On A Wire'; Peter Gabriel: 'Suzanne'; Billy Joel: 'Light As The Breeze'; Jann Arden (the only Canadian on the album): 'If It Be Your Will' (Leonard: "probably one of the best songs I've ever written"); Suzanne Vega: 'Story Of Isaac'; and Martin Gore: 'Coming Back To You'. Tom Robbins contributed ten waxing paragraphs and I noted that while some of the songs copyrights had been updated to 1995, a few had also been newly assigned (from Stranger Music) to 'Bad Monk Publishing'.

Their treatments were less than knock-out, but there was enough there to enthuse Leonard himself to saunter around a few laps of the promotional track: "The truth is, I like this album. I put it on with a lot of trepidation but I can play it in my jeep without fear . . ." he told *Mojo* in November 1995.

Now there's a sight to gladden the heart: a 62-year old non-Buddhist but devoted Zen disciplinarian and songwriter, who'd always thought of himself as a singer, a former pop-icon of the Sixties turned sage-of-the-Nineties, with his foot to the floor, steaming down a mountain road to Los Angeles, California, listening on his in-jeep CD player to a bunch of songs by Leonard Cohen.

Appendix 1

The Tours in detail

Musicians (aka 'The Army') throughout 1970
Leonard Cohen – guitar, vocals
Ron Cornelius – guitar
Charlie Daniels – bass, guitar, violin
Aileen Fowler – vocals*
Bubba Fowler – banjo, guitar
Corlynn Hanney – vocals
Bob Johnston – guitar, keyboards
Sue Mussmano – vocals **

* credited for the 1970 tracks on 'Live Songs'
** not credited on 'Live Songs' for the 1970 tracks, yet mentioned in concert reviews.

1970 tour in Europe
May
  3 – Amsterdam, Netherlands – ?Concertgebouw
  4 – Hamburg, Germany – Musikhalle
  6 – Frankfurt, Germany – Jahrhunderthalle
  8 – Munich, Germany – Circus Krone
  9 – Vienna, Austria – Konzerthaus
10 – London, England – Royal Albert Hall
11 – London, England – ICA (poetry reading)
13 – Paris, France – Olympia

1970 – FESTIVALS
July
25 – USA – Forest Hills, New York – Tennis Stadium
August
  2 – FRANCE – Aix-en-Provence
31 – ENGLAND – Isle of Wight – East Afton Farm

1970 tour in Canada and USA
December
Ottawa, Ontario – Carleton University
Toronto, Ontario – Massey Hall
10 – Montreal, Quebec – Place Des Arts
Berkeley, Calif. – Community Theatre
(the correct order of these, and other as yet unknown, concerts is
    uncertain)

1972 tour in Europe
March
18 – Dublin, Ireland – National Stadium
18 – Dublin, Ireland – River Club, with "Blondel"
19 – Glasgow, Scotland – Kelvin Hall
20 – Manchester, England – Belle Vue
21 – Leeds, England – University
22 – Newcastle, England – City Hall
23 – London, England – Royal Albert Hall
April
 3 – Stockholm, Sweden – Kungliga Tennishall
 4 – Copenhagen, Denmark – Falkoner Teatret
 5 – Hamburg, Germany – Musikhalle
 6 – Frankfurt, Germany – Jahrhunderthalle
 7 – Düsseldorf, Germany – Rheinhalle
 8 – Berlin, Germany – Sportpalast
10 – Vienna, Austria – Konzerthaus
11 – Munich, Germany – Circus Krone
14 – Geneva, Switzerland – Victoria Hall
15 – Amsterdam, Netherlands – Concertgebouw
16 – Brussels, Belgium – Ancienne Belgique
18 – Paris, France – Salle Pleyel
19 – Tel Aviv, Israel – Sports Hall
21 – Jerusalem, Israel – Yad Eliahu Sports Palace

1972 Musicians
Leonard Cohen – guitar, vocals
Ron Cornelius – guitar
Bob Johnston – keyboards
Peter Marshall – bass
David O'Connor – guitar

Jennifer Warnes – vocals
Donna Washburn – vocals

1973
September – October, Israel: various military bases – Leonard 'solo'

Musicians throughout 1974 & early 1975
Leonard Cohen – guitar, vocals
Emily Bindinger – vocals
Erin Dickens – vocals
Jeff Layton – banjo, guitar, mandolin, strings
John Lissauer – keyboards, saxophone, woodwind
Johnny Miller – bass

1974 tour in Europe
September
  1 – Brussels, Belgium – Ancienne Belgique
  5 – Eastbourne, England – Grand Hotel: CBS Convention
  6 – Eastbourne, England – Grand Hotel: CBS Convention
  7 – Paris, France – Parc De La Courneuve
10 – Edinburgh, Scotland – Usher Hall
11 – Glasgow, Scotland – The Apollo
12 – Manchester, England – Free Trade Hall
13 – Newcastle, England – City Hall
14 – Liverpool, England – Empire Theatre
15 – Bristol, England – Hippodrome
16 – Brighton, England – The Dome
17 – Sheffield, England – City Hall
18 – Birmingham, England – Hippodrome
20 – London, England – Royal Albert Hall
22 – Copenhagen, Denmark – Falkoner Teatret
24 – Berlin, Germany – Philharmonie
25 – Düsseldorf, Germany – Philipshalle
26 – Hamburg, Germany – Congress Centrum
28 – Munich, Germany – Circus Krone
29 – Cologne, Germany – Gürzenich (1st show)
29 – Cologne, Germany – Gürzenich (2nd show)
30 – Brussels, Belgium – Ancienne Belgique
October
  1 – Rotterdam, Netherlands – De Doelen
  2 – Amsterdam, Netherlands – Concertgebouw

4 – Heidelberg, Germany – Stadthalle (1st show)
4 – Heidelberg, Germany – Stadthalle (2nd show)
6 – Frankfurt, Germany – Jahrhunderthalle
7 – Vienna, Austria – Stadthalle
8 – The Hague, Netherlands – Concertgebouw
12 – Barcelona, Spain – Palau De La Musica Catalana
13 – Barcelona, Spain – Palau De La Musica Catalana
14 – Madrid, Spain – Teatro Monumental
19 – Paris, France – Olympia
20 – Paris, France – Olympia

Late 1974 Concerts in New York & Los Angeles
November 29 – New York, The Bottom Line – 2 shows
November 30 – New York, The Bottom Line – 2 shows
December 1 – New York, The Bottom Line – 2 shows

later in December – Los Angeles, The Troubadour – 6 shows

Early 1975 tour in Canada and USA
January
2? – Hamilton, Ontario – McMaster University
2? – Waterloo, Ontario – University
28 – London, Ontario – University of Western Ontario
29 or 30? – London, Ontario – Psychiatric Hospital
31 – Toronto, Ontario – Massey Hall
February
1 – Passaic, N.J. – Capitol Theatre
?5 – Philadelphia, Pa. – Irvine Auditorium
7 – New York, NYC – Avery Fisher Hall
9 – Boston, Mass. – Symphony Hall
10 – Montreal, Quebec – Theatre Du Nouveau Monde (1st show)
10 – Montreal, Quebec – Theatre Du Nouveau Monde (2nd show)
Ottawa, Ontario – venue unknown
Minneapolis, Minn. – venue unknown
Vancouver, B.C. – venue unknown
Berkeley, Calif. – Community Theatre
March
4 – Phoenix, Ariz. – Celebrity Theatre
and others, as yet unknown.

190

Late 1975 dates in USA
November
Bryn Mawr, Penn. – The Main Point
Atlanta, Ga – Great South East Music Hall
and others , as yet unknown.

Late 1975 Musicians
Leonard Cohen – guitar, vocals
Steve Burgh – guitar
Carter C.C. Collins – percussion
Erin Dickens – vocals
John Lissauer – keyboards
Johnny Miller – bass
Lorri Zimmerman – vocals

1976 tour in Europe
April
22 – Berlin, Germany – Philharmonie
23 – Berlin, Germany – Philharmonie
24 – Hamburg, Germany – Congress Centrum
25 – Frankfurt, Germany – Jahrhunderthalle
27 – Ludwigshafen, Germany – Friedrich-Ebert-Halle
28 – Münster, Germany – Halle Münsterland
30 – Düsseldorf, Germany – Philipshalle
May
 1 – Cologne, Germany – Messehalle B
 2 – Saarbrücken, Germany – Saarlandhalle
 4 – Mainz, Germany – Rheingoldhalle
 6 – Stuttgart, Germany – Liederhalle
 7 – Stuttgart, Germany – Liederhalle
 8 – Munich, Germany – Circus Krone
 9 – Munich, Germany – Circus Krone
11 – Dublin, Ireland – National Stadium
12 – Oxford, England – New Theatre
13 – Leicester, England – De Montfort Hall
14 – Sheffield, England – City Hall
15 – Glasgow, Scotland – The Apollo
16 – Edinburgh, Scotland – Usher Hall
17 – Newcastle, England – City Hall
18 – Southport, England – Southport Theatre

19 – Manchester, England – Free Trade Hall
20 – Birmingham, England – Town Hall
22 – Plymouth, England – ABC Cinema
23 – Portsmouth, England – Guildhall
24 – Bristol, England – Colston Hall
25 – London, England – Royal Albert Hall
28? – Copenhagen, Denmark – Falkoner Teatret
29 – Oslo, Norway – Chateau Neuf
30 – Gothenburg, Sweden – Scandinavium
31 – Amsterdam, Netherlands – Concertgebouw
June
4 – Paris, France – Olympia
5 – Paris, France – Olympia
6 – Paris, France – Olympia
7 – Paris, France – Olympia
9 – Reims, France – venue unknown
10 – Brussels, Belgium – Ancienne Belgique
14 – Vienna, Austria – Stadthalle
15 – Graz, Austria – Liebenauereishalle
16 – Linz, Germany – Brucknerhaus
18 – Nuremberg, Germany – Meistersingerhalle
19 – Karlsruhe, Germany – Schwarzwaldhalle
21 – Zürich, Switzerland – Kongresshaus
22 – Zürich, Switzerland – Kongresshaus
23 – Strasbourg, France – venue unknown
24 – Nancy, France – venue unknown
25 – Montreux, Switzerland – Casino De Montreux
28 – Besançon, France – venue unknown
29 – Dijon, France – 'Jazz & Folk Festival'
30 – Lyon, France – venue unknown
July
3 – Vienna, Austria – Konzerthaus
4 – Vienna, Austria – Arena
6 – London, England – New Victoria Theatre
7 – London, England – New Victoria Theatre
8 – London, England – New Victoria Theatre

1976 Musicians
Leonard Cohen – guitar, vocals
Cheryl Barnes – vocals

Laura Brannigan – vocals
Sid McGinnes – guitar
Johnny Miller – bass
Luther Rix – drums
Fred Thaylor – keyboards

1979 tour in Europe
October
  7, 8, 9 and 10 – London, England – Rehearsals in Shepperton
    Studios
13 – Gothenburg, Sweden – Scandinavium
14 – Stockholm, Sweden – Konserthuset
15 – Oslo, Norway – Konserthuset
17 – Copenhagen, Denmark – Falkoner Teatret
19 – Avignon, France – Parc des Expositions
20 – Nice, France – Théâtre de Verdure
22 – Paris, France – Pavillon de Paris
24 – Bordeaux, France – Parc d'Exposition
25 – Nantes, France – Parc d'Exposition
26 – Cambrais, France – Palais des Grottes
27 – Antwerp, Belgium – Koningin Elizabethzaal
28 – Brussels, Belgium – Palais des Beaux Arts
29 – Montpelier, France – Palais des Sports
30 – Paris, France – Théâtre des Champs-Elysées
31 – Munich, Germany – ZDF Television Studio
November
  1 – Frankfurt, Germany – Jahrhunderthalle
  2 – Böblingen, Germany – Sporthalle
  4 – Aachen, Germany – Eurogress
  5 – Berlin, Germany – ICC
  6 – Münster, Germany – Halle Münsterland
  8 – Mainz, Germany – Rheingoldhalle
  9 – Bochum, Germany – Ruhrlandhalle
11 – Hannover, Germany – Kuppelsaal
12 – Kassel, Germany – Stadthalle
13 – Bremen, Germany – Stadthalle
14 – Ulm, Germany – Donauhalle
15 – Nuremberg, Germany – Meistersingerhalle
17 – Cologne, Germany – Sporthalle
18 – Düsseldorf, Germany – Philipshalle

19 – Kiel, Germany – Ostseehalle
21 – Hamburg, Germany – Congress Stadium
22 – Braunschweig, Germany – Stadthalle
23 – Hamburg, Germany – Congress Stadium
25 – Freiburg, Germany – Stadthalle
26 – Ludwigshafen, Germany – Friedrich-Ebert-Halle
27 – Lausanne, Switzerland – Théâtre de Beaulieu (?)
28 – Zürich, Switzerland – Kongresshaus (1st show)
28 – Zürich, Switzerland – Kongresshaus (2nd show)
30 – Munich, Germany – Circus Krone

December
1 – Munich, Germany – Circus Krone (1st show)
1 – Munich, Germany – Circus Krone (2nd show)
3 – Bonn, Germany – Beethovenhalle
4 – London, England – Hammersmith Odeon
5 – London, England – Hammersmith Odeon
6 – London, England – Hammersmith Odeon
8 – Birmingham, England – Odeon
9 – Manchester, England – Apollo
10 – Glasgow, Scotland – The Apollo
11 – Edinburgh, Scotland – Odeon
13 – Preston, England – Guild Hall
14 – Dublin, Ireland – National Stadium (1st show)
14 – Dublin, Ireland – National Stadium (2nd show)
15 – Brighton, England – Dome Theatre

1979 Musicians
Leonard Cohen – guitar, harmonica, vocals
Roscoe Beck – bass guitar
John Bilezikjian – oud, mandolin
Bill Ginn – keyboards
Raffi Hakopian – violin
Steve Meador – drums
Paul Ostermayer – wind
Sharon Robinson – vocals
Jennifer Warnes – vocals
Mitch Watkins – electric guitar

Musicians in Australia, Europe and Israel in 1980
Leonard Cohen – guitar, vocals
Roscoe Beck – bass

194

John Bilezikjian – oud, mandolin
Bill Ginn – keyboards
Raffi Hakopian – violin
Steve Meador – drums
Paul Ostermayer – wind
Sharon Robinson – vocals
Mitch Watkins – guitar

1980 tour in Australia
March
  6 – Melbourne – Comedy Theatre
  7 – Melbourne – Comedy Theatre
  8 – Melbourne – Comedy Theatre
  9 – Melbourne – Comedy Theatre
 11 – Adelaide – Apollo Stadium
 13 – Sydney – Capitol Theatre
 14 – Sydney – Capitol Theatre

1980 Bread and Roses Festival
October
  3 – Berkeley, California – Greek Theatre
  5 – Berkeley, California – Greek Theatre
with The Chamber Brothers, and Jennifer Warnes

1980 tour in Europe and Israel
October
 23 – Besançon, France – Rehearsals (Palais des Sports?)
 24 – Besançon, France – Palais des Sports
 25 – Geneva, Switzerland – Victoria Hall
 26 – Zürich, Switzerland – Kongresshaus (1st show)
 26 – Zürich, Switzerland – Kongresshaus (2nd show)
 28 – Lille, France – Palais Saint-Sauveur
 29 – Brussels, Belgium – Palais des Beaux Arts
 30 – Amsterdam, Netherlands – Concertgebouw
November
  1 – Vienna, Austria – Konzerthaus (1st show)
  1 – Vienna, Austria – Konzerthaus (2nd show)
  2 – Munich, Germany – Circus Krone
  3 – Dortmund, Germany – Westfalenhalle II
  4 – Bonn, Germany – Beethovenhalle
  5 – Eppelheim, Germany – Rhein-Neckar-Halle

7 – Frankfurt, Germany – Jahrhunderthalle
8 – Nancy, France – venue unknown (1st show)
8 – Nancy, France – venue unknown (2nd show)
9 – Strasbourg, France – Palais des Congrès et de la Musique
10 – Mulhouse, France – Palais des Sports
12 – St. Etienne, France – Palais des Sports
13 – Lyon, France – Bourse du Travail
14 – Clermont-Ferrand, France – Palais des Sports
16 – San Sebastian, Spain – Velodromo de Anoeta
17 – Barcelona, Spain – Palacio de Deportes
18 – Toulouse, France – Hall Comminges
20 – Berlin, Germany – ICC
21 – Hamburg, Germany – Congress Stadium
22 – Freiburg, Germany – Stadthalle
24 – Tel Aviv, Israel – Mann Auditorium (1st show)
24 – Tel Aviv, Israel – Mann Auditorium (2nd show)

Musicians throughout 1985
Leonard Cohen – guitar, vocals
Richard Crooks – drums
John Crowder – bass, vocals
Ron Getman – guitar, pedal steel, vocals
Anjani Thomas – keyboards, vocals
Mitch Watkins – guitar, keyboards, vocals

Early to mid January: New York, USA – rehearsals

1985 tour in Europe – part 1
January
28 to 30 – Speyer, Germany – Stadthalle, rehearsals
31 – Mannheim, Germany – Rosengarten
February
1 – Münster, Germany – Halle Münsterland
2 – Wiesbaden, Germany – Rhein-Main-Halle
3 – Berlin, Germany – ICC
4 – Hamburg, Germany – Congress Centrum
6 – Oslo, Norway – Central Kino
7 – Helsinki, Finland – Kulttuuritalo
8 – Stockholm, Sweden – Konserthuset
9 – Copenhagen, Denmark – Falkoner Teatret
11 – Rotterdam, Netherlands – De Doelen

12 – Strasbourg, France – Palais des Congrès
13 – Lausanne, Switzerland – Palais de Beaulieu
15 – Bilbao, Spain – Palacio Municipal de Deportes
16 – Madrid, Spain – Pabellon de Deportes del Real Madrid
18 – Cascais, Portugal – Pavilhao Dramatico
22 – Paris, France – Salle Pleyel
23 – Paris, France – Salle Pleyel (1st show)
23 – Paris, France – Salle Pleyel (2nd show)
25 – London, England – Hammersmith Odeon
26 – London, England – Hammersmith Odeon
27 – Manchester, England – Apollo
28 – Birmingham, England – Odeon

March
 2 – Dublin, Ireland – National Stadium (1st show)
 2 – Dublin, Ireland – National Stadium (2nd show)
 4 – Brussels, Belgium – Palais des Beaux Arts
 5 – Basle, Switzerland – Mustermessehalle
 6 – Vienna, Austria – Konzerthaus
 7 – Vienna, Austria – Konzerthaus
 8 – Linz, Germany – Sporthalle
 9 – Munich, Germany – Rudi-Sedlmayer-Halle
10 – Böblingen, Germany – Sporthalle
11 – Cologne, Germany – Sporthalle
13 – Hannover, Germany – Kuppelsaal
14 – Essen, Germany – Grugahalle
16 – Gothenburg, Sweden – Konserthuset
17 – Stockholm, Sweden – Konserthuset
19 – Poznan, Poland – venue unknown
20 – Wroclaw, Poland – Hala Ludowa
21 – Zabrze, Poland – venue unknown
22 – Warsaw, Poland – Sala Kongresowa
24 – Milan, Italy – Teatro Orfeo (1st show)
24 – Milan, Italy – Teatro Orfeo (2nd show)

1985 tour in the USA (part 1) and Canada
April
30 – Philadelphia, Pa. – Walnut Street Theatre
May
 1 – Philadelphia, Pa. – Walnut Street Theatre
 4 – Boston, Mass. – Berklee Performing Centre

5 – New York, NYC – Carnegie Hall
9 – Ottawa, Ontario – NAC Opera
10 – Montreal, Quebec – Salle Wilfrid Pelletier, Place des Arts
11 – Toronto, Ontario – Massey Hall
14 – Winnipeg, Manitoba – Centennial Concert Hall
15 – Vancouver, B.C. – Queen Elizabeth Theatre

1985 tour in Australia and the USA (part 2)
May
21 – Brisbane, Concert Hall, Cultural Centre
24 – Sydney, Entertainment Centre
25 – Melbourne, State Theatre, Victorian Arts Centre
26 – Melbourne, State Theatre, Victorian Arts Centre
27 – Melbourne, State Theatre, Victorian Arts Centre
June
2 – Adelaide, Festival Theatre
5 – Perth, Concert Hall
6 – Perth, Concert Hall
8 – San Francisco, Calif. – Warfield Theatre
9 – Los Angeles, Calif. – Wiltern Theatre

1985 tour in Europe – part 2
June
27 – Helsinki, Finland – Kulttuuritalo
28 – Roskilde, Denmark – Festival
29 – Helsingborg, Sweden – Sofiero Slott
30 – Oslo, Norway – Kalvøya Festival
July
2 – Jerusalem, Israel – Sultan's Pool
4 – Caesarea, Israel – Amphitheatre
6 – Vienna, Austria – Arkadenhof
7 – Graz, Austria – Schlossberg
9 – Montreux, Switzerland – Casino de Montreux
11 – San Sebastian, Spain – Polideportivo de Anoeta
12 – Zaragoza, Spain – Anfiteatro del Rincon de Goya
13 – Guehenno, France – Elixir Festival
15 – Borgholm, Sweden – Slottsruinen
17 – Nice, France – venue unknown
19 – Rome, Italy – Foro Italico
21 – St. Jean De Luz, France – ?Théâtre de la Nature

Appendix 1

Musicians throughout 1988
Leonard Cohen – guitar, keyboard, vocals
Perla Batalla – vocals
John Bilezikjian – oud
Julie Christensen – vocals
Bob Furgo – keyboards, violin
Tom McMorran – keyboards
Steve Meador – drums/electric drums
Bob Metzger – guitar, steel guitar
Steve Zirkel – bass, keyboard, trumpet

1988 tour in Europe
April
2 to 4 – Mainz, Germany – Rehearsals in Eltzer Hof
5 – Mainz, Germany – Rheingoldhalle
6 – Stuttgart, Germany – Liederhalle
7 – Munich, Germany – Philharmonie
9 – Berlin, Germany – ICC
10 – Cologne, Germany – Philharmonie
12 – Mannheim, Germany – Rosengarten
13 – Hannover, Germany – Kuppelsaal
14 – Hamburg, Germany – Congress Centrum
16 – Antwerp, Belgium – Queen Elizabeth Hall
17 – Antwerp, Belgium – Queen Elizabeth Hall
18 – Amsterdam, Netherlands – Music Theatre
19 – Amsterdam, Netherlands – Music Theatre
21 – Aarhus, Denmark – Musikhuset
22 – Gothenburg, Sweden – Scandanavium
23 – Copenhagen, Denmark – Falkoner Teatret
24 – Lund, Sweden – Olympen (1st show)
24 – Lund, Sweden – Olympen (2nd show)
26 – Stockholm, Sweden – Konserthuset
28 – Helsinki, Finland – Ice Hall
30 – Stockholm, Sweden – Konserthuset
May
1 – Oslo, Norway – Konserthuset (1st show)
1 – Oslo, Norway – Konserthuset (2nd show)
3 – Bergen, Norway – Grieghallen
4 – Bergen, Norway – Grieghallen
6 – Stavanger, Norway – Kongeparken

 7 – Oslo, Norway – Konserthuset (1st show)
 7 – Oslo, Norway – Konserthuset (2nd show)
 9 – Madrid, Spain – Palacio De Deportes
10 – Nuremberg, Germany – Meistersingerhalle
11 – Vienna, Austria – Austria Centre
15 – Zürich, Switzerland – Kongresshaus
16 – Zürich, Switzerland – Kongresshaus
17 – Milan, Italy – Teatro Orfeo
20 – San Sebastian, Spain – Velodromo De Anoeta
21 – Palma, Spain – Auditorium
22 – Seville, Spain – Auditirio Prado
23 – Almeria, Spain – Plaza Pueblo
24 – Barcelona, Spain – Palacio De Deportes
27 – Paris, France – Grand Rex
28 – Paris, France – Grand Rex (1st show)
28 – Paris, France – Grand Rex (2nd show)
30 – London, England – Royal Albert Hall
31 – London, England – Royal Albert Hall

June
 1 – London, England – Royal Albert Hall
 4 – Dublin, Ireland – National Stadium (1st show)
 4 – Dublin, Ireland – National Stadium (2nd show)
 5 – London, England – Royal Albert Hall (Prince'sTrust)
 6 – London, England – Royal Albert Hall (Prince's Trust)
 7 – Lisbon, Portugal – Coliseu Recreios
11 – Huesca, Spain – venue unknown
12 – Bilbao, Spain – Palacio De Deportes
15 – Venice, Italy – Teatro di Venezia
16 – Rome, Italy – Teatro Olimpico
19 – Athens, Greece – Licabettus Amphiteatre
24 – Reykjavik, Iceland – Levgardalshøll
26 – Oslo, Norway – Isle Of Calf Festival
28 – Bergen, Norway – Nygardsparken
30 – Stockholm, Sweden – Galarvarvet

July
 2 – Roskilde, Denmark – Festival

1988 tour in the USA (part 1)
July
 5 – New York, NYC – The Ritz

6 – New York, NYC – Carnegie Hall
8 – Berkeley, Calif. – Zellerbach Auditorium
11 – Los Angeles, Calif. – Wiltern Theatre

1988 tour of Canada and the USA (part 2)
October
23 – Edmonton, Alberta – Jubilee Hall
24 – Calgary, Alberta – Jack Singer Concert Hall
26 – Vancouver, B.C. – Queen Elizabeth Theatre
27 – Seattle, Wash. – Paramount Theatre
28 – Portland, Oreg. – Arlene Schnitzer Auditorium
29 – San Francisco, Calif. – The Fillmore
30 – Los Angeles, Calif. – Wiltern Theatre
31 – Austin, Tex. – Opry House
November
1 – Austin, Tex. – Austin City Limits TV Studio
2 – Atlanta, Ga. – Centre Stage
3 – Washington, D.C. – Warner Theatre
4 – Philadelphia, Pa. – Theatre Of The Living Arts
6 – Ann Arbor, Mich. – Michigan Theatre
7 – Chicago, Ill. – Park West
9 – Toronto, Ontario – Massey Hall
10 – Toronto, Ontario – Massey Hall
11 – Ottawa, Ontario – Congress Centre
12 – Quebec, Quebec – Capital Theatre
13 – Montreal, Quebec – Theatre St. Denis
14 – Montreal, Quebec – Theatre St. Denis
15 – Boston, Mass. – Citi
16 – New York, NYC – Beacon Theatre

Musicians throughout 1993
Leonard Cohen – guitar, keyboard, vocals
Perla Batalla – vocals
Jorge Calderon – bass
Julie Christensen – vocals
Bob Furgo – keyboards, violin
Bill Ginn – keyboards
Steve Meador – drums
Bob Metzger – guitars, pedal steel
Paul Ostermayer – keyboards, saxophone

1993 tour in Europe
April
22 to 24 – Holstebro, Denmark – Rehearsals in Hallen
25 – Holstebro, Denmark – Hallen
26 – Holstebro, Denmark – Hallen
27 – Odense, Denmark – Idretshal
29 – Helsinki, Finland – Ice Hall
May
1 – Oslo, Norway – Spektrum
2 – Gothenburg, Sweden – Lisenbergshall
3 – Stockholm, Sweden – Cirkus
4 – Stockholm, Sweden – Cirkus
6 – Copenhagen, Denmark – Falkoner Teatret
8 – The Hague, Netherlands – Congresgebouw
9 – Ghent, Belgium – Expo
10 – London, England – Royal Albert Hall
11 – London, England – Royal Albert Hall
13 – Paris, France – Zenith
14 – Montpelier, France – Zenith
15 – Barcelona, Spain – Palacio Municipal
16 – Madrid, Spain – Palacio De Deportes
18 – Bologna, Italy – Teatro Medico
19 – Milan, Italy – Teatro Smeraldo
21 – Zürich, Switzerland – Kongresshaus
22 – Konstanz, Germany – Rock Am See Festival
23 – Nimjegen, Netherlands – De Vereeniging
25 – Berlin, Germany – Tempodrom
26 – Hamburg, Germany – Stadtpark
27 – Frankfurt, Germany – Alte Oper
28 – Munich, Germany – Circus Krone
29 – Koblenz, Germany – Nurburgring
30 – Vienna, Austria – Ernst-Happel-Stadion

1993 tour in Canada and the USA
June
3 & 4 – Kitchener, Ontario – Rehearsals in Centre in the Square
5 – Kitchener, Ontario – Centre in the Square
6 – London, Ontario – Centennial Hall
7 – Hamilton, Ontario – Hamilton Place
8 – Ottawa, Ontario – Congress Centre

10 – Montreal, Quebec – Theatre du Forum
11 – Quebec, Quebec – Capital Theatre
14 – New York, NYC – Paramount Theatre
16 – Toronto, Ontario – O'Keefe Centre
17 – Toronto, Ontario – O'Keefe Centre
18 – Toronto, Ontario – O'Keefe Centre
19 – Detroit, Mich. – State Theatre
20 – Chicago, Ill. – Park West
22 – Minneapolis, Minn. – State Theatre
24 – Winnipeg, Manitoba – Walker Theatre
25 – Regina, Saskatchewan – Centre Of The Arts
26 – Calgary, Alberta – Jack Singer Hall
27 – Edmonton, Alberta – Jubilee Auditorium
29 – Victoria, B. C. – Royal Theatre
30 – Vancouver, B.C. – Orpheum Theatre

July

1 – Seattle, Wash. – Paramount Theatre
3 – San Francisco, Calif. – Warfield Theatre
5 – Los Angeles, Calif. – Wiltern Theatre
6 – Los Angeles, Calif. – Wiltern Theatre
8 – San Diego, Calif. – Humphries By The Bay
9 – Santa Fe, N. Mex. – Paolo Solari
11 – Austin, Tex. – The Back Yard
12 – Austin, Tex. – Austin City Limits TV Studio
13 – Atlanta, Ga. – The Roxy
15 – Philadelphia, Pa. – Keswick Theatre
16 – Boston, Mass. – Berklee Performing Centre
18 – Washington, D.C. – Lisner Auditorium
20 – Toronto, Ontario – O'Keefe Centre
22 – Thunder Bay, Ontario – Community Auditorium
24 – Winnipeg, Manitoba – Walker Theatre
26 – Saskatoon, Saskatchewan – Centennial Auditorium
27 – Calgary, Alberta – Jack Singer Hall
29 – Vancouver, B.C. – Orpheum Theatre
30 – Victoria, B.C. – Royal Theatre

Appendix 2

Complete list of touring musicians with Leonard Cohen 1970–1993

BARNES, CHERYL – VOCALS, 1976
BATALLA, PERLA – VOCALS, 1988, 1993
BECK, ROSCOE – BASS, 1979, 1980
BILEZIKJIAN, JOHN – OUD, MANDOLIN, 1979, 1980, 1988
BINDINGER, EMILY – VOCALS, 1974,1975 (e)
BRANNIGAN, LAURA – VOCALS, 1976
BURGH, STEVE – GUITAR, 1975 (l)
CALDERON, JORGE – BASS, 1993
CHRISTENSEN, JULIE – VOCALS, 1988, 1993
COLLINS, CARTER C.C. – PERCUSSION, 1975 (l)
CORNELIUS, RON – GUITAR, 1970, 1972
CROOKS, RICHARD – DRUMS, 1985
CROWDER, JOHN – BASS, VOCALS, 1985
DANIELS, CHARLIE – BASS, GUITAR, VIOLIN, 1970
DICKENS, ERIN – VOCALS, 1974,1975 (e),1975 (l)
FOWLER, AILEEN – VOCALS, 1970
FOWLER, ELKIN ('BUBBA') – BANJO, GUITAR, 1970
FURGO, BOB – KEYBOARDS, VIOLIN, 1988, 1993
GETMAN, RON – GUITAR, PEDAL STEEL, VOCALS, 1985
GINN, BILL – KEYBOARDS, 1979, 1980, 1993
HAKOPIAN, RAFFI – VIOLIN, 1979, 1980
HANNEY, CORLYNN – VOCALS, 1970
JOHNSTON, BOB – GUITAR, KEYBOARDS, 1970, 1972
LAYTON, JEFF – BANJO, GUITAR,MANDOLIN, STRINGS, 1974, 1975 (e)
LISSAUER, JOHN – KEYBOARDS, SAXOPHONE, WOODWIND, 1974, 1975 (e), 1975 (l)
MARSHALL, PETER – DOUBLE BASS, 1972

MCGINNES, SID – GUITAR, 1976

MCMORRAN, TOM – KEYBOARDS, 1988

MEADOR, STEVE – DRUMS, 1979, 1980, 1988, 1993

METZGER, BOB – GUITAR, PEDAL STEEL, 1988, 1993

MILLER, JOHNNY – BASS, 1974,1975 (e), 1975 (l), 1976

MUSSMANO, SUE – VOCALS, 1970

O'CONNOR, DAVID – GUITAR, 1972

OSTERMAYER, PAUL – FLUTE, SAXOPHONE, 1979, 1980, 1993

RIX, LUTHER – DRUMS, 1976

ROBINSON, SHARON – VOCALS, 1979, 1980

THAYLOR, FRED – KEYBOARDS, 1976

THOMAS, ANJANI – KEYBOARDS, VOCALS, 1985

WARNES, JENNIFER – VOCALS, 1972, 1979

WASHBURN, DONNA – VOCALS, 1972

WATKINS, MITCH – GUITAR, KEYBOARDS, VOCALS, 1979, 1980, 1985

ZIMMERMAN, LORRI – VOCALS, 1975 (l)

ZIRKEL, STEVE – BASS, KEYBOARDS, TRUMPET, 1988

Appendix 3

Tour-by-Tour Song Lists

Key
* – not written by LC
† – arranged by LC
‡ – not recorded on a LC album

1970
AVALANCHE – solo
BIRD ON THE WIRE
DIAMONDS IN THE MINE
FAMOUS BLUE RAINCOAT
HEY, THAT'S NO WAY TO SAY GOODBYE
JOAN OF ARC
LADY MIDNIGHT
ONE OF US CANNOT BE WRONG
PLEASE DON'T PASS ME BY
SEEMS SO LONG AGO, NANCY
SING ANOTHER SONG, BOYS
SISTERS OF MERCY
SO LONG, MARIANNE
STORY OF ISAAC
SUZANNE
THE PARTISAN*
THE STRANGER SONG – solo
TONIGHT WILL BE FINE
UN AS DER REBBE SINGT*‡
YOU KNOW WHO I AM – solo

1972
AS TIME GOES BY*‡
AVALANCHE – solo

BANKS OF MARBLE*‡
BIRD ON THE WIRE
CHELSEA HOTEL‡
FAMOUS BLUE RAINCOAT
HEY, THAT'S NO WAY TO SAY GOODBYE
JOAN OF ARC
KEVIN BARRY*‡
LADY MIDNIGHT
MINUTE PROLOGUE
ONE OF US CANNOT BE WRONG
PASSING THRU'†
SEEMS SO LONG AGO, NANCY
SING ANOTHER SONG, BOYS
SISTERS OF MERCY
SO LONG, MARIANNE
STORY OF ISAAC
SUZANNE
THE PARTISAN*
THE STRANGER SONG – solo
TONIGHT WILL BE FINE
WE SHALL NOT BE MOVED*‡
YOU KNOW WHO I AM – solo

1974
A SINGER MUST DIE – solo
BELOVED COMRADE*‡
BIRD ON THE WIRE
CHELSEA HOTEL # 2 – solo
DIAMONDS IN THE MINE
DONA NOBIS PACEM*‡
FAMOUS BLUE RAINCOAT
HEY, THAT'S NO WAY GOODBYE
I TRIED TO LEAVE YOU
IS THIS WHAT YOU WANTED
JOAN OF ARC
LADY MIDNIGHT
LEAVING GREEN SLEEVES
LOVE CALLS YOU BY YOUR NAME
LOVER LOVER LOVER
ONE OF US CANNOT BE WRONG

PASSING THRU'†
SEEMS SO LONG AGO, NANCY
SISTERS OF MERCY
SO LONG, MARIANNE
STORY OF ISAAC
SUZANNE
TAKE THIS LONGING
THE BUTCHER
THE PARTISAN*
THE STRANGER SONG – solo
THERE IS A WAR
TONIGHT WILL BE FINE
UN AS DER REBBE SINGT*‡
WHO BY FIRE
WHY DON'T YOU TRY
YOU KNOW WHO I AM – solo

1975
A SINGER MUST DIE – solo
AS DER REBBE ELIMELECH*‡
BIRD ON THE WIRE
CAME SO FAR FOR BEAUTY‡
CHELSEA HOTEL #2 – solo
DIAMONDS IN THE MINE
DON'T GO HOME WITH YOUR HARD-ON
FAMOUS BLUE RAINCOAT
GUERRERO‡ [early IODINE]
HEY, THAT'S NO WAY TO SAY GOODBYE
I GUESS IT'S TIME‡ [early THE SMOKEY LIFE]
I TRIED TO LEAVE YOU
IS THIS WHAT YOU WANTED
JE VEUX VIVRE TOUT SEUL‡ [BIRD ON THE WIRE in French]
JOAN OF ARC
LADY MIDNIGHT
LEAVING GREENSLEEVES
LOVE CALLS YOU BY YOUR NAME
LOVER LOVER LOVER
ONE OF US CANNOT BE WRONG
PASSING THRU'†
RED RIVER VALLEY*‡

SEEMS SO LONG AGO, NANCY
SISTERS OF MERCY
SO LONG, MARIANNE
STORY OF ISAAC
TAKE THIS LONGING
THE BUTCHER
THE PARTISAN*
THE STRANGER SONG – solo
THE TRAITOR SONG‡
THERE IS A WAR
TONIGHT WILL BE FINE
UN AS DER REBBE SINGT*‡
WHO BY FIRE
YOU KNOW WHO I AM – solo

1976
AVALANCHE – solo
BIRD ON THE WIRE
CHELSEA HOTEL #2 – solo
DIAMONDS IN THE MINE
DIE GEDANKEN SIND FREI*‡
DO I HAVE TO DANCE ALL NIGHT‡
EVERYBODY'S CHILD‡
FAMOUS BLUE RAINCOAT
HEY, THAT'S NO WAY TO SAY GOODBYE
I TRIED TO LEAVE YOU
IS THIS WHAT YOU WANTED
JE VEUX VIVRE TOUT SEUL‡ [BIRD ON THE WIRE in French]
JOAN OF ARC
LADY MIDNIGHT
LOVER LOVER LOVER
ONE OF US CANNOT BE WRONG
PASSING THRU'†
SEEMS SO LONG AGO, NANCY
SISTERS OF MERCY
SO LONG, MARIANNE
STORE ROOM‡
STORY OF ISAAC
SUZANNE
TAKE THIS LONGING

THE BUTCHER
THE PARTISAN*
THE STRANGER SONG – solo
THERE IS A WAR
TONIGHT WILL BE FINE
UN AS DER REBBE SINGT*‡
WHO BY FIRE
WHY DON'T YOU TRY
YOU ARE MY SUNSHINE*‡
YOU KNOW WHO I AM – solo

1979
A SINGER MUST DIE – solo
AVALANCHE – solo
BALLAD OF THE ABSENT MARE
BILLY SUNDAY‡
BIRD ON THE WIRE
CHANTE ROSSIGNOL – solo*‡
CHELSEA HOTEL #2 – solo
DIAMONDS IN THE MINE
FAMOUS BLUE RAINCOAT
FIELD COMMANDER COHEN
GUTEN ABEND, GUT' NACHT*‡
HEY, THAT'S NO WAY TO SAY GOODBYE
I TRIED TO LEAVE YOU
IODINE
IS THIS WHAT YOU WANTED
JOAN OF ARC
LADY MIDNIGHT
LOVER LOVER LOVER
MEMORIES
ONE OF US CANNOT BE WRONG
OUR LADY OF SOLITUDE
PASSING THRU'†
RED RIVER VALLEY*‡
SEEMS SO LONG AGO, NANCY
SILENT NIGHT*‡
SISTERS OF MERCY
SISTERS OF MERCY – solo
SO LONG, MARIANNE

STORY OF ISAAC
SUZANNE
SUZANNE – solo
TAKE THIS LONGING
THE GUESTS
THE GYPSY'S WIFE
THE PARTISAN*
THE SMOKEY LIFE
THE STRANGER SONG – solo
THE WINDOW
THERE IS A WAR
THIRSTY FOR THE KISS‡ [early HEART WITH NO COMPANION]
TONIGHT WILL BE FINE
UN AS DER REBBE SINGT*‡
WHO BY FIRE
WHY DON'T YOU TRY

1980
ANOTHER SATURDAY NIGHT*‡
A SINGER MUST DIE – solo
AVALANCHE – solo
BALLAD OF THE ABSENT MARE
BILLY SUNDAY‡
BIRD ON THE WIRE
CHELSEA HOTEL #2 – solo
DIAMONDS IN THE MINE
DO I HAVE TO DANCE ALL NIGHT‡
FAMOUS BLUE RAINCOAT
HEART WITH NO COMPANION
HEY, THAT'S NO WAY TO SAY GOODBYE
I TRIED TO LEAVE YOU
JOAN OF ARC
LADY MIDNIGHT
LOVER LOVER LOVER
MEMORIES
ONE OF US CANNOT BE WRONG
PASSING THRU'†
SEEMS SO LONG AGO, NANCY
SISTERS OF MERCY
SO LONG, MARIANNE

STORY OF ISAAC
SUZANNE
THE GUESTS
THE GYPSY'S WIFE
THE PARTISAN*
THE SMOKEY LIFE
THE STRANGER SONG – solo
THE WINDOW
THERE IS A WAR
TO LOVE SOMEBODY*‡
TONIGHT WILL BE FINE
WHO BY FIRE

1985
A SINGER MUST DIE – solo
AVALANCHE – solo
BIRD ON THE WIRE
CHELSEA HOTEL #2 – solo
COMING BACK TO YOU
DANCE ME TO THE END OF LOVE
DIAMONDS IN THE MINE
FAMOUS BLUE RAINCOAT
HALLELUJAH
HEART WITH NO COMPANION
HEY, THAT'S NO WAY TO SAY GOODBYE
I TRIED TO LEAVE YOU
IF IT BE YOUR WILL
JOAN OF ARC
LOVER LOVER LOVER
MEMORIES
ONE OF US CANNOT BE WRONG – solo
PASSING THRU'†
SISTERS OF MERCY
SISTERS OF MERCY – solo
SO LONG, MARIANNE
STORY OF ISAAC
SUZANNE
SUZANNE – solo
TENNESSEE WALTZ†‡
THE GUESTS

THE GYPSY'S WIFE
THE LAW
THE NIGHT COMES ON
THE PARTISAN*
THE STRANGER SONG – solo
THERE IS A WAR
WHO BY FIRE

1988
A SINGER MUST DIE – solo
AIN'T NO CURE FOR LOVE
AVALANCHE – solo
BIRD ON THE WIRE
CAN'T HELP FALLING IN LOVE*‡
CHELSEA HOTEL # 2 – solo
COMING BACK TO YOU
DANCE ME TO THE END OF LOVE
EVERYBODY KNOWS
FIRST WE TAKE MANHATTAN
HALLELUJAH
HEART WITH NO COMPANION
HEY, THAT'S NO WAY TO SAY GOODBYE
I CAN'T FORGET
I TRIED TO LEAVE YOU
I'M YOUR MAN
IF IT BE YOUR WILL
JAZZ POLICE
JOAN OF ARC
ONE OF US CANNOT BE WRONG
PASSING THRU'†
SISTERS OF MERCY
SO LONG, MARIANNE
STORY OF ISAAC
SUZANNE
TAKE THIS WALTZ
THE GYPSY'S WIFE
THE LAW
THE PARTISAN*
THE STRANGER SONG – solo
THERE IS A WAR

TOWER OF SONG
WHITHER THOU GOEST (a cappella)‡
WHO BY FIRE

1993
A SINGER MUST DIE – solo
AIN'T NO CURE FOR LOVE
ANTHEM
AVALANCHE – solo
BIRD ON THE WIRE
CHELSEA HOTEL # 2 – solo
CLOSING TIME
COMING BACK TO YOU
DANCE ME TO THE END OF LOVE
DEMOCRACY
EVERYBODY KNOWS
FIRST WE TAKE MANHATTAN
HALLELUJAH
I CAN'T FORGET
I TRIED TO LEAVE YOU
I'M YOUR MAN
IF IT BE YOUR WILL
JOAN OF ARC
ONE OF US CANNOT BE WRONG
PASSING THRU'†
SISTERS OF MERCY
SO LONG, MARIANNE
SUZANNE
TAKE THIS WALTZ
THE FUTURE
THERE IS A WAR
TOWER OF SONG
WAITING FOR THE MIRACLE
WHITHER THOU GOEST (a cappella)‡

Appendix 4

Albums

Songs Of Leonard Cohen, 1967
Songs From A Room, 1969
Songs Of Love And Hate, 1971
Live Songs, 1973
New Skin For The Old Ceremony, 1974
Greatest Hits / The Best Of Leonard Cohen, 1975
Death Of A Ladies' Man, 1977
Recent Songs, 1979
Various Positions, 1984
I'm Your Man, 1988
The Future, 1992
Leonard Cohen Live In Concert, 1994

Tracks

A BUNCH OF LONESOME HEROES, Songs From A Room, 1969,
     track 3
A SINGER MUST DIE, New Skin For The Old Ceremony, 1974,
     track 7
AIN'T NO CURE FOR LOVE, I'm Your Man, 1988, track 2
ALWAYS, The Future, 1992, track 8 (written by Irving Berlin, 1925)
ANTHEM, The Future, 1992, track 5
AVALANCHE, Songs Of Love And Hate, 1971, track 1
BALLAD OF THE ABSENT MARE, Recent Songs, 1979, track10
BE FOR REAL, The Future, 1992, track 3 (written by Frederick
     Knight, 1975)
BIRD ON THE WIRE, Songs From A Room, 1969, track 1
BIRD ON THE WIRE, Live Songs (72), 1973, track 4 (introduced in
     French)
BIRD ON THE WIRE, Greatest Hits, 1975 (= 1969), track 4

BIRD ON THE WIRE, Live In Concert (93), 1994, track 2
CAME SO FAR FOR BEAUTY, Recent Songs, 1979, track 4
 (co-writer: John Lissauer)
CHELSEA HOTEL #2, New Skin For The Old Ceremony, 1974,
 track 2
CHELSEA HOTEL #2, Greatest Hits, 1975 (=1974), track 10
CLOSING TIME, The Future, 1992, track 4
COMING BACK TO YOU, Various Positions, 1984, track 2
DANCE ME TO THE END OF LOVE, Various Positions, 1984, track 1
DANCE ME TO THE END OF LOVE, Live In Concert (93), 1994,
 track 1
DEATH OF A LADIES' MAN, Death Of A Ladies' Man, 1977, track 8
 (LC – lyrics; Phil Spector – music)
DEMOCRACY, The Future, 1992, track 6
DIAMONDS IN THE MINE, Songs Of Love And Hate, 1971, track 4
DON'T GO HOME WITH YOUR HARD-ON, Death Of A Ladies'
 Man, 1977, track 6 (LC – lyrics; Phil Spector – music)
DRESS REHEARSAL RAG, Songs Of Love And Hate, 1971, track 3
EVERYBODY KNOWS, I'm Your Man, 1988, track 3 (co-writer:
 Sharon Robinson)
EVERYBODY KNOWS, Live In Concert (93), 1994, track 3
FAMOUS BLUE RAINCOAT, Songs Of Love And Hate, 1971,
 track 6
FAMOUS BLUE RAINCOAT, Greatest Hits, 1975 (= 1971), track 8
FIELD COMMANDER COHEN, New Skin For The Old Ceremony,
 1974, track 4
FINGERPRINTS, Death Of A Ladies' Man, 1977, track 7 (LC –
 lyrics; Phil Spector – music)
FIRST WE TAKE MANHATTAN, I'm Your Man, 1988, track 1
HALLELUJAH, Various Positions, 1984, track 5
HALLELUJAH, Live In Concert (88), 1994, track 7
HEART WITH NO COMPANION, Various Positions, 1984, track 8
HEART WITH NO COMPANION, Live In Concert (88), 1994,
 track 12
HEY, THAT'S NO WAY TO SAY GOODBYE, Songs Of Leonard
 Cohen, 1967, track 7
HEY, THAT'S NO WAY TO SAY GOODBYE, Greatest Hits, 1975
 (= 1967), track 7
HUMBLED IN LOVE, Recent Songs, 1979, track 2
HUNTER'S LULLABY, Various Positions, 1984, track 7

I CAN'T FORGET, I'm Your Man, 1988, track 7

I LEFT A WOMAN WAITING, Death Of A Ladies' Man, 1977, track
    5 (LC – lyrics; Phil Spector – music)

I TRIED TO LEAVE YOU, New Skin For The Old Ceremony, 1974,
    track 8

I'M YOUR MAN, I'm Your Man, 1988, track 4

I'M YOUR MAN, Live In Concert (93), 1994, track 8

IF IT BE YOUR WILL, Various Positions, 1984, track 9

IF IT BE YOUR WILL, Live In Concert (88), 1994, track 11

IMPROVISATION, Live Songs (72), 1973, track 6 (instrumental:
    You know who I am)

IODINE, Death Of A Ladies' Man, 1977, track 2 (LC – lyrics;
    Phil Spector – music)

IS THIS WHAT YOU WANTED, New Skin For The Old Ceremony,
    1974, track 1

JAZZ POLICE, I'M Your Man, 1988, track 6 (co-writer: Jeff Fisher)

JOAN OF ARC, Songs Of Love And Hate, 1971, track 8

JOAN OF ARC, Live In Concert (93), 1994, track 4

LADY MIDNIGHT, Songs From A Room, 1969, track 9

LADY MIDNIGHT, Greatest Hits, 1975 (= 1969), track 5

LAST YEAR'S MAN, Songs Of Love And Hate, 1971, track 2

LAST YEAR'S MAN, Greatest Hits, 1975 (= 1971), track 9

LEAVING GREEN SLEEVES, New Skin For The Old Ceremony,
    1974, track 11

LIGHT AS THE BREEZE, The Future, 1992, track 7

LOVE CALLS YOU BY YOUR NAME, Songs Of Love And Hate,
    1971, track 5

LOVER LOVER LOVER, New Skin For The Old Ceremony, 1974,
    track 3

MASTER SONG, Songs Of Leonard Cohen 1967, track 2

MEMORIES, Death Of A Ladies' Man, 1977, track 4 (LC – lyrics;
    Phil Spector – music)

MINUTE PROLOGUE, Live Songs (72), 1973, track 1

NANCY, Live Songs (72), 1973, track 5 (full title: Seems So Long
    Ago, Nancy)

ONE OF US CANNOT BE WRONG, Songs Of Leonard Cohen
    1967, track 10

ONE OF US CANNOT BE WRONG, Live In Concert (88), 1994,
    track 10

OUR LADY OF SOLITUDE, Recent Songs, 1979, track 7

PAPER-THIN HOTEL, Death Of A Ladies' Man, 1977, track 3 (LC – lyrics; Phil Spector – music)

PASSING THRU, Live Songs (72), 1973, track 2 (written by by Richard Blakeslee, 'arranged' by LC)

PLEASE DON'T PASS ME BY (A DISGRACE), Live Songs (70), 1973, track 8

QUEEN VICTORIA, Live Songs, 1973, track 10 (not live:1972 home-studio recording)

SEEMS SO LONG AGO, NANCY, Songs From A Room, 1969, track 5

SING ANOTHER SONG, BOYS, Songs Of Love And Hate, 1970, track 7 (live, Isle of Wight, 31.8.70)

SISTERS OF MERCY, Songs Of Leonard Cohen, 1967, track 5

SISTERS OF MERCY, Greatest Hits, 1975 (= 1967), track 2

SISTERS OF MERCY, Live In Concert (93), 1994, track 6

SO LONG, MARIANNE, Songs Of Leonard Cohen, 1967, track 6

SO LONG, MARIANNE, Greatest Hits, 1975 (= 1967), track 3

STORIES OF THE STREET, Songs Of Leonard Cohen 1967, track 8

STORY OF ISAAC, Songs From A Room, 1969, track 2

STORY OF ISAAC, Live Songs (72), 1973, track 7

SUZANNE, Songs Of Leonard Cohen, 1967, track 1

SUZANNE, Greatest Hits, 1975 (= 1967), track 1

SUZANNE, Live In Concert (93), 1994, track 13

TACOMA TRAILER, The Future, 1992, track 9 (instrumental; performed by Bill Ginn)

TAKE THIS LONGING, New Skin For The Old Ceremony, 1974, track 10

TAKE THIS LONGING, Greatest Hits, 1975 (= 1974), track 12

TAKE THIS WALTZ, I'm Your Man, 1988, track 5 (lyrics from poem by Lorca, translated by LC)

TEACHERS, Songs Of Leonard Cohen, 1967, track 9

THE BUTCHER, Songs From A Room, 1969, track 7

THE CAPTAIN, Various Positions, 1984, track 6

THE FUTURE, The Future, 1992, track 1

THE GUESTS, Recent Songs, 1979, track 1

THE GYPSY'S WIFE, Recent Songs, 1979, track 8

THE LAW, Various Positions, 1984, track 3

THE NIGHT COMES ON, Various Positions, 1984, track 4

THE OLD REVOLUTION, Songs From A Room, 1969, track 6

THE PARTISAN, Songs From A Room, 1969, track 4 (written by Anna Marley & Hy Zaret,1944; sung partly in French)

THE PARTISAN, Greatest Hits, 1975 (= 1969; written by Anna
    Marley & Hy Zaret, 1944), track 6
THE SMOKEY LIFE, Recent Songs, 1979, track 9
THE STRANGER SONG, Songs Of Leonard Cohen, 1967, track 4
THE TRAITOR, Recent Songs, 1979, track 6
THE WINDOW, Recent Songs, 1979, track 3
THERE IS A WAR, New Skin For The Old Ceremony, 1974, track 6
THERE IS A WAR, Live In Concert (93), 1994, track 5
TONIGHT WILL BE FINE, Songs From A Room, 1969, track 10
TONIGHT WILL BE FINE, Live Songs (70), 1973. track 9
TOWER OF SONG, I'm Your Man, 1988, track 8
TRUE LOVE LEAVES NO TRACES, Death Of A Ladies' Man, 1977,
    track 1 (LC – lyrics; Phil Spector – music)
UN CANADIEN ERRANT (THE LOST CANADIAN), Recent Songs,
    1979, track 5 (written by M.A. Gerin-Lajoie, 1842; sung in French)
WAITING FOR THE MIRACLE, The Future, 1992, track 2
    (co-writer: Sharon Robinson)
WHO BY FIRE, New Skin For The Old Ceremony, 1974, track 9
WHO BY FIRE, Greatest Hits, 1975 (= 1974), track 11
WHO BY FIRE, Live In Concert (88), 1994, track 9
WHY DON'T YOU TRY, New Skin For The Old Ceremony, 1974,
    track 5
WINTER LADY, Songs Of Leonard Cohen, 1967, track 3
YOU KNOW WHO I AM, Songs From A Room, 1969, track 8
YOU KNOW WHO I AM, Live Songs (72), 1973, track 3

Other Recordings By Leonard Cohen

1957

Leonard reads 8 of his own poems: For Wilf And His House (1955);
Beside The Shepherd (1956); Poem (1955); Lovers (1955); The
Sparrows (1955); Warning (1956); Les Vieus (1956); Elegy (1955) – all
of which were published in his 1956 anthology 'Let Us Compare
Mythologies'. Released on 'Six Montreal Poets', by Folkways Records
and Service Corporation . . . FL 9805, in 1957; re-released in 1991 on
cassette by The Smithsonian Institute, on Smithsonian Folkways 09805.

1966

Leonard reads 7 of his own poems: 1. What I'm Doing Here; 2. You
Have The Lovers; 3. Now Of Sleeping; 4. Style (1962); 5. Two Went To
Sleep (1964); 6. Nothing Has Been Broken; 7. These Heroics. All

published in various anthologies, thus: 'Let Us Compare Mythologies' (1956) – No.7; 'The Spice-Box Of Earth' (1961) – Nos. 2 & 3; 'Flowers For Hitler' (1964) – Nos. 1 & 4; 'Parasites Of Heaven' (1966) – Nos. 5 & 6. [Erroneous information given on record sleeve]. Released on 'Canadian Poets 1', by Canadian Broadcasting Corporation in 1966 (no catalogue number on album sleeve).

1970

'Tonight Will Be Fine' from the Isle Of Wight Festival performance 31.8.70. Released on "The First Great Rock Festivals Of The Seventies – Isle of Wight / Atlanta" . . . CBS 66311 (triple vinyl album), in 1971.(Later released, in 1973, minus the long introduction, on 'Live Songs.') 'Suzanne' later released in 1995 – see below.

1974

'Passing Through' – Leonard guests partly on this track, along with Joan Baez et al. Released on 'The Earl Scruggs Revue: Anniversary Special, Volume 1' . . . CBS 80821, in 1975.

1976

'Do I Have To Dance All Night' and 'The Butcher', two tracks, live, recorded at the Olympia, in Paris, June 1976, and issued on a 7" vinyl single in some European countries, including France and Portugal. Released by CBS – 4431, in 1976.

1986

'Take This Waltz', sung by Leonard, with words translated by him from a poem called 'Pequeño vals vienés' by his great idol, Federico Garcia Lorca. Included on an album marking the 50th anniversary of Lorca's death. Released on 'Poetas en Nueva York' . . . CBS 450307 1 (Spanish label); also issued as 'Poets in New York' . . . CBS 450286 1 (Dutch / UK pressing) in 1986. Also available on two different picture-sleeve 7" vinyl singles – 1) from CBS Spain, 650210 7; 2) from CBS Holland, 650210 7. (n.b. a new 'mix' of this track was later included on the 1988 album 'I'm Your Man'.)

1987

'Joan Of Arc' – LC sings a duet with Jennifer Warnes on her album of Cohen covers. Released on 'Famous Blue Raincoat' . . . Cypress Records, PL90048, in1987. Also available on 12" vinyl single: RCA/Cypress, PT 49710 (c/w: First We Take Manhattan/Famous Blue Raincoat), 1987.

1990

'Elvis' Rolls Royce' – Leonard sings lead vocal on this song on the new album by Was(Not Was). The song was written by David and Don Was. Released on 'are you okay?' . . . Fontana 846 351-1, in 1990.

1992

Leonard is featured as the 'spoken voice' on a track called "Eclipse (includes the poem 'Chill Of Death')", set to some of Charlie Mingus' music, produced by Hal Willner, on a tribute album to Mingus (died January 5, 1979). Released on 'weird nightmare – meditations on mingus' – Columbia/Sony, CK 52739 – 2, in 1992; also: A & M 472467 2.

1993

'Born To Lose' – Leonard sings a duet with Elton John on the latter's new album. The song is a 1943 composition by Ted Daffan. Released on 'Duets' . . . Rocket Records 518 478 – 2. Also available as a promotional cd-single.

1994

Leonard reads 'Poem', (the opening text in his new collection 'Stranger Music – Selected Poems and Songs') on a compilation of live-in-the-KCRW FM Radio-Studio-performances . . . December 3, 1993. Released on: 'Rare on Air, Live Performances, Vol.1', Mammoth Records MR0074-2, in 1994.

1994

"I'm Your Man' and 'Coming Back To You' as performed at The Complex, in Los Angeles, April 18, 1993, are included on a compilation of live tracks from "the occasional Sunday morning radio shows Columbia has syndicated for three years . . ." and called 'The Columbia Radio Hour'. Released on: 'the best of the Columbia Records Radio Hour volume 1', Columbia 66466-2, in 1994. (n.b. the complete Cohen performance was issued on a 'demonstration – not for sale' CD (8 tracks) by Columbia, CSK 5249 in 1993.)

1995

'Suzanne' from the 1970 Isle of Wight concert included on a double-disc compilation tribute to that year's festival. Released complete on 'message to love', Castle Communications/Sony Music, EDF 327. Also, partially (verse 1 omitted) on video and laser disc.

Bibliography

Canadian Poetry No.33 (Fall/Winter, 1993), University of Western Ontario, Canada, 1993.

Dorman, Loranne & Rawlins, Clive – Leonard Cohen: Prophet Of The Heart, Omnibus Press, London, 1990.

Gnarowski, Michael (ed.) – Leonard Cohen: The Artist and His Critics, McGraw-Hill Ryerson Limited, Toronto, 1976.

Hutcheon, Linda – Leonard Cohen and His Works (fiction), ECW Press, Toronto, 1989.

Hutcheon, Linda – Leonard Cohen and His Works (poetry), ECW Press, Toronto, 1992.

Morley, Patricia – The Immoral Moralists: Hugh MacLennan and Leonard Cohen, Charles Irwin, Toronto, 1972.

Nadel, Ira – Leonard Cohen: A Life In Art, ECW Press, Toronto/ Robson Books, London, 1994.

Ondaatje, Michael – Leonard Cohen, McClelland and Stewart, Toronto, 1970.

Scobie, Stephen – Leonard Cohen, Douglas & McIntyre, Vancouver, 1978.

The following are also highly recommended:

Adria, Marco – Music Of Our Times: Eight Canadian Singer-Songwriters, James Lorimer & Company Limited, Toronto, 1990. (chapters on Cohen, Gordon Lightfoot, Neil Young, Joni Mitchell, Bruce Cockburn, Murray McLauchlan, Jane Siberry and k.d.lang.)

Bibliography

Fetherling, Douglas – Some Day Soon: Essays on Canadian Songwriters, Quarry Press, Ontario, 1991. (chapters on Cohen, Gordon Lightfoot, Joni Mitchell, Robbie Robertson and Neil Young.)

Fournier, Michael & Norris, Ken (eds.) – take this waltz: A Celebration of Leonard Cohen, The Muses' Company, Quebec, 1994. (poems, essays, messages, reminiscences, stories etc. by Joan Baez, Kris Kristofferson, John Simon, Judy Collins, Harry Rasky and many others to celebrate Leonard's 60th birthday in September 1994.)

There have been a few non-English studies – those listed below are well worth finding:

Graf, Christof – So Long Leonard, Palmyra Verlag, Heidelberg, 1990 (in German.)

Manzano, Alberto – Leonard Cohen, Unilibro, Barcelona, 1978 (in Spanish.)

Sinclair, Rod – Leonard Cohen: In Quest Of Delight, Glydendal, Copenhagen, 1992 (School textbook, in English with Danish vocabulary.)

Vassal, Jacques – Leonard Cohen, Albin Michel, Paris, 1974, rev.1979 (in French.)

1/97 (26909)